The Scales of Weighing Regulatory Costs

ELGAR STUDIES IN LAW AND REGULATION

Series Editor: Roger Brownsword, *Professor of Law, King's College London, UK*

Regulation is a ubiquitous concept in today's world. The proliferation of new technologies necessitates continual re-appraisal of the rules that govern them, whilst globalization increases the complexity of interaction between governance systems on a national, regional and international level. As a field of study, regulation continues to grow and evolve, both in consideration of specific sectors, and at a conceptual level, as the rationale and motivation for regulation are scrutinized.

This new and exciting series is an important forum for original works of scholarship that explore regulation and its interaction with the law. It favours work that has a critical, innovative or analytical perspective and, whilst having a primary focus on legal writing, welcomes approaches that draw on other disciplines. The scope of the series encompasses a wide range of regulatory fields, from biotechnology and ICT to machine learning and AI, from security, food, and environment to health, leisure, and employment. At the same time the series plays host to broader discussions on the nature of risk, governance models, the role of democracy, regulatory theory and many others.

The primary mission of the series is to stimulate the development of original thinking across law and regulation and to foster the best theoretical and empirical scholarship in the field.

Titles in the series include:

Gambling Regulation and Vulnerability
Malgorzata Anna Carran

Regulation of Synthetic Biology
BioBricks, Biopunks and Bioentrepreneurs
Alison McLennan

From Chasing Violations to Managing Risks
Origins, Challenges and Evolutions in Regulatory Inspections
Florentin Blanc

The Scales of Weighing Regulatory Costs
Technology, Geography, and Time
Jamison E. Colburn

The Scales of Weighing Regulatory Costs

Technology, Geography, and Time

Jamison E. Colburn

Pennsylvania State University, USA

Edward Elgar PUBLISHING

Cheltenham, UK • Northampton, MA, USA

Published by
Edward Elgar Publishing Limited
The Lypiatts
15 Lansdown Road
Cheltenham
Glos GL50 2JA
UK

Edward Elgar Publishing, Inc.
William Pratt House
9 Dewey Court
Northampton
Massachusetts 01060
USA

A catalogue record for this book
is available from the British Library

Library of Congress Control Number: 2018945848

This book is available electronically in the **Elgar**online
Law subject collection
DOI 10.4337/9781788113502

MIX
Paper from
responsible sources
FSC® C013056

ISBN 978 1 78811 349 6 (cased)
ISBN 978 1 78811 350 2 (eBook)

Typeset by Columns Design XML Ltd, Reading

Printed and bound in Great Britain by TJ International Ltd, Padstow, Cornwall

Contents

Preface

To move forward sometimes you must go back. An approach pioneered in US law almost 50 years ago viewed regulation's costs through a very different lens from that of regulatory cost-benefit analysis today. In those days, weighing the costs of a regulatory action was a task undertaken for a variety of reasons, some grounded in welfare economics and utilitarian balancing and some not. Rarely was the claim even heard that regulation should only proceed when it was net-on-net "efficient." Today that pervasive substrate is everywhere and rarely unearthed for critical examination. When it is expressed it becomes as polarizing a principle as those it was meant to replace.

This monograph focuses on the measurement and evaluation of regulation's costs across three detailed case studies—cars, electricity, and freight trains. The aim is to regain a little common ground on weighing costs. There is no pretense that they are a representative or comprehensive selection. But what is lost there is hopefully made up in the contextualization of examining calculation methods and principles that have evolved over time, how subtly the relevance of monetized values can morph as a result of that evolution, and why costs of compliance can be so hard to estimate *ex ante*.

The economic concept of "cost" implies within it some end which is being pursued despite the pull of considerations—*reasons*—to the contrary. It implies there is a good that entails a bad. Paired with authority to tailor legal rights, duties, powers, and immunities, this conception implores us to "optimize": to get as much good for bad as we can. Environmental protection has been its chief focus. As Professor Daniel Cole once put it, "that property regime is best which, in the circumstances, would achieve exogenously set societal goals at the lower total cost, where total cost is the sum of compliance, administrative, and residual pollution or consumption costs."[1] I argue in what follows that this too often simplifies the insights being developed beyond their real usefulness.

---

[1] DANIEL H. COLE, POLLUTION AND PROPERTY: COMPARING OWNERSHIP INSTITUTIONS FOR ENVIRONMENTAL PROTECTION 17 (2002).

Too often what the public and practitioners hear about regulatory costs is a bare number (or range) attributed to a discrete governmental choice. It is at least implicitly (and sometimes explicitly) insisted that costs to regulated parties are somehow fixed. Some progression of regulatory steps over years or decades and the social costs that are measurable across that progression are rarely the subject of any talk at all. Much of that analysis would be retrospective and probably more accurate for it. But it would also reveal that we are ingenious at avoiding costs. Economists know this and usually expect it. Finding the *unavoidable* costs of regulation, in short, is the more worthwhile pursuit, even taking economic cost at face value.

But that is the other core premise in what follows. Economics' conception of regulatory costs really ought not to be taken at face value. For it is built on troubled foundations; foundations that professional economists have acute incentives to ignore or to obscure. This is not to impugn anyone's integrity. Foundational troubles are hardly unique to economics. They are matched and even exceeded by those of other social sciences. But troubles of the kind should almost never go unnoticed, especially given what is at stake in today's talk of regulatory costs.

With cryptocurrencies the rage today, it seems worth recalling our money's origins and practical value. Americans' founding fears of central government long kept them bound to local- and state-based currencies—bank notes backed by actual gold and silver which, when spent far from the issuer, invariably drew *ad hoc* discounts from those who accepted them in payment. By the twentieth century, these costs—forgone benefits of a common currency—had brought most Americans around. Among disadvantages in that common currency, though, were unpredictable liquidity shortages. Partly in response, commercial lawyers fashioned what, for a time, was a handy form of liquidity: the *negotiable instrument.* It worked well enough if the party accepting the note had confidence it would be paid. Eventually, negotiable instruments lost much of their utility in the growth of fractional reserve banking, credit card markets, and other sources of liquidity. For that particular flaw of centrally issued currency essentially vanished.

I think this tale is more prevalent in contemporary risk regulation than in the economics done surrounding its supposed costs. There was no magic to negotiable instruments (payment systems students' frustrations notwithstanding!). They were fit for a purpose. But negotiability became more trouble than it was worth because markets simply moved on. What makes regulatory constraints costly can be just as fleeting in the intersection of competition, collective action, and technical change. We would do best to remember always that these things are constantly and dramatically influencing one another.

A final caveat is worth mentioning. There is an inherent arbitrariness in a focus on regulation's *costs*. The distinction between benefits and costs is obviously perspectival: limiting costs can be a benefit and cutting benefits can be a cost. But practical people must suffer such indignities occasionally when trying to clarify or improve applied concepts. That is what this monograph aims for in the weighing of regulation's costs. It is a work of practical reasoning. My thanks for conversations, comments on earlier drafts, and other help go to Todd Aagaard, Mark Aldrich, Dan Farber, John Lopatka, Michael Vandenbergh, the librarians at Penn State Law, the members of a Villanova Law faculty workshop in Spring 2017 and members of a Penn State Law faculty workshop in Fall 2017.

Jamison Colburn
State College, Pennsylvania
March 2018

1. The meanings of regulatory costs

Legislation enabling regulators to govern risk characteristically requires, permits, or forbids the consideration of regulation's costs. Even legislative silences on costs raise the issue given how contentious risk regulation has grown. One need not be an economist to appreciate that most good things come at a cost. But economists typically think that *everything* has a cost—that every opportunity or good in life entails missed opportunities or goods—which can be priced.[1] So what does enabling legislation *mean* when it directs a regulator to consider, or perhaps to minimize, the costs of regulation? This chapter argues that the meaning of cost as a consideration in regulation has changed over time and that it stems from a menu of very different ethical and moral grounds.

Despite a steady diet of cases interpreting statutory signals of this kind, the US Supreme Court has established precious few rules. And as the legal philosopher Scott Shapiro has argued, rules in a legal system tend to have a compensatory aim rooted in distrust: affording government officials "a large degree of interpretive discretion ... provides them with opportunities to expand their powers, reduce restrictions, and further increase their discretion beyond the level contemplated by designers."[2] Europe has not fared much better. Regulatory methods vary so widely

---

[1] Of course, many things have no market price. *See* Martha C. Nussbaum, *The Costs of Tragedy: Some Moral Limits of Cost-Benefit Analysis*, 29 J. LEGAL STUD. 1005 (2000). But some argue this is merely the outset of a grand progression in favor of pricing more. *See, e.g.*, CASS R. SUNSTEIN, RISK AND REASON: SAFETY, LAW, AND THE ENVIRONMENT (2002). Thus, especially if we take economics as "the study of human behavior as a relationship between given ends and scarce means which have alternative uses," LIONEL ROBBINS, AN ESSAY ON THE NATURE AND SIGNIFICANCE OF ECONOMICS 16 (1932), then *economic cost* is a pervasive—perhaps constitutive—element. *See* Roger E. Backhouse & Steve G. Medema, *Defining Economics: The Long Road to Acceptance of the Robbins Definition*, 76 ECONOMICA 805 (2009).

[2] SCOTT J. SHAPIRO, LEGALITY 340 (2011).

among the two systems[3] that general bureaucratic norms on the consideration of costs are almost impossible to detect or to evaluate. This chapter outlines a spectrum of statutory and administrative contexts where regulation's costs may, must, or must not matter to risk regulators. The majority of this is what we would call environmental health and safety regulation. But many of the same problems arise in banking and financial regulation, taxation, trade, healthcare, *etc*. The benefits of risk reduction can come at a cost; perhaps so high a cost that it is deemed prohibitive. Whatever they come to ultimately, though, regulation's costs have always been a kind of countervailing consideration and, thus, a reason to temper, to delay, or to reject some regulatory action all things considered. As the monograph explores in detail, a great deal turns on *how* those costs are estimated and evaluated. But this chapter first introduces the socio-economic and political—the *legislative*—contexts in which the questions arise.

1.1 COSTS AS CONSIDERATION IN RISK REGULATION—A "FACTOR" WITHOUT FOUNDATIONS

For as long as we have thought of legislation as a means to social ends, it has sent conflicting signals: embodied distinct, often competing purposes joined in compromise.[4] Courts and agencies, thus, sort delegative statutes into those that require fixed decisional procedures, those that allow a freer kind of aggregative "factoring" of different purposes or goals, and still other types of delegation less recognizably common.[5] For example, most of the environmental legislation in the United States of the 1970s was reasonably clear that Congress wanted its chief implementing agent, the Environmental Protection Agency (EPA), to consider the costs of its air and water pollution (and other risk) regulations. Nonetheless, overt statutory ambiguities engulfed how, when, and why such costs should be tabulated and considered. Research into the legislative histories of those statutes has repeatedly confirmed that these ambiguities were no

---

[3] *See* Jonathan B. Wiener, *The Real Pattern of Precaution, in* THE REALITY OF PRECAUTION: COMPARING RISK REGULATION IN THE UNITED STATES AND EUROPE 519 (Jonathan B. Wiener et al. eds., 2011).

[4] *See* JEREMY WALDRON, THE DIGNITY OF LEGISLATION (1999).

[5] *See* ROBERT A. KATZMANN, JUDGING STATUTES 11–22 (2014).

mere oversight.[6] So it was often unclear whether the expected costs of a regulation were to be compared to its expected benefits; whether they should just be estimated and considered in some less structured way; or rather that they be used to completely different effect, *e.g.*, to inform later congresses, the public, or still other bureaucratic decision makers. A seemingly interminable debate has dragged on over permitting Congress to "delegate" in this fashion, either as a legal or as a prudential/political matter.[7] Let us consider why.

A pair of cases construing the Occupational Safety and Health Act of 1970 (OSH Act) underscores precisely how imprecise Congress has usually been in its legislation as well as the troubles that creates. Under the statute, the Occupational Safety and Health Administration (OSHA) was to protect workers from "toxic or harmful physical agents" with standards "which most adequately [assure], to the extent feasible, on the basis of the best available evidence, that no employee will suffer material impairment of health or functional capacity even [from] ... regular exposure to the hazard."[8] In short, OSHA's "considerations" were not tightly constrained.[9]

In its rulemaking regulating workplace exposures to benzene, OSHA concluded (as it had in prior rulemakings) that the delegation required it to weigh the costs of technologically attainable reductions of benzene exposure—but not that it must compare the expected benefits and costs of its standard and proceed only if the former outnumbered the latter.[10] A lower court disagreed,[11] and a divided Supreme Court could not form a majority on what relevance, precisely, costs were to have in reducing workplace exposures to benzene.[12] The benzene case, as it has been

---

6 Ambiguity is perhaps the oldest of collective decision-making tools. *See* JON ELSTER, SECURITIES AGAINST MISRULE: JURIES, ASSEMBLIES, ELECTIONS (2013).

7 *See* Thomas W. Merrill, *Rethinking Article I, Section 1: From Non-delegation to Exclusive Delegation*, 104 COLUM. L. REV. 2097 (2004).

8 29 U.S.C. § 655(b)(5).

9 *See* Public Citizen Health Research Group v. Tyson, 796 F.2d 1479, 1494–96 (D.C. Cir. 1986) (recounting and analyzing OSH Act § 6 and the doctrines construing it).

10 *See* Occupational Safety and Health Admin., Dept. of Labor, Occupational Exposure to Benzene, 43 Fed. Reg. 5918, 5920, 5934–40 (1978).

11 *See* American Petro. Inst. v. OSHA, 581 F.2d 493, 503–04 (5th Cir. 1978), *rev'd in part sub. nom.*, Industrial Union Dept., AFL-CIO v. American Petro. Inst., 448 U.S. 607 (1979).

12 *See Industrial Union Dept.*, 448 U.S. at 708–09 & n.27 (Marshall, J., dissenting) (noting plurality and concurrences' differences in rationale and how

remembered, remanded OSHA's standard to it with little guidance beyond a vague, conflicted implication that what the agency had done was somehow contrary to law.[13] So the very next Term a Supreme Court majority waded back into the logjam in a case involving cotton dust, *American Textile Mfrs.*, concluding that the Act did *not* require a structured cost-benefit criterion.[14]

The cotton dust majority compared several similar statutes and found that together they demonstrated that "Congress uses specific language when intending that an agency engage in cost-benefit analysis,"[15] that the OSH Act did not use such language, and that "cost-benefit analysis by OSHA is not required by the statute *because feasibility analysis is*."[16] It was the mirror image of the Benzene plurality's move—analogizing the OSH Act to other, similar statutes.[17] This time, though, a majority in

---

differently they understood the statute, Congress's powers under Article I, and the reviewing courts' functional roles).

[13] *But see* SUNSTEIN, supra note 1 at 195 ("Though the plurality left undecided the question whether the agency must also show a reasonable proportion between costs and benefits, it is clear ... [it] was motivated by the desire to ensure some kind of proportionality between benefits and costs ...").

[14] *See* American Textile Mfrs. Inst. v. Donovan, 452 U.S. 490, 508–09 (1981).

[15] *Donovan,* 452 U.S. at 510–11.

[16] Id. at 509 (emphasis added); *see* id. at 510–12 & n.30 (citing the CAA, CWA, Energy Policy and Conservation Act, Consumer Product Safety Act, and others). Courts invoking this discussion in *Donovan* since have taken "feasible" to mean "technically possible and affordable," City of Portland v. EPA, 507 F.3d 706, 712 (9th Cir. 2007), as requiring the agency to avoid "insuperable financial burdens on the affected industries," Forging Indus. Ass'n v. Secretary of Labor, 773 F.2d 1436, 1453 (4th Cir. 1985), and that the agency demonstrate a "reasonable likelihood that ... costs will not threaten the existence or competitive structure of an industry, even if it does portend disaster for some marginal firms." Public Citizen Health Res. Grp. v. U.S. Dept. of Labor, 557 F.3d 165 (3d Cir. 2009) (*quoting* United Steelworkers of Amer. v. Marshall, 657 F.2d 1189, 1272 (D.C. Cir. 1980)).

[17] The Fifth Circuit in *American Petroleum Inst.* held that any OSHA standard had to address a "significant" risk and had to make a "significant" reduction in that risk if it were going to impose significant costs of compliance in the process. *See* 581 F.2d at 499–505. The court helped itself to that interpretation of the OSH Act by analogizing it to what it called the "precisely similar" Consumer Product Safety Act, id. at 502, citing Aqua Slide 'N' Dive Corp. v. CPSC, 569 F.2d 831 (5th Cir. 1978). Justice Stevens seemed to adopt the Fifth Circuit's approach in his plurality opinion, *see Industrial Union Dept.,* 448 U.S. at 414–15, but Justice Rehnquist's vote for the remand did nothing of the kind, leaving Justice Stevens without a majority.

American Textile Mfrs. unequivocally rejected the cost-benefit interpretation, albeit without clarifying the expected form or content of its so-called "feasibility analysis." Subsequent lower court cases took this "feasibility" approach to have distinct features, most notably the need to examine and evaluate regulatory burdens rather closely.[18]

There are good reasons not to align costs against benefits in some synthetic calculus the elements of which are often so disparate. For one thing, as often as Congress or the European Commission has referenced cost in their risk regulation delegations, they have seldom included anything remotely resembling a mandate for cost-benefit analysis.[19] For another, syntheses of the kind are only as reliable as their weakest terms.[20] More importantly, however, the concept of cost itself is deceptively perspectival: a "cost" to one cohort is often mirrored by an equal and opposite benefit to another. The number that represents that cost, on the other hand, conveys nothing of the kind. That essential *negotiability* has been embodied perhaps most poignantly in the calculation of a "social cost of carbon" (SCC), *i.e.*, climate change damages on a

---

[18] *See* Sections 2.2 and 2.3.

[19] The EU Commission's "Regulatory Scrutiny Board" and "Better Regulation Guidelines" have undergone a rapid evolution from their debut in 2002 as a series of loosely connected, abstract principles into a mandate for "EU policies and laws so that they achieve their objectives *at minimum cost*." European Commission, Commission Staff Working Document: Better Regulation Guidelines 4 (SWD (2017) 35) (emphasis added), *available at* https://ec.europa.eu/info/sites/info/files/better-regulation-guidelines.pdf. *Cf.* Alberto Alemanno, *How Much Better is Better Regulation?*, 6 EUR. L. RISK REG. 344, 350–51 (2015) (arguing that the EU Commission's cost-benefit mandate has the potential to reopen legislative purposes, compromises, and to force new allocations of institutional control throughout the EU). But this shift to cost-benefit analysis of Commission initiatives may be increasingly limited by the lack of inter-institutional consensus regarding such analyses' *relevance* to final EU directives and regulations. *See* id. at 351–55.

[20] *Cf.* Adam M. Finkel, *The Cost of Nothing Trumps the Value of Everything: The Failure of Regulatory Economics to Keep Pace with Improvements in Quantitative Risk Analysis,* 4 MICH. J. ENVTL. & ADMIN. L. 91, 105 (2014) ("the problem with the weak link in a designed product is not simply the creation of a vulnerability at which the entire product is most likely to fail catastrophically; less well-appreciated is the fact that, in hindsight, all of the time and expense spent on refining the stronger links beyond the quality of the weakest one were wasted.").

marginal, per-ton basis.[21] Transforming marginal tons of greenhouse gas (GHG) emissions into a SCC compressed the myriad perspectives, claims, and counterclaims bearing on the risk/regulatory balance at issue into a supposedly singular measure. That quantity, dubbed a *cost* of not averting emissions, was really just camouflage for the myriad of immensely contestable judgments underlying it. Much as a negotiable instrument embodies all of the possible claims under the law to some underlying asset within a single writing, the SCC estimates purported to do so for each and every single ton of GHG emissions the planet over. That calculation of *cost* substituted contestability with cardinality, ostensibly in the name of *improving* analysis.[22]

So how are costs to be assessed and evaluated if *not* by being done up into a single measure to be leveled against the correlative benefits? A spectrum of answers has emerged from practice, each grounded ultimately in its own ethical footings.[23] What relevance can be attached to costs when they are *not* part of a cost-benefit calculus?[24] Since the OSHA cases it has been abundantly clear that considering regulation's costs is a step which regulators may and do take in various directions. Courts have occasionally interpreted ambiguous statutory directives like

---

[21] *See* INTERAGENCY WORK GROUP, TECHNICAL SUPPORT DOCUMENT: SOCIAL COST OF CARBON FOR REGULATORY IMPACT ANALYSIS UNDER EXECUTIVE ORDER 12866 (Feb. 2010), *available at* https://www.epa.gov/sites/production/files/2016-12/documents/scc_tsd_2010.pdf.

[22] It was not *so* long ago that the conjuring of cardinal measures of welfare from indeterminate collections of diverse individuals, each with their own subjective probabilities and preferences, was immensely controversial. *See* John C. Harsanyi, *Cardinal Welfare, Individualistic Ethics, and Interpersonal Comparisons of Utility*, 63(4) J. POL. ECON. 309 (1955).

[23] *See, e.g.*, Gregory C. Keating, *Pressing Precaution Beyond the Point of Cost-Justification*, 56 VAND. L. REV. 653 (2003); David M. Driesen, *Distributing the Costs of Environmental, Health, and Safety Protection: The Feasibility Principle, Cost-Benefit Analysis, and Regulatory Reform*, 32 B.C. ENVTL. AFFS. L. REV. 1 (2005); MATTHEW D. ADLER & ERIC A. POSNER, NEW FOUNDATIONS OF COST-BENEFIT ANALYSIS (2006); RICHARD L. REVESZ & MICHAEL A. LIVERMORE, RETAKING RATIONALITY: HOW COST-BENEFIT ANALYSIS CAN BETTER PROTECT THE ENVIRONMENT AND OUR HEALTH (2008); Dov Waisman, *Equity and Feasibility Regulation*, 50 U. RICH. L. REV. 1263 (2016).

[24] Even stripping the question of its technical freight and opposing "goods" to "bads" in the simplest sense, the goodness of uncertain prospects can become deceptively complex just in the selection of the proper metrics of "good." *See* JOHN BROOME, WEIGHING GOODS: EQUALITY, UNCERTAINTY AND TIME (1991). When the technical problems of pricing are brought back in, such complexities can easily overtake the value of the analytical exercise itself.

the one above to require cost-benefit analysis.[25] And precedents to that effect lie about today ready for the next analogy.[26] Such a legal mandate, however, puts risk regulators to a task the sense of which remains deeply contested.

Risk regulation's *benefits* come, if anywhere, in the reduction of risk. That must be some function of identifiable *hazards* and the means of their containment.[27] Quantifying this sum has long bedeviled environmental, health, and safety regulators.[28] This is not least because risk is both a positive (probabilistic) and a normative concept.[29] To be put at risk

---

[25] A pair of opinions, *see Aqua Slide 'N' Dive*, 569 F.2d 831; D.D. Bean & Sons v. CPSC, 574 F.2d 643 (1st Cir. 1978), established a now entrenched judicial construction of the Consumer Product Safety Act's mandate to the Consumer Product Safety Commission that CPSC prepare a cost-benefit analysis for any of its product safety measures. *See* Zen Magnets LLC v. CPSC, 841 F.3d 1141, 1147–48 (10th Cir. 2016).

[26] *See, e.g.*, Business Roundtable v. SEC, 647 F.3d 1144, 1148–52 (D.C. Cir. 2011) (construing Investment Company Act requirement that SEC determine whether its regulations will "promote efficiency, competition and capital formation" to require marginal cost-benefit analysis); New Mexico Growers Ass'n v. U.S. Fish & Wildlife Serv., 248 F.3d 1277, 1285 (10th Cir. 2001) (interpreting Endangered Species Act § 4(b)(2)'s requirement that FWS consider "the economic impact of specifying" listed species' critical habitat as requiring "a full analysis of all of the economic impacts of a critical habitat designation, regardless of whether those impacts are attributable co-extensively to other causes"); Corrosion Proof Fittings, Inc. v. EPA, 947 F.2d 1201, 1214–17 (5th Cir. 1991) (construing the Toxic Substances Control Act § 6(c)(1)(D)'s requirement that EPA analyze "the reasonably ascertainable economic consequences" of its rule by citing *Aqua Slide*, 569 F.2d 831, as requiring EPA to use cost-benefit analysis).

[27] *See* Marjolein B.A. van Asselt & Ortwin Renn, *Risk Governance*, 14 J. RISK RES. 431, 436–38 (2011) (calling attention to the uncertainty, complexity and ambiguity of risk grounded in the plurality of hazards, the uncertainties of causation, prediction, and variation, *etc.*); CHRISTOPHER HOOD ET AL., THE GOVERNMENT OF RISK: UNDERSTANDING RISK REGULATION REGIMES 3–4 (2001).

[28] Isolating and monetizing regulation's benefits has long been an identifiable subfield. *See, e.g.*, A. MYRICK FREEMAN III, THE BENEFITS OF ENVIRONMENTAL IMPROVEMENT: THEORY AND PRACTICE (1979).

[29] The general problem of induction aside, *risk* has invited as much attention from philosophers of science and mind over the last century as it has from economists and economic theory. Risks are inherently forward looking, albeit with informational roots in the past and present. *See* MICHAEL V. FRANK, CHOOSING SAFETY 14–26 (2008). Despite early hopes that so much attention would eventually yield shared probabilistic frameworks for evaluation, risk has

is to be done some form of *harm*.[30] Often, though, the nature and not just the degree of that harm depends on the probabilities at issue. And risk regulation's costs may distribute independently of any of that. The costs of risk regulation have nothing necessarily in common with its benefits—not its agents, events, causes, or consequences. There is, for example, the wholly discrete and independent sum of *government's* costs of action in risk regulation.[31] Stated formally, thus, if expected risk $\boldsymbol{r}$ is the sum of all possible hazards (h) up to n hazards in the absence of choice option $\boldsymbol{\varphi}$, where p is each hazard's probability—

$$(\boldsymbol{r})^{exp} = \sum_{exp} \{h^1(p) + h^2(p) + h^3(p) \ldots n\}$$

—then $\boldsymbol{\varphi}$'s costs bear no necessary relationship to the risks faced by those weighing ϕ against other options.[32] We should say that $\boldsymbol{\varphi}$'s costs are a sum exogenous to $\boldsymbol{r}$ with distinct probabilistic, epistemic, and cognitive challenges.[33] So the costs and benefits of any given risk regulation may

remained a divisive and lumpy field. "If we were all-knowing and present everywhere all the time, we'd be able to see all possible outcomes of all our possible decisions and actions. Risk arises from our inability to reliably predict the future." Id. at 22.

[30] *Cf.* JOHN OBERDIEK, IMPOSING RISK: A NORMATIVE FRAMEWORK (2017) (presenting the argument that to impose risk on others is to deprive them of autonomy to which they are at least presumptively entitled); Claire Finkelstein, *Is Risk a Harm?*, 151 U. PA. L. REV. 963 (2003) (offering a conditional "yes"). To be put at risk by collective decision making is to be done the harm by a collective—some mechanisms of which can be more problematic than others. *See* HENRY S. RICHARDSON, DEMOCRATIC AUTONOMY 234–37 (2002).

[31] *See* Chapter 6, Section 6.2.

[32] Stating a sum of φ's *costs* can highlight the existence of discrete vectors. Thus, cost = C_i ($\boldsymbol{a}$, z), where $\boldsymbol{a}$ is a parameter or vector of parameters describing some option φ, z is a vector of parameters summarizing the current economic equilibrium, and C_i ($\boldsymbol{a}$, z) is the associated costs borne by the agent i. *See* William A. Pizer & Raymond Kopp, *Calculating the Costs of Environmental Regulation, in* 3 HANDBOOK OF ENVIRONMENTAL ECONOMICS 1307, at 1309–10 (Karl-Göran Mäler & Jeffrey R. Vincent eds., 2005).

[33] The challenges of prediction will distribute independently, and perhaps unevenly, in these distinct calculations. That creates its own methodological choices. *See* COLIN HOWSON & PETER URBACH, SCIENTIFIC REASONING: THE BAYESIAN APPROACH (3d ed. 2006) (arguing that all rational inquiries, especially recognizably "scientific" inquiries, possess ineradicable subjectivities and that the choice of probabilistic methods must be made according to the best all-things-considered assessments, case by case). As Sunstein and others routinely note, having to make such choices will then introduce various cognitive biases. *See* SUNSTEIN, supra note 1 at 33–49.

(and perhaps should) comprise two theoretically and practically distinct analyses, each with their own forms of uncertainty and variability, types of proof and relevant expertise, and, most especially, their own independent conclusions.[34]

For whatever reason, delegative legislation has long been characteristically vague on how and whether to combine these inquiries.[35] (The study of the political dynamics therein has itself been practically stalemated for reasons beyond our scope.[36]) When Congress deliberates over new legislation, each chamber and the President consider delegating the authority to govern discrete, salient risks against a potentially infinite array of risks and uncertainties.[37] These are, in American constitutional terms, compound *political* questions of estimation, prioritization, and

---

[34] The orthodox concession—that without monetization, costs and benefits remain incommensurable—obscures this separability thesis. *Cf.* HOOD ET AL., supra note 27 at 70–89 (explaining a general approach to risk regulation grounded in a "market failure hypothesis"); PRESIDENTIAL/CONGRESSIONAL COMMISSION ON RISK ASSESSMENT AND RISK MANAGEMENT, 2 RISK ASSESSMENT AND RISK MANAGEMENT IN REGULATORY DECISION-MAKING 19–29 (1997) (treating risk as the product of hazard times exposure). Furthermore, as our national academies have found repeatedly in studying hazards like toxins, segregating elements of the search/investigation is often vital to success. *See, e.g.*, NATIONAL RESEARCH COUNCIL, SCIENCE AND JUDGMENT IN RISK ASSESSMENT 4–5 (1994) (listing hazard identification, dose response assessment, exposure assessment, and risk characterization as the divisible elements in understanding the risks of hazardous air pollutants).

[35] Prevailing Supreme Court doctrine maintains that delegative legislation ambiguous on the "precise question" at issue in a challenge to agency action normally should be interpreted as authorizing any "reasonable" agency interpretation thereof where the agency's interpretation is embodied in some action having the "force of law." *See* Chevron, U.S.A., Inc. v. Natural Resources Defense Council, Inc., 467 U.S. 837, 842044 (1984); United States v. Mead Corp., 533 U.S. 218, 227–31 (2001); City of Arlington v. FCC, 133 S. Ct. 1863, 1868–75 (2013).

[36] Arrow, Borda, and Condorcet voting paradoxes, like the many theorems they have spawned, implicitly question the democratic legitimacy of legislation and have done so for the bulk of its existence. *See* DENNIS C. MUELLER, PUBLIC CHOICE III 2–6 (2003). The theorems long resisted empirical testing, *see* GERRY MACKIE, DEMOCRACY DEFENDED 23–71 (2003), but a relative balance of empirical confirmations versus disconfirmations today has left a veritable stalemate in the study of legislative delegation and democratic autonomy. *See* STEVEN P. CROLEY, REGULATION AND PUBLIC INTERESTS: THE POSSIBILITY OF GOOD REGULATORY GOVERNMENT 14–76 (2008).

[37] *See, e.g.*, ADRIAN VERMEULE, LAW'S ABNEGATION: FROM LAW'S EMPIRE TO THE ADMINISTRATIVE STATE (2016).

institutionalization.[38] Yet reviewing courts consistently find that, once a statute *has* delegated authority to some administrator, the ensuing decisions—regardless of their origins in an opaque text forged in political compromise—are fully subject to judicial review for consistency with "the law."[39] We may call this the *Overton Park* consensus for the landmark precedent that announced it.[40] Upon review such decisions are typically scrutinized for demonstrable arbitrariness, routinely testing the boundaries between administrative and judicial competence.[41] For what is *arbitrary* in the context of contemporary risk regulation?

The Securities and Exchange Commission's (SEC) corporate governance rulemakings came to just this intersection some years ago.[42] Across a line of cases, the Court of Appeals for the District of Columbia Circuit, a court that had long made clear that it would scrutinize the *evidence* for

---

[38] A "political" question in American terms is one without "judicially discoverable and manageable standards for resolving it." Baker v. Carr, 369 U.S. 186, 217 (1962).

[39] In Citizens to Preserve Overton Park v. Volpe, 401 U.S. 402 (1971), the Supreme Court held that even legislation created from inscrutable compromise, delegating to the agency the duty to assess "feasible or prudent alternative[s]," id. at 405, created "law to apply" and thus judicially reviewable agency action consistent with the Administrative Procedure Act (APA), 5 U.S.C. § 551 *et seq. See* id. at 416–19. *Overton Park*'s legacy, arguably, has been to substitute judicial for political review along several margins. *See* Peter L. Strauss, *Citizens to Preserve Overton Park v. Volpe—Of Politics and Law, Young Lawyers and the Highway Goliath, in* ADMINISTRATIVE LAW STORIES 259 (Peter L. Strauss ed., 2006).

[40] The US Supreme Court's most noted accounts of the arbitrariness review standard(s) grew more or less directly from *Overton Park. See* Merrick B. Garland, *Deregulation and Judicial Review*, 98 HARV. L. REV. 505, 541 (1985).

[41] *Cf.* VERMEULE, supra note 37 (arguing that law and legal theory from the early twentieth century to the present and for the foreseeable future must grapple with the interface of judicial and administrative authority).

[42] *See* John C. Coates IV, *Cost-Benefit Analysis of Financial Regulation: Case Studies and Implications*, 124 YALE L.J. 882, 890–902 (2015) (*discussing* Chamber of Commerce v. SEC, 412 F.3d 133 (D.C. Cir. 2005); Business Roundtable v. SEC, 647 F.3d 1144 (D.C. Cir. 2011); Nat'l Ass'n of Mfrs. v. SEC, 748 F.3d 359 (D.C. Cir. 2014)).

SEC's economic findings,[43] confronted SEC's economic analysis, challenged for having drawn "arbitrary" inferences from inconclusive evidence.[44] The claim was that SEC failed to quantify costs—costs the agency had said were not quantifiable.[45] In *Chamber of Commerce v. SEC*,[46] the Court "subtly elevated the statutory mandate for the SEC to 'consider' efficiency, competition and capital formation to [an] independent obligation to *determine* (as best it can) the economic consequences of proposed rules."[47] Subtle or not, though, judicial interventions like this can have profound consequences.[48]

Consider the use of disclosures to discourage the sourcing of materials from "conflict" locations like the Democratic Republic of Congo.[49] The civil war there has been particularly brutal and resistant to resolution. Congress had directed SEC to require any person manufacturing a product where "conflict minerals are necessary to the functionality or production of [that] product" to disclose that fact in standard SEC filings and SEC obliged, promulgating a series of disclosure duties.[50] The disclosures SEC elected to require would be burdensome to assemble, with estimated compliance costs of $3–4 billion upfront and roughly $200–600 million annually thereafter.[51] When it came time to estimate the *benefits* of the disclosure rule—disclosures being the tool chosen to

---

[43] *See* Bruce Kraus & Connor Raso, *Rational Boundaries for SEC Cost-Benefit Analysis*, 30 YALE J. REG. 289, 298–300 (2013) (*discussing* Timpanaro v. SEC, 2 F.3d 453 (D.C. Cir. 1993)).

[44] *See, e.g., Business Roundtable*, 647 F.3d at 1148–56.

[45] *See* Coates, supra note 42 at 891–96, 912–26. One proposal, given how little confidence SEC had in direct estimations of costs of financial regulation, was to fashion a model, albeit one that would by necessity be extraordinarily complex. *See* id. at 943–47.

[46] 412 F.3d 133 (D.C. Cir. 2005).

[47] Kraus & Raso, supra note 43 at 305 (emphasis in original) (*discussing Chamber of Commerce*, 412 F.3d at 143).

[48] *Cf.* Kraus & Raso, supra note 43 at 292 (noting that challenges were "100 percent successful to date" where they have attacked SEC rulemakings on grounds of inadequate cost-benefit analysis).

[49] Congress included a mandate in the Dodd-Frank Wall Street Reform and Consumer Protection Act to SEC that SEC require disclosures from certain types of firms with business in covered countries. *See* Securities and Exchange Commission, Final Rule—Conflict Minerals, 77 Fed. Reg. 56274, 56277–78 (2012).

[50] *See* Pub. L. No. 111-203, 124 Stat. 1376, at § 1502 (2010), codified in relevant part at 15 U.S.C. §§ 78m(p), 78m note.

[51] *See* Securities and Exchange Commission, Final Rule—Conflict Minerals, 77 Fed. Reg. 56274, 56334 (2012).

alert markets to the uses of "conflict minerals" so that market actors could avoid them—SEC was deeply uncertain. Indeed, it "was 'unable to readily quantify' the 'compelling social benefits' the rule was supposed to achieve: reducing violence and promoting peace and stability in the Congo."[52] Lacking data on how effective the disclosures could or would be in real markets,[53] it opted instead to rely on "Congress's judgment that supply-chain transparency would promote peace and stability by reducing the flow of money to armed groups."[54] Was that arbitrary?[55] Certainly SEC might have surveyed Americans to discover what they were *willing to pay* to peaceably resolve the war in Congo.[56] It chose not to do so. Was it arbitrary to deny a *de minimis* exemption from the disclosure requirements? Surely SEC might have decided that Congress did not intend to impose heavy compliance costs on someone playing virtually *no* role in the Congo's multifaceted, long-enveloping tragedy. It chose not to do so.

On both counts the reviewing court found that SEC had *not* been arbitrary—that it had good and sufficient reasons for its rule.[57] But what

---

[52] National Ass'n Mfrs. v. SEC, 748 F.3d 359, 364 (D.C. Cir. 2014) (*quoting* Conflict Minerals Rule, 77 Fed. Reg. at 56350)).

[53] *See Nat'l Ass'n Mfrs.*, 748 F.3d at 364.

[54] *See* id.

[55] A general authority to review agency action not otherwise withdrawn specifically by statute is available from APA § 10. The broadest grounds for setting aside agency action in that statute is that the action is adjudged "arbitrary, capricious, an abuse of discretion or otherwise not in accordance with law." Id. at § 706(2)(A). In this case, the five-member Commission voted three to two to make the rule. *Nat'l Ass'n Mfrs.*, 748 F.2d at 363.

[56] Americans' expressed willingness to pay to avoid the harms of Congo's civil war might be relevant. *See* Eric A. Posner & Cass R. Sunstein, *Moral Commitments in Cost-Benefit Analysis*, *available at* https://papers.ssrn.com/sol3/papers.cfm?abstract_id=2930450 at 17–19. Then again, the collection and use of such data may well have been to dismiss Congress's evaluation of avoiding conflict minerals—a choice which itself could be judged "arbitrary" or "not in accordance with law." *Cf. State Farm*, 463 U.S. at 52 (holding that, where a rule's benefits accrue as to the risk the statute targets, rescinding that rule requires at least an explanation in keeping with the statute's purposes and text).

[57] *See Nat'l Ass'n Mfrs.*, 748 F.3d at 364. Contemporary moral theory typically takes as given some substantive theory of rational action, whether as a matter of individual or collective agency. *See* DAVID SCHMIDTZ, RATIONAL CHOICE AND MORAL AGENCY (1995). US federal courts rarely resort to such theory, at least explicitly—although struggles with the rules of recognition applicable to agency reasons are quite common. *See* Jacob Gersen & Adrian Vermeule, *Thin Rationality Review*, 114 MICH. L. REV. 1355 (2016).

had SEC's decision procedure been?[58] How did it justify its ignorance of the benefits of its rule? Would it have been prohibitively costly to have collected data showing its rules' costs *were* justified by their benefits?[59] Would Americans' expressed "willingness to pay"[60] have been that data? To be sure, SEC had good reason to pause on the strategic ramifications of taking such an approach.[61] Data of the kind rarely come with their own assurances of accuracy, whatever the costs of their collection.[62]

SEC might have answered that the disclosure requirements were justified because they were the *right* or just thing to do.[63] Lurking, often, is a right/wrong boundary—foreign as that dichotomy can seem to economics—in talk of costs and "willingness to pay."[64] All-things-considered justifications that turn to some extent on fairness or justice are pervasive in life. Utilitarianism's most powerful synthesis struggled

---

[58] SEC need not have resorted to "economic" reasoning to have followed *some* decision procedure. *See, e.g.*, John Rawls, *Outline of a Decision Procedure for Ethics*, 60(2) PHIL. REV. 177 (1951). This is the only way that competent agents can gain assurances that they have tallied the reasons for and against relevant options, though. Id. at 185–96.

[59] In many contexts, the government's own "decision costs" are a relevant decisional factor. *See* Gersen & Vermeule, supra note 57 at 1390–96.

[60] So-called "willingness-to-pay" data, from surveys or other means, put a price to benefits that lack direct pricing information. *See* SUNSTEIN, supra note 1 at 180.

[61] Cognitive psychologists have revealed important shortcomings in survey research. *See* DANIEL KAHNEMAN, THINKING, FAST AND SLOW (2011); *cf.* John C. Harsanyi, *Morality and the Theory of Rational Behavior, in* UTILITARIANISM AND BEYOND 39 (Amartya Sen & Bernard Williams eds., 1982) (arguing that rational prudence must include at least a minimal account of the "social setting" of the decision wherein others' preferences are uncertain). "The concept of rational behaviour arises from the empirical fact that human behaviour is to a large extent goal-directed behaviour." Id. at 42. Assuming SEC's *goals* included minimizing its own costs, conducting willingness-to-pay survey research in support of a rule might not have been "means-ends rational"—to say nothing of that research's problems with accuracy. *See* Wendy E. Wagner, *Administrative Law, Filter Failure, and Information Capture*, 59 DUKE L.J. 1321, 1351–65 (2010) (describing causes and consequences of "information excess" in regulation).

[62] *See, e.g.*, MATTHEW D. ADLER & ERIC A. POSNER, NEW FOUNDATIONS OF COST–BENEFIT ANALYSIS 166–73 (2006) (noting several problems with "willingness-to-pay" data, especially the potential for strategic misrepresentations).

[63] *See, e.g.*, CASS R. SUNSTEIN, FREE MARKETS AND SOCIAL JUSTICE 96 (1997) ("[E]ven a system that generally respects freedom of contract may block exchanges on several grounds.").

[64] *See, e.g.*, Harsanyi, supra note 61 at 40–41.

mightily with the existence of some ostensibly "ultimate" good exceeding all other goods.[65] Judging goodness and rightness separately puts considerable stress on their distinction.[66] Yet the good and the right may be different (in philosophy if not economics) even if they are practically impossible to disentangle.[67]

So even conceding that goodness fully decides rightness, the metaphor of *weighing* the good and bad of an option remains deceptively simplistic.[68] Like any metaphor, it suppresses differences to highlight similarities. We like to weigh *factors*, each with its own valence in our evaluative frameworks.[69] But just as any set of things' weight can be their thinnest commonality, considerations for and against an option are rarely the only *reasons* pertaining to that option.[70] Principals and agents, for

---

[65] *See* HENRY SIDGWICK, THE METHODS OF ETHICS 391–407 (7th ed. 1907) (Hackett 1981); *cf.* J.B. SCHNEEWIND, SIDGWICK'S ETHICS AND VICTORIAN MORAL PHILOSOPHY 310–28 (1977) (explaining Sidgwick's struggle).

[66] *Cf.* ADLER & POSNER, supra note 62 at 52–61 (arguing that welfare as a metric of goodness need not be morally exclusive and fielding the common objections to the use of welfare as a moral criterion); SCHMIDTZ, supra note 57 at 98–106.

[67] Properly Kantian or Rawlsian principles of rightness—even merely "intuitionistic" agreements to the same effect—could have justified the Dodd-Frank Act's posture toward DRC's civil war. *See, e.g.*, JOHN RAWLS, JUSTICE AS FAIRNESS: A RESTATEMENT 5–9, 13–14 (2001) (*discussing* the ideals of a society as a "fair system of cooperation," the "well-ordered society" and how Kant viewed justice as a global obligation); DEREK PARFIT, 1 ON WHAT MATTERS 377–80 (2011) (defending a "Kantian" version of "rule consequentialism").

[68] On weighing and how it contrasts with "lexical priority" views, *see* Michael Huemer, *Lexical Priority and the Problem of Risk*, 91 PAC. PHIL. Q. 332 (2010); *but cf.* BROOME, supra note 24 at 7 ("Not all teleological judgement need be much like weighing … . It is consistent with teleology to think that some considerations dominate others lexically."). Still, the weighing metaphor—which some find problematic on metaethical grounds, *see, e.g.*, DOUGLAS A. KYSAR, REGULATING FROM NOWHERE 38–45 (2010)—need not account for *all* the ways in which costs matter.

[69] *See, e.g.*, SHELLY KAGAN, NORMATIVE ETHICS 17–22 (1998) (observing that normative, "commonsense" ethics can be divided into "factors" such as the good, doing harm, and honesty, and "foundations" in either teleology or deontology).

[70] Whether we take the class of all reasons, *i.e.*, as favorers or disfavorers, *see* T.M. SCANLON, WHAT WE OWE TO EACH OTHER 17 (1998), or rather split the range of reasons into distinct kinds having different bases of normativity, *see, e.g.*, JOHN SKORUPSKI, THE DOMAIN OF REASONS (2011), every reason can be judged as such both for its validity and its sufficiency. Unidimensional weighing collapses that distinction.

example, often have much thicker relationships than any particular choice can reflect. Thus, taking the private costs of complying with the SEC's Congo standards as (relatively) high and the uncertain benefits as being (mostly) overseas, the sum of SEC's reasons may have seemed to be against making that rule.[71] Congress, however, had decided for its own reasons to direct SEC to require disclosures, whatever good SEC thought might come of it.[72] How was SEC to serve Congress? Its being Congress's agent entailed that question. Of course, a *de minimis* exemption was not necessarily ruled out by the legislation.[73] For all could be told, Congress simply ignored that option. But it seems that SEC decided that the lack of cause-to-effect ties linking US capital investment to suffering in central Africa was insufficient reason for a *de minimis* exemption.[74] As SEC seemed to suggest, costs may do better as some kind of proxy for justice or fairness in this context than as a metric for utility or welfare.[75] Particularly in contexts where a fair system of

---

[71] How to count (or weigh) the good of foreign nationals against that of American citizens and/or how to consider the "diminishing marginal utility" of goods like money income relative to goods like security or safety entail severe operational and epistemological troubles, severely complicating most economic methods. *See, e.g.*, Kenneth J. Arrow, *Some Ordinalist-Utilitarian Notes on Rawls' Theory of Justice*, 70(9) J. PHIL. 245 (1973).

[72] Teleological approaches depart from other approaches, we might say, in their evaluation of acts, choices, *etc.*, by the goodness or the badness thereof. Goodness determines rightness for teleological approaches. *See* BROOME, supra note 24 at 6–13. And "[t]he standard sort of teleology is *maximizing*." Id. at 6. But this entailment is both strength and weakness, especially where the goods being weighed are not (or may not be) additive. *See* Shelly Kagan, *The Additive Fallacy*, 99(1) ETHICS 5 (1988).

[73] *But see* 748 F.3d at 366 ("Having established that conflict minerals are frequently used in minute amounts, the Commission could reasonably decide that a per-issuer exception could 'thwart' the statute's goals by leaving unmonitored small quantities of minerals aggregated over many issuers.").

[74] Assigning weights to *moral* reasons may be a uniquely problematic exercise. *See* Michael Philips, *Weighing Moral Reasons*, 96 MIND 367 (1987). Furthermore, any theory of "doing harm" will rest on causal foundations which become question-begging beyond the simplest cases of act/consequence. *See, e.g.*, Carolyn R. Morillo, *Doing, Refraining, and the Strenuousness of Morality*, 14(1) AMER. PHIL. Q. 29 (1977). And as Section 2.1 demonstrates, consequentialist reasons are pervasive in contemporary risk regulation.

[75] Utility as a measure of "good" has long wrestled with peoples' preferences for fairness and justice. *See* John Broome, *Utility*, 7 ECON. & PHIL. 1 (1991). American courts rather pragmatically ignore the basic concept of cost's conflation of the two. *See, e.g.*, U.S. EPA v. EME Homer City Gen., 134 S. Ct. 1584 (2014) (upholding EPA's use of abatement costs to assign proportional

cooperation is at stake, indeed, utility and welfarism can obscure the relevance of costs as choice factors.[76] If I need others' help to accomplish my goals, for example, I must deal with them as they *are*—not as I believe they should rationally be.[77] If they think my behavior unfair, my calculation of costs or benefits will be beside the point. In the SEC's case, while the reviewing court found "exhaustively analyzed" costs, "immeasurable" benefits, and laudable goals, the path to final reasonableness did not begin or end with a cost-benefit criterion.[78]

So what sort of consideration *must* cost be when it arises in delegated risk regulation? In a secular world, costs are characteristically confined to those costs befalling *persons*, whether natural or legal. But which persons?[79] Championing or mandating cost-benefit analysis in risk regulation presupposes that *cost* is a coherent (economic) concept.[80] But is it? If projected costs can be avoided and not experienced, were they ever really "costs"? Economics has more trouble with that question than you might think. A projected cost is an odd thing. Costs are innately sensitive to temporal position, *i.e.*, past, present, future. For example, an earlier era of "reasonable" price regulation came to a close without ever really

---

responsibility to upwind states for downwind nonattainment of uniform national standards).

[76] A powerful exploration of the rifts exposed in utilitarianism by the "universalization" of acts and consequences is DAVID LYONS, FORMS AND LIMITS OF UTILITARIANISM (1965).

[77] *See* id. at 177–97. If the "others" whose cooperation is needed comprise discrete social groups or firms, formal rationality can become an even bigger obstacle. *See, e.g.*, THE FIRM AS A COLLABORATIVE COMMUNITY: RECONSTRUCTING TRUST IN THE KNOWLEDGE ECONOMY (Charles Heckscher & Paul S. Adler eds., 2006).

[78] *Nat'l Ass'n Mfrs.*, 748 F.3d at 369–70.

[79] A once prominent critique of fully secularized ethics cast it as no more than "emotivism" and argued that, notwithstanding the dominance of secular ethics since the Enlightenment, it is essentially incoherent. *See* ALASDAIR MACINTYRE, AFTER VIRTUE (2d ed. 1984). A more lasting critique of the project of "commonsense morality"—including utilitarian-welfarist ethics—is Derek Parfit's *Reasons and Persons* (1986). Skepticism of welfarist ethics since Parfit has often taken aim at how the relevant people to be protected are selected and identified. *See, e.g.*, KYSAR, supra note 68; JOHN BROOME, WEIGHING LIVES (2004).

[80] In their "textbook" of the subject, Mishan and Quah offer no introduction, preface, or glossary entry and, in a part devoted to "basic concepts," presume agreement on the tenets of welfare economics in explaining specific types of "cost." *See* E.J. MISHAN & EUSTON QUAH, COST-BENEFIT ANALYSIS (5th ed. 2007).

resolving whether the "costs" to be recouped through prices should be calculated on an average or on a marginal basis.[81] Marginal cost accounting ignores the past—because nothing can be done about it![82] From that experience to the present, regulation's costs have proven a protean field of concepts which has both expanded and contracted its place in risk regulation.[83] Indeed, as this monograph explores, economic cost as a consideration in regulation hides within it a series of seemingly intractable choices about what to measure, when, and how.

Finally, cost-benefit analysis—an increasingly professionalized economic decision procedure—is rarely legislated in terms. More often, legislation directs regulators simply to *consider* costs.[84] Thus, reviewing courts are most apt to hold that, given such legislative ambiguity, costs are to be estimated and evaluated by those who are delegated the authority.[85] And although our "commonsense" talk of right and wrong often defaults to a form of "factor balancing" in which foundational issues are bracketed and factors favoring or disfavoring a choice are "weighed" against other factors,[86] this says nothing necessarily about

---

[81] *See* ALFRED E. KAHN, THE ECONOMICS OF REGULATION: PRINCIPLES AND INSTITUTIONS 63–75 (2d ed. 1988).

[82] Confining cost accounting to only those costs that can be avoided is arguably the business firm's strategic imperative. *See* Robin Cooper & Robert S. Kaplan, *Measure Costs Right: Make the Right Decisions*, HARV. BUS. REV. 96 (Sept.–Oct. 1988).

[83] In their classic account Revesz and Livermore argue that, although cost-benefit analysis was, as then practiced, "biased against regulation," "those biases are not inherent to the methodology." RICHARD L. REVESZ & MICHAEL A. LIVERMORE, RETAKING RATIONALITY 10 (2008). Indeed, in their view for many kinds of regulation, "the use of cost-benefit analysis is a requirement of basic rationality." Id. at 12. In an earlier classic McGarity juxtaposed what he called "techno-bureaucratic rationality" with "comprehensive analytical rationality," with the latter tending toward the economist's professional ethos and the former toward the engineer's. *See* THOMAS O. MCGARITY, REINVENTING RATIONALITY: THE ROLE OF REGULATORY ANALYSIS IN THE FEDERAL BUREAUCRACY 4–16 (1991). Chapter 3 explores that division in detail.

[84] Each of the case studies in Chapters 4, 5 and 6 explore specific legislative mandates in context.

[85] *See, e.g.*, New York v. Reilly, 969 F.2d 1147, 1150 (D.C. Cir. 1992) (construing provision requiring that costs be taken into consideration and concluding that "[b]ecause Congress did not assign the specific weight [EPA] should accord each of these factors," it is up to the agency's sound discretion).

[86] *See, e.g.*, SHELLY KAGAN, NORMATIVE ETHICS 17–22 (1998) (dividing the understanding of normative, "commonsense" ethics into "factors" and "foundations").

what any particular legislative delegation must necessarily mean. Society may care about risk regulation's costs for different reasons.

1.2 THREE REASONS TO ESTIMATE AND TO EVALUATE COSTS

Cost's role in the pursuit of public welfare has been, in practice, the core concern.[87] Cost in this tradition is a quantity to be minimized if regulation's (net) benefits are to be maximized.[88] This kind of utilitarian or *teleological* criterion is endemic to orthodox economics[89] and, by extension, to contemporary cost-benefit analysis.[90] Its challenges stem from specifying the public's "goods," weighing disparate goods—especially goods as valued by different people at different times or places—and assessing the realized "opportunity costs" of acquiring one good instead of others.[91]

But cost also might indicate a kind of *imprecision* or uncertainty in an agent's focus or purpose, implicating different concerns. Even assuming a more or less utilitarian theory of legislation, the principal–agent dynamics in delegations involving risk can reveal critical insights into the public's good.[92] Cost in this light can be a surrogate for means–ends

---

[87] *See* ADLER & POSNER, supra note 62 at 9–24.

[88] *See, e.g.*, REVESZ & LIVERMORE, supra note 83 at 12–13; SUNSTEIN, supra note 1 at 19–22; MCGARITY, supra note 83 at 17–25; THEODORE M. PORTER, TRUST IN NUMBERS: THE PURSUIT OF OBJECTIVITY IN SCIENCE AND PUBLIC LIFE 148–89 (1995).

[89] *See, e.g.*, PAUL A. SAMUELSON & WILLIAM D. NORDHAUS, ECONOMICS (19th ed. 2009). "Social" cost in this tradition is whatever lost opportunities or charges taken result from public policy choices. *See, e.g.*, CHARLES D. KOLSTAD, ENVIRONMENTAL ECONOMICS 22 (2000) (asserting that total US expenditures on pollution abatement "are approximately 2% of gross domestic product (GDP)"). Properly "social" costs can be very difficult to identify in practice, though, as Chapters 2 and 3 explore in detail.

[90] *See, e.g.*, REVESZ & LIVERMORE, supra note 83 at 12–13; MISHAN & QUAH, supra note 80 at 10; ADLER & POSNER, supra note 62 at 1–8.

[91] *See* ELIZABETH ANDERSON, VALUE IN ETHICS AND ECONOMICS (1993); BROOME, supra note 24; J.A. Mirrlees, *The Economic Uses of Utilitarianism, in* UTILITARIANISM AND BEYOND 63 (Amartya Sen & Bernard Williams eds., 1982); WILLIAM J. BAUMOL & WALLACE E. OATES, THE THEORY OF ENVIRONMENTAL POLICY 14–32 (2d ed. 1988).

[92] Professor Boyd demonstrated this long-run process at work—perhaps unintentionally—in tracing the rise of risk-focused regulation in the US from fits and starts to an "administrative law of unreasonable risk." *See* William Boyd,

irrationality: In a world of uncertain and dynamic utilities and risks, we often use the information at hand as a rough guide to discerning our own *true* ends or purposes.[93] The matter can be immensely more complex when ends are to be given by an internally plural principal (not the agent) in punctuated expressions like legislation. Cost is still, in this regard, a tool for serving ends or purposes. But its real use is to keep the interactivity of means and ends tractable, evident, and current.

Finally, regulatory costs might be an altogether different sort of consideration: a decisional input which, though not itself directly relevant or representative, maintains a kind of back pressure in the decision domain. In this mediative role, costs can serve to buffer the inevitable frictions between efficiency and fairness. For example, the US Congress has often directed regulators to set "performance standards"[94] that require the best performance "feasible" or which is *achievable* by the affected (market) actors. In that context, cost-as-burden mixes considerations of fairness and efficiency, as Chapter 3 explains and two later case studies explore in detail.

Without knowing which of these roles costs are to play, though, decision makers will struggle with precisely how they are to be tabulated and evaluated.[95] Indeed, even where cost is but an ingredient of cost-benefit welfarism, its varied uses have often confounded decision makers.

Genealogies of Risk: Searching for Safety, 1930s–1970s, 39 ECOL. L.Q. 895 (2012). Another example worth considering is the European Union's pivot toward climate change and the impact that that had on the EU's overall risk governance principles. *See* Veerle Heyvaert, *Governing Climate Change: Towards a New Paradigm for Risk Regulation*, 74 MOD. L. REV. 817 (2011). Professor Heyvaert tracks the role of "fictional certainty" in contemporary EU risk regulation, id. at 821, and how climate change's twin problems of mitigation and adaptation undermined that, forcing an institutionally fragmented system to come back together in governing the different elements of climate risk as a disordered whole.

93 *See, e.g.*, SCHMIDTZ, supra note 57 at 58–66 (describing the kinds of ends that are adopted for the sake of acquiring settled ends). "Instrumental or static rationality involves seeking effective means to given ends. The essence of reflective rationality is that, although it involves means–end reasoning, it goes beyond instrumental rationality because it does not take ends as given." Id. at 70.

94 A "performance standard" specifies an outcome while leaving the measures to achieve that outcome open for the regulated party/ies to select. *See* Cary Coglianese, *The Limits of Performance-Based Regulation*, 50 U. MICH. J.L. REF. 525, 526–31 (2017).

95 Given the difficulties of weighing moral factors against one another, *see, e.g.*, Michael Philips, *Weighing Moral Reasons*, 96 MIND 367 (1987) (showing that moral weights differ by circumstances), if cost can be either a fairness or

The "feasibility analysis" OSHA named in *American Textile Mfrs.*[96] as an alternative to cost-benefit analysis is still debated for whether and how it actually *differs* from the simple comparison of costs to benefits.[97] OSHA has long maintained that its feasibility analysis is *not* cost-benefit analysis and reviewing courts have uniformly agreed.[98] Yet OSHA strives to monetize both costs *and* benefits all the same.[99] EPA monetizes costs and benefits in most of its "technology-based" standards, often refining the standard to maximize the difference.[100] More recent "breakeven" variants of cost-benefit analysis[101] presume that cost estimates can and should occupy some privileged position in regulatory decisions—that, in essence, only benefits' surpassing costs can warrant regulatory action.[102] Yet we have good reasons to doubt such monistic thinking in general[103] and such a strict cost/benefit criterion in particular.[104] Only where

---

efficiency consideration, how or even whether it aligns with other reasons for a proposed action may be deeply uncertain. Section 2.1.1 elaborates.

[96] *See* supra notes 9–18 and accompanying text.

[97] *See, e.g.*, Driesen, supra note 23; Amy Sinden *et al.*, *Cost-Benefit Analysis: New Foundations on Shifting Sand*, 3 REG. & GOVERNANCE 48 (2009); Matthew Adler & Eric A. Posner, *New Foundations of Cost-Benefit Analysis: A Reply to Professors Sinden, Kysar, and Driesen*, 3 REG. & GOVERNANCE 72 (2009); Jonathan S. Masur & Eric A. Posner, *Against Feasibility Analysis*, 77 U. CHI. L. REV. 657 (2010); David M. Driesen, *Two Cheers for Feasible Regulation: A Modest Response to Masur and Posner*, 35 HARV. ENVTL. L. REV. 313 (2011).

[98] *See, e.g.*, Public Citizen Health Research Group v. U.S. Dept. of Labor, 557 F.3d 165, 177 (3d Cir. 2009).

[99] *See Note—OSHA's Feasibility Policy: The Implications of the "Infeasibility" of Respirators*, 129 HARV. L. REV. 2235, 2237–42 (2016).

[100] See Chapters 4 and 5.

[101] *See, e.g.*, Daniel Farber, *Breaking Bad? The Uneasy Case for Regulatory Breakeven Analysis*, 102 CAL. L. REV. 1469 (2014).

[102] "[B]reakeven analysis is a kind of conditional cost-benefit analysis that asks, 'How high would the benefits have to be for the regulation to be justified?'." Farber, id. at 1470.

[103] *See* ANDERSON, supra note 91 (articulating and defending a pluralistic theory of value in ethics and economics).

[104] Whether lost opportunities or charges incurred are a "cost" or a "benefit" will often come down to point of view and, supposing they involve individuals of varied points of view, may raise the prospect of reciprocal yet asymmetric benefits/costs. *See, e.g.*, Cass R. Sunstein, *Incommensurability and Kinds of Valuation: Some Applications in Law, in* INCOMMENSURABILITY, INCOMPARABILITY, AND PRACTICAL REASON 234 (Ruth Chang ed., 1997) (arguing that different agents often value the same things in incommensurable ways, preventing comparisons of their gains and losses).

benefits are as easy to estimate or as determinate as costs can such methods even purport to be analytical, *i.e.*, substantively impartial, tools.[105]

In sum, costs—or, more precisely, our collective sense of cost as a decisional factor in risk regulation—has done without foundations. Cost considerations have been a collection of notions bearing family resemblances but lacking any fixed or immutable foundations. This may explain their longevity and vitality, but it should alert us to their penchant to morph subtly, even undetectably, into very different influences. Section 1.3 sketches the principal role of judicial review in that experience.

1.3 AN INSTITUTIONAL DIMENSION: JUDICIAL REVIEW OF COST AS A CONSIDERATION

Especially in an American context, the weighing of costs in regulation cannot be backed out of the totality of experience for study without first understanding judicial review's place as such. By some accounts judicial review or the prospect thereof saturates the average regulatory decision in America, coloring its timing, procedural form, and content.[106] And, to be sure, the review of factored determinations and factor-constrained policymaking more generally is the subject of a vast professional literature. But this literature does not as a whole show any set of linear or causal relationships. Indeed if anything it underscores the turbulence and unpredictability in judicial review—how courts and agencies interpret statutes differently, how they each handle proof problems, and the wide variety of impacts these forces exert on administration.[107] In the relatively rare instances where court/agency interactions become serious

105 *See* Finkel, supra note 20 at 106–11; David M. Driesen, *Cost-Benefit Analysis and the Precautionary Principle: Can They be Reconciled?*, 2013 MICH. ST. L. REV. 771, 807–11.

106 *See, e.g.*, Elizabeth Magill & Adrian Vermeule, *Allocating Power Within Agencies*, 120 YALE L.J. 1032 (2011); Louis J. Virelli III, *Deconstructing Arbitrary and Capricious Review*, 92 N. CAR. L. REV. 721 (2014).

107 Gersen and Vermeule's empirical study of arbitrariness reviews in the US Supreme Court found that the vast majority of cases are decided in the agency's favor and that, as a result, agencies are only required to make decisions on the basis of reasons—not on the basis of objectively good reasons. *See* Gersen & Vermeule, supra note 57 at 1358. But that contrasts with a much less lopsided advantage for the agency in the courts of appeal which Miles and Sunstein found in 2008. *See* Thomas Miles & Cass R. Sunstein, *The Real World of Arbitrariness Review*, 75 U. CHI. L. REV. 761 (2008). They also found that "[w]hen agency

inter-branch conflicts,[108] it is often judicial opinions that "assur[e] compliance below while avoiding accountability above."[109] That is, discerning the real grounds of such a decision can be challenging to say the least.[110] It is one thing to note that all agency choices, when challenged in a timely fashion by affected parties with standing to bring a lawsuit, must be grounded in *reasons*—no matter the precise standard of review.[111] It is something else again to explain the requisite grounds, force, or normativity of those reasons within and across specific agency contexts.[112] And yet agency "reasonableness" is the limit in estimations and evaluations of costs which we will encounter over and over in this

---

decisions are liberal, Democratic appointees are significantly more likely to vote to uphold them than when they are conservative. By contrast, Republican appointees are significantly more likely to uphold conservative agency decisions." Id. at 813. And, of course, arbitrariness review is just one among several different forms of review.

108 As Professor Vermeule has argued repeatedly and at length, courts and agencies rarely come into conflict—relative to their baseline activities—and rarer still is the court order that constrains an agency more than minimally. *See* VERMEULE, supra note 37; ADRIAN VERMEULE, THE SYSTEM OF THE CONSTITUTION (2011); ADRIAN VERMEULE, JUDGING UNDER UNCERTAINTY: AN INSTITUTIONAL THEORY OF LEGAL INTERPRETATION 118–48 (2006).

109 Antonin Scalia, *Vermont Yankee: The APA, the D.C. Circuit, and the Supreme Court*, 1978 SUP. CT. REV. 345, 372. Then-Professor Scalia was referring to a lower court's efforts to guide agencies without being corrected by a higher court.

110 *See* id. at 372–75. "It is surely ironic that our judicial system has managed to develop a system of review for definitive administrative statements of intent, but not for functionally similar pronouncements by the courts themselves." Id. at 374.

111 *See, e.g.*, David Zaring, *Reasonable Agencies*, 96 VA. L. REV. 135 (2010) (arguing that the Court's many different standard of review doctrines have converged to a kind of "reasonableness" review).

112 *Cf.* Peter L. Strauss, *"Deference" is too Confusing—Let's Call Them* "Chevron *Space" and* "Skidmore *Weight,"* 112 COLUM. L. REV. 1143, 1145 (2012) (arguing that deference, like discretion, is a highly variable, if not empty, concept and that what courts are doing in hearing agency statutory interpretations breaks out into two very different kinds of judicial oversight). "Th[e] 'reasoned decision-making' requirement pervades administrative law. The simplicity of the phrase itself, however, misleadingly masks the nuances of its application. It is used to describe judicial review that ranges in intensity from searching hard look to lenient super deference." Emily Hammond Meazell, *Super Deference, the Science Obsession, and Judicial Review as Translation of Agency Science*, 109 MICH. L. REV. 733, 741 (2011) (internal citations omitted).

study. Sketching some better contours of this "reasonableness" constraint, thus, is part of this study's burden.

In truth, the US Supreme Court has had an unfortunate tendency to conflate distinct questions when describing or applying its various "standards" of review. Costs in regulation are at least an issue of (1) policymaking judgment, (2) statutory interpretation, and (3) factual proof gathered as such. They may raise other issues, but regulatory costs entail at least these three. Organized by statute to review distinct issues of discretion, law, and fact as they arise in "formal" or "informal" agency adjudications or rulemakings,[113] US federal courts are supposed to resist the temptation to fashion new agency obligations, whether of a procedural or substantive character.[114] Record requirements for formal proceedings, for example, should not be imposed upon informal proceedings and review standards appropriate to issues of fact are not to be applied to exercises of discretion.[115] Still, fuzzy boundaries remain the norm.[116]

---

[113] A "formal" adjudication or rulemaking is conducted "on the record" such that all relevant testimony, exhibits, and other information on which the agency relies is gathered into and recorded in a complete catalogue. "Informal" proceedings have a less structured record and can include "off the record" sources, albeit at the peril of undermining whatever factual support the rule may need upon challenge. *See* William F. Pedersen, *Formal Records and Informal Rulemaking*, 85 YALE L.J. 38 (1975); Sierra Club v. Costle, 657 F.2d 298, 400–410 (D.C. Cir. 1981).

[114] *See* Perez v. Mortgage Bankers' Ass'n, 135 S. Ct. 1199 (2015); Allentown Mack Sales & Serv., Inc. v. NLRB, 522 U.S. 359, 366–67 (1998); Vermont Yankee Nuclear Power Corp. v. Natural Resources Defense Council, Inc., 435 U.S. 519, 546–49 (1978); United States v. Allegheny-Ludlum Steel, 406 U.S. 742, 756–57 (1972); Citizens to Preserve Overton Park v. Volpe, 401 U.S. 402 (1971); SEC v. Chenery, 332 U.S. 194, 202–07 (1947).

[115] *See generally* A GUIDE TO JUDICIAL AND POLITICAL REVIEW OF FEDERAL AGENCIES (John F. Duffy & Michael Herz eds., 2005). The Supreme Court's unfortunate tendency mentioned may stem from its origins in and habits of employing common law methods. *See* John F. Duffy, *Administrative Common Law in Judicial Review*, 77 TEX. L. REV. 113 (1999). Whatever the causes, the Court has superintended a long, consistent march toward the "administrative state" so fitfully demonized in American politics today. *See* JERRY L. MASHAW, CREATING THE ADMINISTRATIVE CONSTITUTION (2012).

[116] "It is not infrequent that the available data do not settle a regulatory issue, and the agency must then exercise its judgment in moving from the facts and probabilities on the record to a policy conclusion. Recognizing that policymaking in a complex society must account for uncertainty, however, does not imply that it is sufficient for an agency merely to recite 'substantial uncertainty' as a justification for its actions." Motor Vehicle Mfrs. Ass'n v. State Farm Mut. Ins. Co., 463 U.S. 29, 52 (1983).

For decades the consensus has been that review for administrative "arbitrariness" extends at least (and perhaps at most) to whether the agency's decision was based on the relevant factors, to whether a "clear error of judgment" occurred, and to whether the "reasoned basis" for the action could fairly be discerned from the administrative record required by law.[117] For almost as long, the Supreme Court has maintained that an agency delegated authority by statute is entitled to real judicial deference in interpreting that statute.[118] But because all of that is predicated upon, and mostly constituted by *legislation*, the normal vagueness of ordinary language and the untidy decision-making processes of Congress are all that separate an agency's jurisdiction to regulate from what is beyond its reach.[119] In other words, law constraining when and how costs must or must not be weighed by an agency can often only be differentiated from the *discretion* vested in that same agency by a knife's edge.[120]

When EPA's authority to set national ambient air quality standards (NAAQS) without considering the costs thereof was challenged, the Supreme Court was inundated with "hundreds of pages of briefing … submitted on the issue,"[121] much to the effect that if EPA *could* take that initiative itself, the Clean Air Act (CAA) should be held unconstitutional.[122] In rejecting the challenge, the Court unanimously held that CAA § 109(b)'s failure even to mention costs in directing EPA to establish NAAQS led to a "natural," "textual" inference that costs should be excluded therefrom.[123] What keeps this episode so timely today is the path the Court took to reading CAA § 109(b) to bar cost considerations. The statute erected no *explicit* barrier to factoring cost into the stringency

---

[117] *See, e.g.*, Bowman Transp., Inc. v. Arkansas-Best Freight Sys., Inc., 419 U.S. 281, 284–86 (1974); *State Farm*, 463 U.S. at 43.

[118] *See* Chevron U.S.A. v. Natural Resources Defense Council, Inc., 467 U.S. 837 (1984).

[119] *See, e.g.*, Mayo Found. for Med. Educ. & Research v. United States, 562 U.S. 44, 48–58 (2011); City of Arlington v. FCC, 133 S. Ct. 1863, 1867–774 (2013).

[120] *Cf.* Stephen Breyer, *Judicial Review of Questions of Law and Policy*, 38 ADMIN. L. REV. 363, 379 (1986) ("It is difficult, after having examined a legal question in depth with the object of deciding it correctly, to believe both that the agency's interpretation is legally wrong, *and* that its interpretation is reasonable.").

[121] Whitman v. American Trucking Ass'ns., 531 U.S. 457, 465 (2001).

[122] *See Whitman*, 531 U.S. at 465–67. The principal authority to this effect was the fractured coalition for remanding the rulemaking to OSHA in the *Benzene* case. *See* Section 1.1 supra.

[123] *See Whitman*, 531 U.S. at 469–71.

of its NAAQS. It simply made no mention of cost while at the same time requiring that the NAAQS be "based on"[124] a factual document setting out "air quality criteria" which "accurately reflect the latest scientific knowledge useful in indicating the kind and extent of all identifiable effects on public health or welfare."[125] Equally suggestive was CAA § 108, which separately requires EPA to communicate techniques and costs of pollution abatement to the states that are charged with attaining the NAAQS.[126] In *Whitman*, those suggestions were sufficient to bar costs from consideration. An earlier lower court precedent, *Lead Industries Ass'n v. EPA*,[127] reached the same conclusion by a similar path.[128] The Court in *Whitman* adopted *Lead Industries*' interpretation and most of its approach.[129] Indeed, it went further, stating that "to prevail in their present challenge, respondents must show a textual commitment of authority to the EPA to consider costs in setting NAAQS under § 109(b)(1)."[130]

Notably, though, the Court's *Chevron* holding that *reasonable* agency interpretations of ambiguous delegations ordinarily should govern[131]—decisive in another aspect of the *Whitman* case[132]—played no role on the factoring of costs. Now this may do little more than confirm that calling something a "factor" is but a placeholder until the number and ranking of *all* relevant factors is settled.[133] But the very reasoning in *Massachusetts v. EPA*[134] touting the CAA's structured decision making and how

---

[124] 42 U.S.C. § 7409(b)(1).

[125] 42 U.S.C. § 7408(a)(2).

[126] *See* 42 U.S.C. § 7408(b)(1).

[127] 647 F.2d 1130 (D.C. Cir. 1980).

[128] *See Lead Industries*, 647 F.2d at 1148–62.

[129] *See Whitman*, 531 U.S. at 464–71. Justice Scalia paid no attention to the CAA's legislative history.

[130] *Whitman*, 531 U.S. at 468.

[131] Chevron, U.S.A., Inc. v. Natural Resources Defense Council, Inc., 467 U.S. 837 (1984).

[132] *See Whitman*, 531 U.S. at 481–83 (setting aside as unreasonable EPA's interpretation of Clean Air Act nonattainment provisions under *Chevron* step two).

[133] For example, in *Judulang v. Holder*, 132 S. Ct. 476 (2011), the Court rejected a long-standing agency policy toward deportable aliens by belittling the weight of the one valid reason for the policy the agency could give: the policy saved it time and money. *Cf. Judulang*, 132 S. Ct. at 489–90 ("Cost is an important factor for agencies to consider in many contexts. But cheapness alone cannot save an arbitrary agency policy").

[134] 549 U.S. 497 (2007).

considerations expressly named in the statute generally work to exclude other factors by omission[135] most assuredly characterized the *Whitman* opinion.[136]

Contrast that with *Entergy Corp. v. Riverkeeper*.[137] There the Court confronted a mandate in the Clean Water Act (CWA) authorizing EPA to set performance standards requiring "that the location, design, construction, and capacity of cooling water intake structures reflect the best technology available for minimizing adverse environmental impact."[138] EPA had determined that this mandate permitted it to prepare and use a cost-benefit analysis in setting the standards.[139] The courts had to decide if that was a *permissible* or "reasonable" construction of the CWA. As then-judge Sotomayor concluded in an opinion for the Second Circuit Court of Appeals, it was not—or at least EPA's record did not show through evidence or explanation that it had factored costs rationally into its decision.[140]

An oddity of that CWA mandate was a jurisdictional cross-reference to other CWA sections which *did* expressly name and situate cost as a decision factor.[141] In the Supreme Court, the cross-reference and the CWA's failure to specify exactly *how* costs should factor into the standards were decisive in overruling the Second Circuit. It seemed to

---

135 *See Massachusetts*, 549 U.S. at 532–35; Richard J. Pierce, Jr., *What Factors Can an Agency Consider in Making a Decision?*, 2009 MICH. ST. L. REV. 67, 77–79 (2009) (noting *Massachusetts*' peculiar regard for the CAA's unique alignment of decisional factors).

136 *Massachusetts* was, in this connection, reminiscent of Union Electric Co. v. EPA, 427 U.S. 246 (1976). *Union Electric* held that the CAA § 110(a)(2) mandate to EPA that it approve measures in state implementation plans "as may be necessary" to attain applicable NAAQS vested no authority in EPA to reject a plan for being "economically or technologically infeasible." Id. at 256–69.

137 556 U.S. 208 (2009).

138 33 U.S.C. § 1326(b).

139 *See* U.S. EPA, National Pollutant Discharge Elimination System—Final Regulations to Establishment Requirements for Cooling Water Intake Structures at Phase II Existing Facilities, 69 Fed. Reg. 41576, 41650–664 (2004).

140 *See* Riverkeeper, Inc. v. EPA, 475 F.3d 83, 97–105 (2d Cir. 2007). "[O]n the record before us, it is impossible to tell whether the EPA based its decision on [what it deemed] permissible cost-effectiveness analysis or exceeded its authority by relying impermissibly upon a cost-benefit analysis." Id. at 104.

141 *See* 33 U.S.C. § 1326(b) ("Any standard established pursuant to [CWA §§ 301 or 306] applicable to a point source shall require … ."); *cf.* Riverkeeper, Inc. v. EPA, 358 F.3d 174, 186 (2d Cir. 2004) ("That cross-reference is an invitation to look to section 306 for guidance in discerning what factors Congress intended the EPA to consider in determining the 'best technology available.'").

the Supreme Court majority that "the phrase 'best technology available,' even with the added specification 'for minimizing adverse environmental impact,'" did not "unambiguously preclude cost-benefit analysis."[142] And yet, like his opinion in *Whitman*, Justice Scalia's majority opinion in *Entergy* essentially ignored *Chevron*. The *Entergy* majority focused on the merest text of the provision: the plausible and necessary inferences from its syntax. In a concurrence Justice Breyer took pains to apply the *Chevron* framework and demonstrate various contextual ambiguities and the consequent delegation to EPA in filling out the analysis of "best technology available."[143] And for Justices Stevens, Souter, and Ginsburg in dissent, EPA's cost-benefit analysis was just wrong for CWA § 316(b) because of how "narrow," "skewed," and ultimately inconsistent with the legislation's purposes that analysis had been.[144]

Together, *Whitman* and *Entergy* combined dashed whatever hopes persisted for some simple default rules in the weighing of regulation's costs—including the presumption that complex risk regulation statutes that delegate vest the real discretion in the agency.[145] The Supreme Court has repeatedly showed itself to be deeply divided over whether, why, and how cost shall be factored into regulation and has offered nothing like a simple, general primer for interpreting the Statutes at Large.

There are few assurances to be found in the late personnel changes on the Court. What can be said with confidence is that the Court's arbitrariness review doctrines are and will remain a favored means of challenging agencies' choice of decisional inputs, the investigation and documentation of any relevant quantities involved, *and* of challenging the legal significance of individuated factors like cost in risk regulation.[146] The Court's precedents operationalize challenges both to the means/ends rationality and to the policymaking discretion inherent in deciding what form and quantity of evidence can justify risk regulation in the face of

---

142 *Entergy*, 556 U.S. at 219–26 (emphasis added).

143 *See* id. at 231–36 (Breyer, J., concurring in part and dissenting in part).

144 *See* id. at 238–40 (Stevens, J., joined by Souter & Ginsburg, JJ., dissenting). EPA encountered great difficulties monetizing the rule's benefits and was quite credibly skewered for having grossly exaggerated its costs. *See* Doug Kysar, *Fish Tales, in* Reforming Regulatory Impact Analysis 190, 192 (Winston Harrington *et al.* eds., 2009).

145 *See, e.g.*, Sunstein, supra note 1 at 191–216.

146 The case studies of Chapters 4, 5, and 6 explore this institutional dimension of weighing costs at length. The US Supreme Court has steadily signaled at least these three distinct aspects of review to the lower federal courts. *See* Farber, supra note 101 at 91–111.

any inefficiencies, uncertainties, costs of compliance, *etc.*[147] Indeed, reviewing courts rarely need to separate those various elements out in their analysis given the wide ambit contemporary legal systems afford to rooting out official "arbitrariness" of all kinds. The aggregate result defies synthesis given the fact specificity of each case and context. It may be accurate to say that the Supreme Court itself has conducted these reviews in largely deferential tones.[148] But that past does precious little to predict the future, especially as lower federal courts are now constantly invited to scrutinize regulatory cost estimations and evaluations.

[147] *See* Citizens to Preserve Overton Park v. Volpe, 401 U.S. 402, 408–20 (1971); Bowman Transp., Inc. v. Arkansas-Best Freight Sys., Inc., 419 U.S. 281, 289–94 (1974); Baltimore Gas & Elec. Co. v. Natural Resources Defense Council, 462 U.S. 87, 97–105 (1983); Motor Vehicle Mfrs. Ass'n v. State Farm Mut. Auto. Ins. Co., 463 U.S. 29, 41–57 (1983); FCC v. Fox Television Stations, Inc., 129 S. Ct. 1800, 1822–24 (2009) (Kennedy, J., concurring in part); Judulang v. Holder, 132 S. Ct. 476, 487–90 (2011).

[148] *See generally* Gersen & Vermeule, supra note 57.

2. The ambiguities of social cost accounting

Legislation delegating authority to regulate risk has etched a recurring pattern for the past five or so decades. Especially in the US, but increasingly in Europe too, the pattern includes (1) the targeting of some discrete, salient threat to the public; (2) charging a (relatively) permanent governmental agent with the reduction or confinement of the threat(s); and (3) demanding that any resultant regulatory "costs" thereof be minimized to some (usually nebulous) degree.[1] This chapter describes these contours in more detail with the help of prominent examples as a first step to understanding the relevance of regulatory costs.

2.1 SOCIAL COST IN THE LEGAL LEXICON

From its inception, welfare economics struggled with comparing values between persons.[2] If two people value some good differently, transferring

[1] Noted accounts of this pattern include DAVID VOGEL, THE POLITICS OF PRECAUTION (2012) (advancing and testing a variety of explanatory factors accounting for "policy divergences" in the EU and US over several commonly salient risk areas); Timur Kuran & Cass R. Sunstein, *Availability Cascades and Risk Regulation*, 51 STAN. L. REV. 683 (1999); CARNEGIE COMM'N ON SCIENCE, TECH. & GOVERNMENT, RISK AND THE ENVIRONMENT: IMPROVING REGULATORY DECISION-MAKING (1993); STEPHEN BREYER, BREAKING THE VICIOUS CIRCLE: TOWARD EFFECTIVE RISK REGULATION (1993) (denouncing the disproportionate attention that especially salient risks garner and advocating more attention to regulatory costs); ULRICH BECK, RISK SOCIETY: TOWARDS A NEW MODERNITY (Mark Ritter trans., 1992) (observing increasingly corporatist tendencies in the study and governance of risks inherent in a modern society); and BRUCE A. ACKERMAN & WILLIAM T. HASSLER, CLEAN COAL—DIRTY AIR (1981).

[2] *See* KENNETH J. ARROW, SOCIAL CHOICE AND INDIVIDUAL VALUES 9–21 (2d ed. 1963); I.M.D. LITTLE, A CRITIQUE OF WELFARE ECONOMICS 51–66 (2d ed. 1957); LIONEL ROBBINS, AN ESSAY ON THE NATURE AND SIGNIFICANCE OF ECONOMIC SCIENCE 132–34 (2d ed. 1935). Arrow's famed "impossibility theorem" assumed individual preferences were *complete orderings* on its way to proving that no acceptably "democratic" procedure exists for aggregating these

it to the higher valuer can create more "welfare" out of thin air without *producing* anything. Inhibiting or voiding these transfers can seem like a lost opportunity—or a *cost*.[3] Of course, for anything not priced by markets—so-called "externalities" or "public" goods supplied by society to all for free—transfers of the sort necessitate their own "fundamental theorem(s)" of optimizing.[4] And with the proliferation of such "second-best" theorems comes the prospect that (suboptimal) reality will block any such optimization.[5] Finally, pains and lost opportunities fully offset by gains elsewhere might count as no (net) cost at all. So was the path

---

orderings into a social preference ordering. *See* id. at 17–18. That turned out to be a most contentious assumption.

[3] Assuming losses do not outnumber gains, Pareto (among others) had argued that transfers like this should continue to some "optimum." Identifying and quantifying losses and gains to the ends of such preference optimization then became the problem to which welfare economists turned. *See* George J. Stigler, *The Development of Utility Theory*, 33 J. POL. ECON. 369 (1950); ARROW, supra note 2 at 22–25. For them, prices overtook metaphysics as the field of study. *See* GEORGE J. STIGLER, THE THEORY OF PRICE 46–83 (3d ed. 1966). The troubles with that sort of "optimizing" have always been apparent in worlds with skewed distributions of wealth. *See* LITTLE, supra note 2 at 84–116; J. DE V. GRAAF, THEORETICAL WELFARE ECONOMICS 75–92 (1971). Whether social welfare is best pursued by overall optimizing ("efficiency") in a competitive equilibrium or by maximizing total growth, though, was a question long ago shunted aside by welfarist orthodoxy. *See* HLA MYINT, THEORIES OF WELFARE ECONOMICS 1–14 (1948).

[4] *See* Mark Blaug, *The Fundamental Theorems of Modern Welfare Economics, Historically Contemplated*, 39(2) HIST. POL. ECON. 185, 192–97 (2007); William J. Baumol & Charles J. Wilson, *Introduction, in* I WELFARE ECONOMICS xv (William J. Baumol & Charles J. Wilson eds., 2001).

[5] This "second-best" enjoys no general presumption that its optima are better than third-best optima, *etc.* To make such welfare comparisons requires context-specific knowledge. *See* Robert G. Lipsey & Kelvin Lancaster, *The General Theory of Second Best*, 24(1) REV. OF ECON. STUDS. 11 (1956); LITTLE, supra note 2 at 258–73; JAN DE V. GRAAF, THEORETICAL WELFARE ECONOMICS 55–70 (1957). A fundamental theorem of welfare economics is that, in the absence of externalities and public goods, any competitive equilibrium must be "Pareto optimal." A second theorem, arguably circular in its implications, is that redistributive transfers can correct for the market failures of the first theorem's exceptions. Baumol & Wilson, supra note 4 at xxxi. The circularity is perhaps indicative of welfarism's deeper failings. *Cf.* Lipsey & Lancaster, supra at 31 (arguing that economic systems' successive levels of optimization may require the impossible for Pareto optimality to hold).

from Pareto to Kaldor-Hicks.[6] If the focus remains on actualized experience, however, lost opportunities are always personal. (Any opportunity is what you make of it!) And the social is never personal. So prescriptions for minimizing "social" costs long foundered in paradoxes of personhood or of redistribution and the unreality of conditions needed to assure that markets will function as advertised.[7]

The stock evasions of these troubles[8] eventually grew untenable as expanded provision of public goods,[9] increasing turbulence in the economy,[10] and the collapse of the Keynesian macroeconomic consensus[11]

---

[6] *See* Blaug, supra note 4 at 192–95; DE V. GRAAF, supra note 5 at 7–27; LITTLE, supra note 2 at 84–116.

[7] *See* Frank H. Knight, *Some Fallacies in the Interpretation of Social Cost,* 38(4) Q. J. ECON. 582 (1924); Nancy Ruggles, *The Welfare Basis of the Marginal Cost Pricing Principle,* 17(1) REV. ECON. STUDS. 29 (1949); Nancy Ruggles, *Recent Developments in the Theory of Marginal Cost Pricing,* 17(2) REV. ECON. STUDS. 107 (1949); LITTLE, supra note 2 at 274–79; AMARTYA K. SEN, COLLECTIVE CHOICE AND SOCIAL WELFARE (1970); J.A. Mirrlees, *An Exploration in the Theory of Optimum Income Taxation,* 38(2) REV. ECON. STUDS. 175 (1971). A culmination came in Coase's *The Problem of Social Cost,* a paper not only confined to a fictional world without "transaction costs," but which advanced what amounted to a tautology within that world. *See* Donald H. Regan, *The Problem of Social Cost Revisited,* 15(2) J. LAW & ECON. 427 (1972).

[8] *Cf.* MARK BLAUG, ECONOMIC THEORY IN RETROSPECT 573 (5th ed. 1997) (*discussing* orthodoxy among "old" welfare economists avoiding talk of interpersonal comparisons of welfare and other challenges to its integrity); MYINT, supra note 3 at xiii (denying any part of "welfare economics" involves interpersonal comparisons which were regarded as unscientific and more about "value judgments").

[9] Public goods' production and consumption—ignored in Pigou's opus *The Economics of Welfare*—entail a divergence between private and social costs that cannot be bridged (except perhaps at the ballot box). *See* ARROW, supra note 2 at 38–45. For this and other reasons, as "national income" became "gross national product" and then "gross domestic product" in the system of national accounts, aggregating private costs grew less indicative of "social welfare." *See* Abram Bergson, *National Income and Welfare, in* ESSAYS IN NORMATIVE ECONOMICS 131–56 (1966). That coincided roughly with the shift in focus from welfare to growth.

[10] On the turn toward government management of "the economy" through the tools of national accounting, *see* DIANE COYLE, GDP: A BRIEF BUT AFFECTIONATE HISTORY 11–57 (2014).

[11] *See* BLAUG, supra note 8 at 641–88; COYLE, supra note 10 at 63–66; *see also* J.R. Hicks, *The Scope and Status of Welfare Economics,* 27(3) OXFORD ECON. PAPERS 307, 311–21 (1975).

put all economic reasoning under a microscope.[12] But in that breach economics turned its focus to *production* and what could be done to improve all standards of living through economic expansion, *i.e.*, growth and development. As the post-war boom continued fashioning what Lizabeth Cohen dubbed the "consumers' republic," with corporate, labor, and government interests all collaborating to segment consumption markets under the banner of prosperity, a conspiracy of surpluses saved economists from having to answer the toughest questions about welfare and welfarism.[13] So identifying properly *social* costs—costs in the aggregate—remained as much a philosophical and ethical matter as an economic one.

With increased attention to metrics like gross domestic product (GDP) and nationwide unemployment, the "science" of "human behavior as a relationship between ends and scarce means which have alternative uses"[14] focused on stimulating and fulfilling demand, leaving behind the definitional wars over welfare.[15] Welfare economics, in short, was overcome by *growth* economics and its own failure to offer much *economic* guidance to those aiming to improve social welfare.

By the late 1960s and early 1970s, however, the legal system—particularly tort and contract remedies—had plunged into the methodological quagmire of welfare economics all the same.[16] If a tortfeasor's

---

[12] *See, e.g.*, Amartya K. Sen, *Social Choice Theory: A Re-Examination*, 45(1) ECONOMETRICA 53 (1977); Amartya K. Sen, *Personal Utilities and Public Judgments: Or What's Wrong with Welfare Economics*, 89(355) ECON. J. 537 (1979).

[13] *See* LIZABETH COHEN, A CONSUMERS' REPUBLIC: THE POLITICS OF MASS CONSUMPTION IN POSTWAR AMERICA (2002).

[14] LIONEL ROBBINS, AN ESSAY ON THE NATURE AND SIGNIFICANCE OF ECONOMIC SCIENCE 15 (1932). *See* Roger E. Backhouse & Steve G. Medema, *Defining Economics: The Long Road to Acceptance of the Robbins Definition*, 76 ECONOMICA 805, 813–15 (2009).

[15] *See* H. Spencer Banzhaf, *Quantifying the Qualitative: Quality-Adjusted Price Indexes in the United States, 1915–61*, 33 HIST. POL. ECON. 345 (2001). On the growth of "growth" economics in the US, *see* ROBERT J. GORDON, THE RISE AND FALL OF AMERICAN GROWTH: THE U.S. STANDARD OF LIVING SINCE THE CIVIL WAR 319–28 (2016) (observing a shift in US economic growth theory toward a focus on "evolutionary" changes measured by aggregate statistics like GDP and inflation). On the original split of growth from welfare economics, *see* John R. Hicks, *The Valuation of Social Income*, 7 ECONOMICA 105 (1940).

[16] Scholarly attention to tort law's distributive and efficiency effects, *see, e.g.*, GUIDO CALABRESI, THE COSTS OF ACCIDENTS: A LEGAL AND ECONOMIC ANALYSIS (1970); RICHARD A. POSNER, ECONOMIC ANALYSIS OF LAW (1972), and several judicial experiments with the availability and scope of equitable remedies, *see, e.g.*, Spur Industries, Inc. v. Del E. Webb Dev. Co., 494 P.2d 700

"production" (whatever it was[17]) was creating (monetized) value by employing people, fulfilling consumption demands, and turning a profit, the good of halting it to right some other wrong being done by that production had to at least offset the bad of forgoing those (measurable) benefits.[18] This sounded as much utilitarian as welfarist.[19] A resurgent preference for damage remedies over injunctive relief was justified in

---

(Ariz. 1972); Boomer v. Atlantic Cement 257 N.E.2d 870 (N.Y. 1970), had by then highlighted a societal interest in denying ostensibly "costly" tort relief.

[17] The so-called "production boundary," a staple of growth economics, has gone through several transformations in the history of the field. *See* Itsuo Sakuma, *The Production Boundary Reconsidered*, 59(3) REV. INCOME & WEALTH 556 (2013). Roughly, it differentiates the production of value from simple transfers (or "rents"). From beginnings in Smith, Ricardo and other classical economists, though, this "boundary" became highly problematic, not least in its confusing profit for productivity. *See* Sections 2.1.1 and 3.2.

[18] *See, e.g.*, Guido Calabresi, *Transaction Costs, Resource Allocation and Liability Rules—A Comment*, 11 J. LAW & ECON. 67 (1968); Anthony T. Kronman, *Specific Performance*, 45 U. CHI. L. REV. 351 (1978). This thinking was pervasive, if also latent, in the post-war-era legal curricula of top US law schools. *See* William N. Eskridge, Jr. & Philip P. Frickey, *An Historical and Critical Introduction to* The Legal Process, *in* HENRY M. HART, JR. & ALBERT M. SACKS, THE LEGAL PROCESS: BASIC PROBLEMS IN THE MAKING AND APPLICATION OF LAW li (William N. Eskridge, Jr. & Philip P. Frickey eds., 1994). A wave of work in the 1960s and early 1970s combined economic with utilitarian reasoning. *See, e.g.*, P.S. ATIYAH, ACCIDENTS, COMPENSATION AND THE LAW (1970); James E. Krier, *The Pollution Problem and Legal Institutions: A Conceptual Overview*, 18 U.C.L.A. L. REV. 429 (1971); George P. Fletcher, *Fairness and Utility in Tort Theory*, 85 HARV. L. REV. 537 (1972); GUIDO CALABRESI & PHILIP BOBBITT, TRAGIC CHOICES 31–50 (1978); NEIL K. KOMESAR, IMPERFECT ALTERNATIVES: CHOOSING INSTITUTIONS IN LAW, ECONOMICS, AND PUBLIC POLICY (1994). In retrospect, that *ad hoc* mixing of decision factors stands out. *See* Douglas Laycock, *The Neglected Defense of Undue Hardship (and the Doctrinal Train Wreck in* Boomer v. Atlantic Cement), 4(3) J. TORT L. (2012).

[19] *Compare* Duncan Kennedy, *Cost-Benefit Analysis of Entitlement Problems: A Critique*, 33 STAN. L. REV. 387 (1981) (arguing that the cost-benefit analysis of utilitarian and welfarist origins is incoherent and incapable of generating determinate legal rules or standards), *with* LITTLE, supra note 2 at 6–14 (critiquing Pigou's *The Economics of Welfare* and calling it "utilitarian economics" while questioning its coherence). Of course, quite problematically, Pigou had calculated social costs by summing all direct and indirect private costs in market prices, a method that amounts to a merely "partial" analysis: "[w]here the divergences between private and social costs are pervasive throughout the economy," BLAUG, supra note 8 at 582, market prices are actually *no* measure of satisfactions (or "utility").

precisely these terms.[20] And risk regulation eventually followed suit,[21] amenable as it has been to "economic analysis" of its configurable aspects.[22] The obscured concept of "social cost" tucked within was portrayed alternatively as both economic function and ethical duty, with the methodological troubles that had for so long stymied welfare economists politely ignored.[23]

Of course, this amalgamation quietly obscured the prospect that the production in question could be *both* good for the transacting parties and bad for their society's wealth and welfare.[24] For what remained missing

---

[20] *See, e.g.*, Doug Rendleman, *The Inadequate Remedy at Law Prerequisite for an Injunction*, 33 U. FLA. L. REV. 346 (1981).

[21] *See, e.g.*, STEPHEN BREYER, REGULATION AND ITS REFORM (1982); W. KIP VISCUSI, RISK BY CHOICE: REGULATING HEALTH AND SAFETY IN THE WORKPLACE (1983).

[22] *See, e.g.*, YORAM BARZEL, ECONOMIC ANALYSIS OF PROPERTY RIGHTS 86–89 (1989) (*discussing* a "Hobbesian" delineation of legal rights that enhances pre-existing economic rights).

[23] *See, e.g.*, POSNER, supra note 16 at 3 ("Cost to the economist is 'opportunity cost'—the benefit forgone by employing a resource in a way that denies its use to someone else"); CALABRESI, supra note 16 at 26 (arguing that the "principal function of accident law is to reduce the sum of the costs of accidents and the costs of avoiding accidents"). This was the evident view of "social cost" in the earliest work on optimizing pollution controls. *See, e.g.*, J.H. DALES, POLLUTION PROPERTY AND PRICES: AN ESSAY IN POLICY-MAKING AND ECONOMICS 6 (1968) ("[P]ollution of all kinds is always economically beneficial to some people to some extent. When a factory discharges untreated wastes into a water course, it is presumably adopting the cheapest way of disposing of its unwanted materials."); Anthony C. Fisher & Frederick M. Peterson, *The Environment in Economics: A Survey*, 14(1) J. ECON. LIT. 1, 25 (1976) (concluding that market failures cause most environmental damage and that Pigovian taxes are the economist's preferred tool); *cf.* STIGLER, supra note 3 at 165–68 (describing the scope of "external economies" and their exclusion from price-theoretic economic models).

[24] It obscured the prospect that valuing goods in the aggregate will sometimes entail considerations wholly absent from individual choice. *Cf.* PARTHA DASGUPTA, AN INQUIRY INTO WELL-BEING AND DESTITUTION 11 (1993) (noting that welfare economic theories of competitive equilibrium, externality, efficiency, the commons, and public goods must all be reconstructed to reflect basic material "needs" in poor, rural societies where human reproduction serves as both capital and consumption); Partha Dasgupta, *Saving and Fertility: Ethical Issues*, 23 PHIL. & PUB. AFFS. 99, 109–27 (1994) (arguing that utilitarianism only ever works analytically without the existence of actual persons having real life histories and plans, that unborn generations necessarily overlap each other, and that parental motivations intermixing savings and investment choices can

from its concept of "social" cost was any theory of the *social* distinguishing it from the personal or positional.[25] Indeed, even its concept of the personal is now thought to have gone badly askew.[26] As many times as cost-benefit hawks have delved into their tools for quantification from a purely static picture of Pareto's social costs,[27] they cannot escape the fact that costs imposed on others are never just *costs*.[28] They cannot escape the fact that societal detriment presumes a perspective or standing that is societal.[29] And if individual "utility functions" (or "preference orderings") cannot strictly add up to legally prescriptive social welfare accounts as Bentham had hoped,[30] welfarism gives no hope of resolving the contentious questions surrounding the aggregation of even those gains and losses that can be priced.[31] With no methods to identify or to count properly social costs, there can be no talk of social cost minimization.

---

generate socially disastrous outcomes). Contrary to some accounts, this has had formative effects on the standard tools of today. *See, e.g.*, CHARLES D. KOLSTAD, ENVIRONMENTAL ECONOMICS 5–7 (2000) (distinguishing the contemporary field of "environmental" economics by its belief that goods are valuable according to "multiple scarce factors" as well as "how much value individual people place on the final good" and that both positive and normative explanatory work characterizes the field).

[25] In the broadest sense, as Arrow and colleagues argued in 2012, if an economy is risking its own *sustainability* as judged by our best measurements of wealth, *e.g.*, growth accounting incorporating population growth, technological change and all forms of capital, then the "optimum" or "efficient" development of that economy must both be in doubt. *See* Kenneth J. Arrow *et al.*, *Sustainability and the Measurement of Wealth*, 17 ENVT. & DEV. ECON. 317 (2012).

[26] *See, e.g.*, Richard H. Thaler, *From Homo Economicus to Homo Sapiens*, 14(1) J. ECON PERSPS. 133 (2000).

[27] *See, e.g.*, EDWARD M. GRAMLICH, A GUIDE TO BENEFIT-COST ANALYSIS 31 (2d ed. 1990); E.J. MISHAN & EUSTON QUAH, COST-BENEFIT ANALYSIS 4–6 (5th ed. 2007).

[28] *See* DAVID M. DRIESEN, THE ECONOMIC DYNAMICS OF ENVIRONMENTAL LAW 20–21 (2003).

[29] *Cf.* id. at 23 ("[Cost-benefit analysis] assumes that imposition of costs upon existing polluters, whatever the environmental effects, causes a societal economic detriment. It equates the economic interests of polluters with those of society. The assumption of identity between polluter and societal economic interests produces a static approach to economic considerations.").

[30] *See* JOHN E. ROEMER, THEORIES OF DISTRIBUTIVE JUSTICE 14–50 (1996)

[31] Welfarism's strictest answer—that a society's welfare functions are to be constructed by collective decision making, much as an individual's welfare function might be set—then ran aground of social choice theory's emergent

2.1.1 The Perspectival Social Cost

Social costs should be those costs that befall society in general. From that premise, however, they seem to assume answers to deeply contested questions. Adequately deterring a polluting agent,[32] for example, requires an understanding of pollution, agency, deterrence, and adequacy from properly *collective*—not merely personal or positional—priorities.[33] Achieving that perspective has proven far more difficult than the utilitarian-welfarist traditions acknowledge. In fact, these traditionalists bootstrapped their way out of two debates they were losing just as legal welfarists were proposing social cost accounting as a powerful new tool for law.[34] Welfare economics' Achilles' heels were and have remained its footings in the quagmire of interpersonal value comparisons[35] and its static (not dynamic) analytical tools.[36] (Welfarism also confuses the

---

challenges to collective decision making. *See* ARROW, supra note 2 at 104–05; William Vickery, *Utility, Strategy and Social Decision Rules*, 74 Q.J. ECON. 507 (1960).

[32] *See* Maureen Cropper & Wallace E. Oates, *Environmental Economics: A Survey*, 30 J. ECON. LIT. 675, 678–85 (1992).

[33] *Cf.* id. at 678 ("The standard approach in the environmental economics literature characterizes pollution as a public 'bad' that results from 'waste discharges' associated with the production of private goods."). For any aggregate of persons persisting over time, *e.g.*, in a "society," what is good, bad, right, wrong, efficient, or inefficient will evolve, perhaps dramatically, entailing far more information gathering for collective evaluations—potentially beyond its worth to that aggregate—than standard welfarist tools usually offer. *See* Peter J. Hammond, *Utilitarianism, Uncertainty and Information, in* UTILITARIANISM AND BEYOND 85 (Amartya Sen & Bernard Williams eds., 1982).

[34] One amalgamated approach took to comparing the "surplus value" created by the subject production to the surpluses gained from its amendment (or prohibition) eliminating the targeted externalities. *See* WILLIAM J. BAUMOL & WALLACE E. OATES, THE THEORY OF ENVIRONMENTAL POLICY (1975); PAUL BURROWS, THE ECONOMIC THEORY OF POLLUTION CONTROL (1979); *cf.* KOLSTAD, supra note 24 at 68–74 (observing that this approach was "not easy to implement"). This particular amalgamation influenced several legal-theoretic debates of the time. *See, e.g.*, Guido Calabresi & A. Douglas Melamed, *Property Rules, Liability Rules, and Inalienability: One View of the Cathedral*, 85 HARV. L. REV. 1089, 1094 & n.12 (1972) (*discussing The Problem of Social Cost*).

[35] *See, e.g.*, Lionel Robbins, *Richard T. Ely Lecture—Economics and Political Economy*, 71(2) AMER. ECON. REV. 1, 19–24 (1981); PARTHA DASGUPTA, HUMAN WELL-BEING AND THE NATURAL ENVIRONMENT 13–23 (2001).

[36] *See* Baumol & Wilson, supra note 4 at xlii; JOHN R. HICKS, METHODS OF DYNAMIC ECONOMICS 1–10 (1985).

relatively small set of Pareto-relevant "externalities" for the immense universe of the unpriced[37]—an error of devastating proportions given its ambitions.[38])

For its part, utilitarianism was ironically both too morally exacting and not sensitive enough to individual persons.[39] It too was unable to fashion a plausible aggregative perspective from so many agent-relative perspectives. Overcoming these challenges remains work to be done for welfare-utilitarianism. Proposed solutions have ever since bogged down in polarizing debates over the means of valuation, the tools of collective decision making, and their coordinated use.[40] And that frames the question: what are regulation's "costs"?

2.1.2 Goods (and Costs): Counting in Three Dimensions

As John Broome once argued, any "good" will have at least three dimensions: (1) a state of nature or society, (2) concerned people, and (3) a certain time.[41] This makes any maximization of good(s) subject to

---

37 *See, e.g.*, WILLIAM D. NORDHAUS, INVENTION, GROWTH AND WELFARE (1969); James M. Buchanan & William Craig Stubblebine, *Externality*, 29(116) ECONOMICA 371 (1962); *see also* Tibor Scitovsky, *Two Concepts of External Economies*, 62 J. POL. ECON. 143 (1954).

38 *See* SEN, supra note 7 at 78–86; RICHARD H. THALER, QUASI-RATIONAL ECONOMICS (1991).

39 *See, e.g.*, JOHN RAWLS, A THEORY OF JUSTICE (1971); J.J.C. SMART & BERNARD WILLIAMS, UTILITARIANISM: FOR AND AGAINST (1973). A retrospective on Rawls, Williams, David Lyons and other philosophers whose work of that era aimed chiefly at rejecting or constraining utilitarianism (and welfare economics) is AMARTYA SEN, THE IDEA OF JUSTICE (2009).

40 *See* Lee Anne Fennell, *The Problem of Resource Access*, 126 HARV. L. REV. 1471, 1478–93 (2013); AMARTYA SEN, COLLECTIVE CHOICE AND SOCIAL WELFARE 1–41 (2d ed. 2017). After any collective chooses its valuation or decision-making rules, there remain the (substantial) problems of implementation in the face of strategic action. *See* Eric Maskin, *Nash Equilibrium and Welfare Optimality*, 66 REV. ECON. STUDS. 23 (1999).

41 *See* JOHN BROOME, WEIGHING GOODS: EQUALITY, UNCERTAINTY AND TIME 25 (1991). Broome calls his states of nature the *locations* of good, id. at 23, and holds that the assumption that state-by-state comparison is adequate entails assuming "separability" between states—that "the value of what happens in one location is independent of what happens in other locations." Id. Exploring that assumption comprises the bulk of the book's original work. *See also* JOHN BROOME, WEIGHING LIVES 118–31, 187–96, 254–64 (2004).

three kinds of uncertainty.[42] And it means that counting in only one dimension is sure to be, at best, partial. Committing to counting without knowing how to do so in all three dimensions is morally risky. Take, for example, the global effort to stop stratospheric ozone degradation. Its architects sought to safeguard a feature of Earth's atmosphere shielding it from excess UVB solar radiation. The causal processes involved, the requisite breadth and depth of cooperation, and who would benefit (most) from the efforts all precluded any accounting of "externalities," welfare maximization, or collective responsibilities and would have derailed the so-called Montreal Protocol had any of that been important.[43] The sum total of human and international cooperation in that instance is thought by decision theorists and economists alike to have *succeeded* despite all of the incalculables.[44] But what if that cooperation had turned on the parties' first finding a collectively "optimal" level of abatement? Each party, presumably, would have first had to resolve individually the probabilities of several possible outcomes—sowing a certain randomness into *any* aggregative decision procedure to follow.[45] Aggregating that collection of estimates need not have yielded a coherent bundle, either.[46]

---

[42] If goods are, in the general case, plotted along a three-dimensional grid of locations, with each location a person at a time in some state of nature, comparing alternatives will distribute goods across that grid. Different alternatives will distribute points differently. BROOME, WEIGHING GOODS, supra note 41 at 27. Similarly, the questions of how (and whether) goods distributed across the dimensions make up the *overall* good should, ideally, be answered three dimensionally. But this is not to say from whose point of view some "overall" good is or can be evaluated. *See* John M. Taurek, *Should the Numbers Count?*, 6(4) PHIL. & PUB. AFFS. 293 (1977).

[43] *See* Robert J. Goodin, *International Ethics and the Environmental Crisis*, 4 ETHICS & INT'L AFFS. 191 (1990).

[44] *See* SCOTT BARRETT, ENVIRONMENT & STATECRAFT: THE STRATEGY OF ENVIRONMENTAL TREATY-MAKING (2003). Organic halogen compounds are immensely useful chemicals. A subset, chlorofluorocarbons used as refrigerants, dry cleaning solvents, propellants, *etc.*, became the targets of global phase-outs, essentially as cheaper, less harmful substitutes became available. These uses and harms distributed variably throughout the world, though.

[45] *See* ARROW, supra note 2 at 8–11; AMARTYA SEN, COLLECTIVE CHOICE AND SOCIAL WELFARE 97 (2d ed. 2017).

[46] *Cf.* BROOME, supra note 41 at 130–48, 152–63 (arguing that "probability-relative good," when combined with so-called Pareto optimization for a general good in the presence of prospects discounted differently by different individuals, puts individual preference maximization in conflict with maximizing the general good). Specifically, did the substitution of the chemicals at issue and the costs of doing so exceed the costs of unabated ozone-depleting chemicals' use over the

For example, what if the parties first had to identify some threshold of necessary cooperation toward their common ends?[47] That would have highlighted the marginal leverage each party could then have gained when/if its contribution became determinative, sowing still more instability into the process.[48] And can we even say *in hindsight* that the utility, *i.e.*, usefulness, traded off in 1987 between certain of the Earth's solar-reflective capacities and use of the damaging chemicals across the planet was at least even or better?[49] In some parts of the world, uses of such substances are (and were) far more valuable than they are on average.

Multidimensional goods mean that social optimizing calculations can be practically impossible. Though that does not necessarily deny the appeal of markets (markets can surely hedge compound uncertainties and arbitrage expected costs[50]), it questions any identity between market outcomes and inclusive good maximization or cost minimization. And the bulk of the work on "instrument choice" in risk regulation has taken

---

interval in which those chemicals' utility would have led to their continued production? *Cf.* BARRETT, supra note 44 at 286–90 (concluding that the parties to the Montreal Protocol must have decided that compliance was in their interest—but that no obvious proof to that effect could be constructed).

[47] Unilateral action against the chemicals without sufficient cooperation would have remained ineffective in every case. Of course, a sufficient sum of contributions can become an equilibrium that is then maintained by social forces. *See* Mark Granovetter, *Threshold Models of Collective Behavior*, 83(6) AMER. J. SOC. 1420 (1978).

[48] *See, e.g.*, ANTHONY DOWNS, AN ECONOMIC THEORY OF DEMOCRACY (1957).

[49] Even putting aside the problems of quantitatively scaling utility from actual behaviors, *cf.* Daniel Ellsberg, *Classic and Current Notions of "Measurable Utility,"* 64 ECON. J. 528 (1954) (challenging the measurability of distinct utility functions as suggested by welfarists), the "goods" secured by stratospheric ozone are an unwieldy aggregate that, regardless of the maximand (happiness, well-being, human capacities, *etc.*), not only lacked any ready surrogate(s) for such tabulation. By its immensity it necessarily commingled goods over time—likely over generations given the chemicals' latency in the atmosphere—and over geographically diverse areas (despite a polar vortex concentrating most of the observable effects in the southern hemisphere).

[50] *See* Sanford J. Grossman & Joseph E. Stiglitz, *On the Impossibility of Informationally Efficient Markets*, 70 AM. ECON. REV. 393 (1980) (using a model stock market to show that "equilibrium" is unattainable unless traders enter the market on the basis of competing subjective estimates of uncertainty).

that identity on faith.[51] Because so many choices lack sufficient information about their states, concerned persons, and/or timing, *actual* goods typically escape the confines of instrument choice's social cost accounting tools. The extremal value analyses so central to the maximizing within that accounting fail.[52] Maximizing the estimable gains of affected persons, *if it is to be a means of maximizing collective well-being*, assumes a type of weighing across dimensions that fails conceptually.[53]

Utilitarianism faces a similar fate: "utilitarianism, both in theory and practice, is alarmingly good at combining technical complexity with simple-mindedness."[54] Just as the immensity of unpriced goods and prospects, unpriced indifference, and the unpredictable interactions thereof through time taint aggregative evaluations grounded in *observed* prices (or behaviors), so too is the utilitarian insistence on the commensurability of utility gains deeply compromised by our firm convictions about justice, fairness, and generations.[55] For something like environmental or consumer safety risks, where societies are constantly deliberating the right/wrong and cost/benefit balances, where no final answers

---

[51] *See* Kenneth R. Richards, *Framing Environmental Policy Instrument Choice*, 10 DUKE ENVTL. L. & POL'Y 221, 230–32, 254–72 (2000).

[52] Extremal value analysis derives from the statistics of deviations from a mean or median. Virtually all of the marginalist techniques in the instrument choice literature entail its use. As Broome demonstrates in painstaking detail, with individuated probability estimates of what is or will be "good" states of affairs, a marginalist evaluation of multiple goods devolves to combining disparate subjective probability estimates—a notoriously difficult mathematical pursuit. *See* BROOME, supra note 41 at 122–48. Some of welfarism's architects seem to have anticipated these obstacles. *See, e.g.*, Frank P. Ramsey, *Truth and Probability, in* THE FOUNDATIONS OF MATHEMATICS AND OTHER LOGICAL ESSAYS 156 (Routledge 1931).

[53] *See* BROOME, supra note 41 at 215–20.

[54] SMART & WILLIAMS, supra note 39 at 149. Williams continued: "[s]imple-mindedness consists in having too few thoughts and feelings to match the world as it really is. … The important issues that utilitarianism raises should be discussed in contexts more rewarding than that of utilitarianism itself." Id. at 149–50; *see also* ROEMER, supra note 30 at 127–62 (tracing a series of now-standard objections to utilitarian ethics wherever a population is not fixed and individual convictions about distributive justice are prevalent).

[55] *See* DANIEL H. COLE, POLLUTION AND PROPERTY: COMPARING OWNERSHIP INSTITUTIONS FOR ENVIRONMENTAL PROTECTION 93–95 (2002) (noting the problematic nature of prices as information); RICHARD TUCK, FREE RIDING 119–55 (2008) (challenging the coherence of utilitarian "maximands" where cooperative action is needed to maximize anything). Preferences can be evil, mistaken, *etc.*, just as the "goodness" of a state of affairs must be experienced

on "optimal" savings or investment are long-lived, where "market failure" is pervasive and the nature and scope of "public" goods are so deeply contested, and where individual optimizations are so often flawed,[56] all of the foregoing give good reasons to discount welfarism's social cost accounting.[57] How *steep* that discount ought to be in any given case is the practical question.

Welfarists never expected much progress against their social costs from a fully judicialized approach.[58] The tools available in court are blunt and limiting.[59] Common law courts' jurisdictional limits and the expected

---

from *some* point of view. *See* Taurek, supra note 42 (challenging the intuition that choosing to save one instead of five lives is a "wrong" to any of the five individually). In short, a single "utility function" or preference ordering has nothing necessarily to say about *social* welfare or utility in general. Yet, as Ken Arrow put it in reviewing *A Theory of Justice*,

> [t]he implicit ethical basis of [welfare economics] is some version of utilitarianism. ... The basic theorem of welfare economics: that, under certain conditions, the competitive economic system yields an outcome that is optimal or efficient ... depends on the identification of the utility structures that motivates the choices made by economic agents with the utility structures used in judging the optimality of the outcome of the competitive system (Kenneth J. Arrow, *Some Ordinalist-Utilitarian Notes on Rawls's* Theory of Justice, 70(9) J. PHIL. 245, 246 (1973)).

The identity condemns both because, while "philosophers have been more prone to analyze what individuals should want [and] economists have been content to identify 'should' with 'is' for the individual (not for society)," id., neither has yet overcome the unpredictability of consequences or the complex grounds of "goodness" in a pluralistic society that persists over time.

56 *See, e.g.*, Richard H. Thaler, *Mental Accounting Matters*, 12 J. BEHAV. DEC.-MAKING 183 (1999).

57 *See, e.g.*, Karl W. Kapp, *Environmental Disruption and Social Costs: A Challenge to Economics*, 23 KYKLOS 833 (1970); NICHOLAS GEORGESCU-ROEGEN, THE ENTROPY LAW AND THE ECONOMIC PROCESS (1971); Adam B. Jaffe *et al.*, *A Tale of Two Market Failures: Technology and Environmental Policy*, 54 ECOL. ECON. 164 (2005); DOUGLAS E. BOOTH, HOOKED ON GROWTH: ECONOMIC ADDICTIONS AND THE ENVIRONMENT (2004); SEN, supra note 45 at 4–36, 80–93, 269–81. Some early utilitarian-economic work on pollution controls adverted to these obstacles. *See, e.g.*, ALLEN V. KNEESE & BLAIR T. BOWER, MANAGING WATER QUALITY: ECONOMICS, TECHNOLOGY, INSTITUTIONS 4–8 (1968).

58 *Cf.* POSNER, supra note 16 at 343 ("The party optimizes his litigation expenditures by spending up to the point where a dollar in such expenditures increases the expected value of the litigation to him by just a dollar.").

59 *See, e.g.*, *Developments in the Law—Injunctions*, 78 HARV. L. REV 994, 1005 (1965) ("Injunctive relief may provide the plaintiff with a means to extort a

"leakage" from their reach long anchored the consensus.[60] (Cognitive biasing inherent in decision making from particulars later hardened it.[61]) For the civil defendant who made a plausible showing of hardship in having to change operations, courts would weigh a menu of variables including the parties' relative culpabilities, available opportunities to mitigate damages, the public interest, *etc*.[62] Yet just as the hope of social cost minimization was dwindling, a sea change occurred: Risk regulation was tectonically shifted from the judicial to the administrative process. And the resulting mandates to administrative agencies like EPA, OSHA, the Consumer Product Safety Commission (CPSC), the National Highway Traffic Safety Administration (NHTSA), the Federal Railroad Administration (FRA), and others embodied many of these same confusions.

---

money settlement disproportionate to the harm threatened."). As the New York Court of Appeals observed in *Boomer*, "[e]ffective control of air pollution is a problem presently far from solution even with the full public and financial powers of government. In large measure adequate technical procedures are yet to be developed and some that appear possible may be economically impracticable. It seems apparent that the amelioration of air pollution will depend on technical research in great depth; on a carefully balanced consideration of the economic impact of close regulation; and of the actual effect on public health. It is likely to require massive public expenditure and to demand more than any local community can accomplish and to depend on regional and interstate controls. A court should not try to do this on its own ..." (*Boomer*, 257 N.E.2d at 871).

60 Inter-jurisdictional "competition" for residents and capital became the welfare economist's take on such dynamics. *Cf.* WALLACE E. OATES, FISCAL FEDERALISM 54 (1972) (hypothesizing that unless cost savings can be realized from the centralized provision of goods, "Pareto-efficient levels of consumption of the good" will be supplied in each local jurisdiction allowed to compete for residents). If environmental quality is thought of as a "local" public good, it might be the subject of inter-local competition for residents and investment. *See* Charles M. Tiebout, *A Pure Theory of Local Expenditures*, 64 J. POL. ECON. 416 (1956). But beyond Tiebout's simple model, environmental quality quickly escapes analysis in its infinitely varied social, spatial, and temporal scales.

61 *See, e.g.*, Frederick Schauer, *Do Cases Make Bad Law?* 73 U. CHI. L. REV. 883 (2006); Richard Stewart, *Crisis in Tort Law? The Institutional Perspective*, 54 U. CHI. L. REV. 184 (1987); Neil Komesar, *In Search of a General Approach to Legal Analysis: A Comparative Institutional Alternative*, 79 MICH. L. REV. 1350 (1981).

62 *See* Laycock, supra note 18 at 207; Daniel A. Farber, *Equitable Discretion, Legal Duties, and Environmental Injunctions*, 45 U. PITT. L. REV. 513 (1984). Laycock had earlier recorded a similar drift in the application of the "irreparable injury" test for the granting of tort injunctions. *See* Douglas Laycock, *The Death of the Irreparable Injury Rule*, 103 HARV. L. REV. 687 (1990).

2.2 A LEGISLATIVE BIG BANG: THE STATUTORY MANDATES TO CONSIDER COSTS

The deluge of statutory delegations from 1970 to 1976 still shapes American risk regulation today. From the Clean Air Act of 1970 (CAA) and the Occupational Safety and Health Act of the same year to the Consumer Product Safety Act, the Safe Drinking Water Act of 1974 (SDWA)[63] and the Toxic Substances Control Act of 1976 (TSCA),[64] the legislative direction given to the administering agency(ies) was to reduce risk to the greatest extent "feasible," "achievable," or by the best techniques "available." Many, like CAA, SDWA, and TSCA have been amended significantly since.[65] But these updates have diverged less in their precision (or lack thereof) regarding the costs to be weighed than in the *timing* or exact *relevance* of those considerations by Congress's agents. Overwhelmingly, the statutes direct their agency administrators to take the costs of compliance into account in setting any of their standards but specify little else.

The CAA is renowned for its national ambient air quality standards (NAAQS), which are set without regard to costs.[66] They ground the Act's reputation for "technology forcing"—a demand that regulated parties meet its standards regardless.[67] Yet technological innovation became the

---

[63] Pub. L. No. 93-523, 88 Stat. 1660 *et seq.* (1974), *codified at* 42 U.S.C. §§ 300f–300j-26.

[64] Pub. L. No. 94-469, 90 Stat. 2003 *et seq.* (1976), *codified at* 15 U.S.C. §§ 2601–29.

[65] The SDWA Amendments of 1996 were a complete overhaul as was TSCA's Frank Lautenberg Chemical Safety for the 21st Century Act, Pub. L. No. 114-182, 130 Stat. 448 (2016), *codified at* 15 U.S.C. §§ 2601 *et seq.*

[66] *See* Whitman v. Amer. Trucking Ass'ns, 531 U.S. 457, 465–68 (2001); *see also* Massachusetts v. EPA, 549 U.S. 497, 532–33 (2007); Honeywell Int'l, Inc. v. EPA, 374 F.3d 1363, 1372–73 (D.C. Cir. 2004).

[67] *See* Train v. Natural Resources Defense Council, Inc., 421 U.S. 60, 91 (1975); *see* D. Bruce La Pierre, *Technology-Forcing and Federal Environmental Standards*, 62 IOWA L. REV. 771, 773–74 (1977); Note—*Forcing Technology: The Clean Air Act Experience*, 88 YALE L.J. 1713 (1979). Much (but not all) of the "technology-forcing" talk of the 1970s reflected the Act's ambient environmental quality standards. *See* Chapter 4, Section 4.1.1.

core of the CAA—regulatory inducement of that innovation its animating impetus through dozens of more specific implementing elements.[68] A history of the US EPA could surely be told as that of its pushing air pollution control's technological frontiers while tacitly weighing the expected costs of doing so.[69] Two formative, ostensibly nationwide studies of "the cost of clean air" informed those deliberations at the very outset.[70] They document estimative techniques that evolved quickly. In the first report, a summary calculation of fractional charges on expected gross output within the Act's scope (a handful of targeted sectors) transitioned, in the second report, to a more direct estimation of those targets' practical technological needs.[71] That single move foreshadowed much of the CAA's lived experience with evaluating regulation's costs.[72] Section 2.2.1 focuses on this peculiarity within one of our modern pillars of risk regulation.

2.2.1 "Achievable" Performance: Rise of the Clean Air Act

For some level of air pollution abatement to be practicable or *cost-achievable* it must be accessible to the targeted polluter(s) given their market position(s). CAA provisions directing that air pollution be abated with all "available" or "achievable" technology include CAA § 111's new (stationary) source performance standards (NSPSs),[73] CAA § 112's national emission standards for "hazardous air pollutants" (HAPs),[74]

---

68 *See, e.g.*, David P. Currie, *The Mobile Source Provisions of the Clean Air Act*, 46 U. CHI. L. REV. 811, 816–18 (1979); Krier, supra note 18 at 438–43.

69 *Cf.* Michael A. Livermore & Richard L. Revesz, *Rethinking Health-Based Environmental Standards*, 89 N.Y.U.L. REV. 1184 (2014) (arguing that costs are implicitly factored into NAAQS); Daniel A. Farber, *Taking Costs into Account: Mapping the Boundaries of Judicial and Agency Discretion*, 40 HARV. ENVTL. L. REV. 87 (2016).

70 *See* FIRST REPORT OF THE SEC. HEALTH, EDUC. & WELFARE, THE COST OF CLEAN AIR (June 1969) (hereafter "COST OF CLEAN AIR I"); SECOND REPORT OF THE SEC. HEALTH, EDUC. & WELFARE, THE COST OF CLEAN AIR, S. DOC. 91-65 (March 1970) (hereafter "COST OF CLEAN AIR II").

71 *See* COST OF CLEAN AIR II, supra note 70 at 2.

72 *See* Chapter 4, Sections 4.1–4.2.

73 *See* 42 U.S.C. § 7411(a)(1).

74 *See* 42 U.S.C. § 7412(d).

CAA § 129's solid waste incinerator standards,[75] CAA § 165's preconstruction requirements,[76] CAA § 173's nonattainment permit requirements,[77] CAA § 111(d)'s residual existing source standards,[78] CAA § 202(a)(3)'s new motor vehicle standards,[79] CAA § 211's reformulated gasoline standards for nonattainment areas,[80] CAA § 213's non-road and CAA § 231's aircraft engine standards,[81] and CAA § 407(b)'s utility boiler nitrogen oxides controls.[82] Though costs are targeted in different ways in these provisions,[83] they all aim in their own way to identify *cost-achievable* input, process, and/or capital changes to abate pollution.[84] Because of the fact-specificity of such determinations and because of the subtly different statutory phrasings, few (if any) default rules have emerged since 1970 by which the technological frontiers of pollution abatement may or must be judged pursuant to the CAA.[85]

---

75 *See* 42 U.S.C. § 7429(a)(2).

76 *See* 42 U.S.C. § 7475(a). Preconstruction review for "attainment" areas and pollutants includes the selection of the "best available control technology" for the source, "taking into account energy, environmental, and economic impacts and other costs," which EPA finds on a source-by-source basis is "achievable … through application of production processes and methods, systems, and techniques including fuel cleaning, clean fuels, or treatment or innovative fuel combustion techniques … ." Id. at § 7479(3).

77 *See* 42 U.S.C. §§ 7503(a), 7501(3). CAA § 172 also requires all implementation plans in nonattainment areas to require "reasonably available control technology" of any existing sources. Id. at § 7502(c)(1).

78 *See* 42 U.S.C. § 7411(d).

79 *See* 42 U.S.C. § 7521(a)(3).

80 *See* 42 U.S.C. § 7545(k).

81 *See* 42 U.S.C. §§ 7547, 7571.

82 *See* 42 U.S.C. § 7651f(b).

83 CAA §§ 111(a)–(b), 112(d), 129(a)(2), 169(3), 202(a)(3), 211(k), 213(a)(3) and 407(b) each mentions cost(s) explicitly among their choice factors whereas provisions like CAA §§ 111(d) and 171(3) do not. Provisions like CAA § 231 reference the standard's "technological feasibility," *see* 42 U.S.C. § 7571(a)(1)(B), although that tends to be rare in the CAA.

84 *See* Jamison E. Colburn, *Technology-Based? Cost Factoring in US Environmental Standards*, 7 MICH. J. ENVT'L & ADMIN. L. 83, 92–106 (2018).

85 *See, e.g.*, EPA v. EME Homer City Gen., L.P., 134 S. Ct. 1584, 1606–07 (2014) (Ginsburg, J.) (holding EPA may consider costs of abatement in determining which upwind states "contribute significantly" to downwind nonattainment); Michigan v. EPA, 135 S. Ct. 2699, 2707 (2015) (Scalia, J.) (holding that EPA must afford "at least some attention to cost" in determining whether it is "appropriate and necessary" to regulate electricity generating boilers' pollution); Massachusetts v. EPA, 549 U.S. 497, 528–35 (2007) (finding that text and structure of CAA "forecloses" any interpretation other than that GHGs including

Standards keyed to economic "feasibility,"[86] as it is often called, can confuse means and ends. Especially where legislation explicitly names the availability of technology as a factor to be weighed (as so much US legislation of the era did), it focuses the standard setter upon the details of production and the incumbent firms that happen to be in business at the time.[87] That standards could not spring from such processes without either locking in certain defined solutions or inducing the regulated parties to collude against stringency became a common refrain.[88] The key variables always at issue were cost avoidance and timing. There is no avoiding either of these variables, but there are a great many ways to recombine them.[89]

Market actors often respond strategically to constraints. Yet the possibility that a standard itself induces such adaptation, perhaps shrinking its own cost-of-compliance figures, suggests a kind of *endogeneity* or causal reciprocity between the standard-setting and the conduct being governed.[90] Because feasibility of this kind can be estimated with respect

---

carbon dioxide are "air pollutants" as defined, regardless of practical consequences of so interpreting the statute).

[86] *See, e.g.*, United Steelworkers of America, etc. v. Marshall, 647 F.2d 1189, 1264–65 (D.C. Cir. 1980); Industrial Union Dept., AFL-CIO v. Hodgson, 499 F.2d 467, 477 (D.C. Cir. 1974) (linking the "to the extent feasible" proviso in OSH Act § 6(b)(5) to the cost-availability of technological or other workplace precautions to reduce risk).

[87] This was a source of great debate surrounding those 1970s statutes. *See, e.g.*, ALLEN V. NEESE & CHARLES L. SCHULTZE, POLLUTION, PRICES AND PUBLIC POLICY 58–64 (1975). Many economists were convinced the laws ignored the competitive incentives afoot. *Cf.* id. at 63 ("If 'best available' is taken to mean the best equipment installed in any plant—the apparently logical interpretation ... then such equipment would immediately become the standard for the industry. The interpretation could go further to include technology that has been developed but not yet implemented. But then who in industry would seek an innovation that added to [their] costs, even if it sharply reduced pollution?").

[88] *See generally* Winston Harrington *et al.*, *Comparing Instrument Choices, in* CHOOSING ENVIRONMENTAL POLICY: COMPARING INSTRUMENTS AND OUTCOMES IN THE UNITED STATES AND EUROPE 1 (Winston Harrington *et al.* eds., 2004); William A. Pizer & Raymond Kopp, *Calculating the Costs of Environmental Regulation, in* 3 HANDBOOK OF ENVIRONMENTAL ECONOMICS 1307 (Karl-Göran Mäler & Jeffrey R. Vincent eds., 2005).

[89] *See* Chapter 4.

[90] If technological innovation can lower the marginal cost of pollution abatement while regulation increases the cost of unabated pollution, *any* standard has the potential to change affected firms' payoffs and therefore their best strategy(s). *See* David Popp *et al.*, *Energy, the Environment, and Technological*

to a single firm, facility, or even a process unit, it need not necessarily be a "dynamic" estimate. What is cost-accessible on average across a range of firms over an interval of time will obviously differ from that of a single firm or facility. But whether this fit is from site-to-solution or from sector-to-solution, *cost achievability*—not overall societal efficiency—has been the CAA's focal, yet easily obscured, concern.[91] And from the earliest efforts, the uncertainties of cost avoidance have affected those analyses and their use by regulators, courts, and the public.

In *International Harvester v. Ruckelshaus*,[92] the CAA had mandated cuts in "light duty vehicle" pollution to be imposed beginning in model year 1975 if not postponed by EPA with a finding that the necessary technology was not "available" (among other things).[93] Congress projected that the (seemingly drastic) cuts it mandated would be achievable as pollution abatement technology improved and the automakers were

Change, in 2 HANDBOOK ON THE ECONOMICS OF INNOVATION 873, 876–86 (Bronwyn H. Hall & Nathan Rosenberg eds., 2010). Nonetheless, "[t]he generation of knowledge through the innovative process contrasts sharply with the negative externalities from pollution. Because of the public goods nature of knowledge, a firm that invests in or implements a new technology typically creates benefits for others while incurring all the costs." Id. at 877. Thus, "[w]hile all investment is characterized by uncertainty, the uncertainty associated with the returns to investment in innovation is often particularly large." Jaffe *et al.*, supra note 57 at 167.

91 This drew significant welfarist criticism from the start. *See, e.g.*, ALLEN V. KNEESE & CHARLES L. SCHULTZE, POLLUTION, PRICES AND PUBLIC POLICY 69–84 (1975).

92 478 F.2d 615 (D.C. Cir. 1973).

93 *See* 478 F.2d at 623–24 (*quoting* then-Section 202(b)(5)(D), 42 U.S.C. § 1857f-1(b)(5)(D)). The 1970 amendments required a 90% reduction in two pollutants, "hydrocarbons" and carbon monoxide, by model year 1975 over the controls in place in 1970 but then 90% reductions in nitrogen oxides one model year later as well. Legislated at the end of calendar year 1970, this supposedly gave manufacturers about 43 months' lead time. EPA first had to "translate" 1970's loose standards into detailed, testable requirements. *See* Natural Resources Defense Council, Inc. v. Ruckelshaus, 359 F. Supp. 1028, 1030–31 (D.D.C. 1972). Given the realities of mass production, the state of the technology in development at the time, and the need to certify compliant models almost a year in advance of their assembly and sale, however, this approach had the counterintuitive effect of locking domestic firms onto a very small sample of "bolt on" solutions early in the process. *See* John B. Heywood, *Future Emission Control Technology, in* FRANK P. GRAD ET AL., THE AUTOMOBILE AND THE REGULATION OF ITS IMPACT ON THE ENVIRONMENT 279, 280 (1975).

forced to evolve.[94] As it turned out, after battling the manufacturers over the scope of the "light duty vehicle" category,[95] EPA would *not* postpone, forcing a showdown before the reviewing court.[96] In this first big test of the cost-achievability idea, thus, a reviewing court had to assess balancing of the proffered budget constraints of incumbent firms, the engineering of the product(s) at issue and the conceivable technological improvements thereof, and how to give the correct push along the risk-reducing course Congress had suggested.[97] For mobile sources, Congress had put the onus on the manufacturers to show that their abatement options were not commercially feasible (among other things).[98] Key to that approach was understanding the degree to which their products and/or processes could be changed if abatement equipment itself proved insufficient. In a passage that has been quoted repeatedly since, the court aligned the choice as follows:

> [w]e are inclined to agree with [EPA] that as long as feasible technology permits the demand for new passenger automobiles to be generally met, the basic requirements of the Act would be satisfied, even though this might occasion fewer models and a more limited choice of engine types. The

---

94 *See* JAMES E. KRIER & EDMUND URSIN, POLLUTION AND POLICY: A CASE ESSAY ON CALIFORNIA AND FEDERAL EXPERIENCE WITH MOTOR VEHICLE AIR POLLUTION, 1940–1975 206–08 (1977); Currie, supra note 68 at 816–19; JACK DOYLE, TAKEN FOR A RIDE: DETROIT'S BIG THREE AND THE POLITICS OF POLLUTION 62–79 (2000).

95 *See* 478 F.2d at 638–40.

96 *See* 478 F.2d at 650. The opinion in *International Harvester* only remanded the refused postponement—although the practical result of the remand was a postponement. It has long been argued that the flaw in the 1970 CAA was its draconian penalty for noncompliant vehicles—an effective ban on their sale. Graduated fines on a per-vehicle basis would have been a more targeted and, thus, more plausible threat for EPA to make. *See* KNEESE & SCHULTZE, supra note 91 at 64; Currie, supra note 68 at 818–20. Later amendments made that change.

97 The D.C. Circuit would return to this list of factors repeatedly with CAA § 202 rulemakings. *See* Natural Resources Defense Council, Inc. v. U.S. EPA, 655 F.2d 318, 324–36 (D.C. Cir. 1981); Natural Resources Defense Council, Inc. v. Thomas, 805 F.2d 410, 419–34 (D.C. Cir. 1986); Natural Resources Defense Council, Inc. v. Reilly, 983 F.2d 259, 261–73 (D.C. Cir. 1993); Sierra Club v. EPA, 325 F.3d 374, 377–83 (D.C. Cir. 2003).

98 The exact balance EPA was to strike included considering the public health and welfare, good-faith efforts by the manufacturers, "that effective control technology, processes, operating methods, or other alternatives are not available or have not been available," and the results of a particular National Academy of Sciences study. *International Harvester*, 478 F.2d at 623–24.

driving preferences of hot rodders are not to outweigh the goal of a clean environment.[99]

Once the 1970 CAA set this system in motion, though, the incumbent firms began coordinating their resistance—pressuring EPA, Congress, and the public, and ultimately the reviewing court. They argued that, using their "available" technology—catalytic conversion of a standard combustion engine's by-products—achieving the reductions was not commercially feasible.[100] The collective effort mounted also aimed to show that EPA's standards would significantly disadvantage these firms relative to their foreign competitors.[101] They projected the price increases any solutions would mean to consumers, which interested Congress.[102] The automakers even suggested their own bankruptcies—which eventually interested the reviewing courts.[103] Yet where the American firms' solutions had all exhibited serious troubles,[104] several foreign manufacturers had discovered new solutions in engine design.[105] They even sought to take advantage of the American firms' unwillingness (or inability) to adapt.[106] Ignoring the parties' identities, this was exactly the kind of technology-forcing Congress aimed to spur. Of course, then, as now, *foreign* competitors' triumph in a race to innovate was hardly seen as victory.[107] This is a now-routine snag in balancing regulatory costs to which we return in Chapter 4. The American automobile sector would

---

[99] 478 F.2d at 640. This "general demand" theory of commercial feasibility came to define the CAA's approach to mobile sources and other source categories as well. *See* Chapter 4, Section 4.2.

[100] *See* Chapter 4, Section 4.1.1.

[101] *See Int'l Harvester*, 478 F.2d at 636–38; DOYLE, supra note 94 at 73–74. Doyle traces that history back to the antitrust conspiracy case the U.S. Department of Justice had filed in 1968 against Ford, GM and Chrysler for conspiring not to compete in the research, development, manufacture, and sale of pollution control technology. *See* id. at 29–49.

[102] *See* DOYLE, supra note 94 at 115–26 (detailing a $750,000 ad campaign funded by Ford, General Motors, and Chrysler in 1975 asserting that fuel economy would suffer and purchase prices would increase between $150 and $400).

[103] *See Int'l Harvester*, 478 F.2d at 636–38.

[104] 478 F.2d at 625 ("The problem [EPA] faced in making a determination that technology was available … was that actual tests showed only one car with actual emissions which conformed to the standard … . No car had actually been driven 50,000 miles, the statutory 'useful life' of a vehicle … .").

[105] *See* DOYLE, supra note 94 at 93.

[106] *See* Chapter 4, Section 4.3.

[107] *See* La Pierre, supra note 67 at 794–98; DOYLE, supra note 94 at 99–126.

keep losing market share to foreign competitors notwithstanding EPA's (court- or Congressionally ordered) sensitivity to their air pollution challenges.[108] But one net result from that first encounter with "achievability" was to draw regulators' attention to goals beyond mere "end-of-pipe" solutions.[109] And another statute, the Clean Water Act, has exemplified the challenges entailed in that approach over a long run.

2.3 THE CLEAN WATER ACT: EFFICIENCIES FROM A PHASED APPROACH?

Overall, the CWA's strategy was to phase out the consideration of cost in the setting of its performance standards, gradually ratcheting up their stringency in pursuit of a "zero discharge" national goal.[110] This signaled to regulated parties that constraints were coming *before* they were bound to comply.[111] That overall strategy was derailed by later legislative amendments, turning what had been a stepped pursuit of ending discharges into a bewildering array of standard-types bearing uncertain

---

[108] *See* DOYLE, supra note 94 at 217–334. The sport utility and light-duty truck markets were the only interruptions in an otherwise continuous loss of market share from the 1970s to the present. *See* id. at 395–460. The private equity specialists charged with restructuring Chrysler and General Motors certainly believed mismanagement was a more important cause of the industry's troubles than was a hostile regulatory climate. *See, e.g.*, STEVEN RATTNER, OVERHAUL: AN INSIDER'S ACCOUNT OF THE OBAMA ADMINISTRATION'S EMERGENCY RESCUE OF THE AUTO INDUSTRY (2010) (describing mismanagement and failures to adapt as the long-term causes of Detroit's decline and the American firms' eventual insolvencies in 2008–09).

[109] *See* Leslie Sue Ritts & Ben Snowden, *The Regulation of Hazardous Air Pollutants, in* THE CLEAN AIR ACT HANDBOOK 249, 289–90 (Julie R. Domike & Alec C. Zacaroli eds., 4th ed. 2016).

[110] *See* Amer. Frozen Food Inst. v. Train, 539 F.2d 107, 116–24 (D.C. Cir. 1976); E.I. du Pont de Nemours & Co. v. Train, 430 U.S. 112, 116–22 (1977); Weyerhaueser Co. v. Costle, 590 F.2d 1011, 1031–49 (D.C. Cir. 1978); Ass'n of Pac. Fisheries v. EPA, 615 F.2d 794, 805–20 (9th Cir. 1980); EPA v. Nat'l Crushed Stone Ass'n, 449 U.S. 64, 70–83 (1980). Reviewing courts commonly invoked Senator Muskie's words to this effect, which appeared prominently in an *ex post* legislative history of the 1972 amendments prepared by the Congressional Research Service.

[111] That offers regulated parties flexibility they may use to avoid costs. *See* Richards, supra note 51 at 248.

relationships to cost minimization and pollution prevention.[112] CWA standards demanding that pollution be abated at least as much as the available technology could accomplish include CWA §§ 301 and 306's "best practicable control technology currently available" (BPT),[113] "best conventional pollutant control technology" (BCT),[114] "best available technology economically achievable" (BATEA),[115] for *existing* and "best available demonstrated control technology" (BADT)[116] for *new* point source dischargers.[117] It also includes CWA § 307(a)'s toxic pollutant standards,[118] CWA § 316(b)'s "best technology available" standards for cooling water intakes,[119] and CWA § 402(p)'s "maximum extent practicable" standard for municipal and industrial stormwater discharge control.[120]

Courts generally interpreted the progression from BPT to BATEA as the ratcheting of cost back from being a dominant to being a peripheral consideration, up to whatever point the costs of a solution were not "wholly disproportionate" to its effectiveness.[121] And they were told

---

[112] *See* Emily L. Sherwin, *The Bubble Concept in Water Pollution Control*, 60 B.U. L. REV. 686, 693–96 (1980); A. Myrick Freeman III, *Technology-Based Effluent Standards: The U.S. Case*, 16(1) WATER RESOURCES RES. 21, 23–26 (1980).

[113] *See* 33 U.S.C. § 1311(b)(1)(A).

[114] *See* 33 U.S.C. § 1311(b)(2)(E). The so-called BCT "cost test" that arose out of the 1977 amendments grew from EPA's work to specify the cost of certain benchmark technologies for the common pollutants of total suspended solids, biochemical oxygen demand, and oil/grease. *See* U.S. EPA, Best Conventional Pollutant Control Technology; Reasonableness of Existing Effluent Limitation Guidelines, 44 Fed. Reg. 50732 (1979).

[115] *See* 33 U.S.C. § 1311(b)(2)(A).

[116] *See* 33 U.S.C. § 1316(a)(1).

[117] Unlike the CAA, which consolidates review of such standard-settings in one court (the D.C. Circuit), the CWA's special statutory review provision allows any court of appeals to hear challenges to these technology-based standard-settings. *See* 33 U.S.C. § 1369(b)(1).

[118] *See* 33 U.S.C. § 1317(a)(1).

[119] *See* 33 U.S.C. § 1326(b).

[120] *See* 33 U.S.C. § 1342(p)(3)(B); *see* Tualatin Riverkeepers v. Oregon Dept. of Envtl. Quality, 230 P.3d 559 (Or. App. 2010).

[121] *See* Amer. Frozen Food Inst. v. Train, 539 F.2d 107, 116–24 (D.C. Cir. 1976); Weyerhaeuser Co. v. Costle, 590 F.2d 1011, 1024–28, 1044–47 (D.C. Cir. 1978); BASF v. Wyandotte Corp. v. Costle, 598 F.2d 637, 656–57 (1st Cir. 1979); Ass'n of Pac. Fisheries v. EPA, 615 F.2d 794, 803–20 (9th Cir. 1980); Natural Resources Defense Council, Inc. v. U.S. EPA, 822 F.2d 104, 109–26 (D.C. Cir. 1987); Chem. Mfrs. Ass'n v. EPA, 870 F.2d 177, 203–06, 226–27,

often enough that the cost variation between retrofitting existing and enhancing new capital is always of the same sign,[122] even as important game-theoretic insights suggested that differentiating between old and new capital introduces a host of unwanted distortions.[123] Because each of the factored determinations were to be made permit by permit, absent an applicable sectoral standard, and no permit could be weakened by any later-adopted sectoral standard,[124] confusion eventually set in over the differentiation of the standards based on pollutants, certain high-priority sectors, and other sub-classifications.[125]

Judicial doctrine had established that BPT for categories and classes of existing sources meant "the *average of the best* existing performance by plants of various sizes, ages, and unit processes within each industrial category."[126] In contrast, by the time new source standards were under

---

261–63 (5th Cir. 1989); BP Exploration & Oil Co. v. EPA, 66 F.3d 784, 789–91 (6th Cir. 1995).

[122] *See Chem. Mfrs. Ass'n*, 870 F.2d at 262. Cost-of-compliance variability among regulated parties was the cause of much commentary. *See, e.g.*, Freeman, supra note 112 at 24–26; ACKERMAN & HASSLER, supra note 1. It remained so long after the CWA standard-setting abated. *See, e.g.*, Jonathan S. Masur & Eric A. Posner, *Toward a Pigouvian State*, 164 U. PA. L. REV. 93 (2015); T.H. TIETENBERG, EMISSIONS TRADING: PRINCIPLES AND PRACTICE 27 (2d ed. 2005); Harrington *et al.*, supra note 88 at 7–8; WILLIAM J. BAUMOL & WALLACE E. OATES, THE THEORY OF ENVIRONMENTAL POLICY (2d ed. 1988).

[123] *See* Richard L. Revesz & Allison L. Westfahl Kong, *Regulatory Change and Optimal Transition Relief*, 105 NW. U. L. REV. 1581 (2011); Robert N. Stavins, *Vintage-Differentiated Environmental Regulation*, 25 HARV. ENVTL. L. REV. 29 (2006); Dallas Burtraw *et al.*, *Economics of Pollution Trading for SO_2 and NO_x*, 30 ANN. REV. ENV'T. & RES. 253 (2005).

[124] This "best professional judgment" (BPJ) permitting became a pervasive element of the Act. *See, e.g.*, Trustees for Alaska v. EPA, 749 F.2d 549, 552–54 (9th Cir. 1984); U.S. EPA, NPDES PERMIT WRITERS' MANUAL § 5.2.3.5 (Sept. 2010). EPA counsels permit writers to use methods "consistent with the statistical approach EPA has used to develop effluent guidelines," including calculating maximum daily discharges "by multiplying the long-term average achievable by implementation of the model technology or process change by a daily variability factor determined from the statistical properties of a lognormal distribution." Id.

[125] *See* Ridgway M. Hall, Jr., *The Evolution and Implementation of EPA's Regulatory Program to Control the Discharge of Toxic Pollutants to the Nation's Waters*, 10(3) NAT. RES. LAWYER 507 (1977); ROBERT W. ADLER ET AL., THE CLEAN WATER ACT TWENTY YEARS LATER 138–70 (1993).

[126] *See* American Meat Inst. v. EPA, 526 F.2d 442 (7th Cir. 1975) (emphasis added) (*quoting* Sen. Edmund Muskie, in *A Legislative History of Water Pollution Control Act Amends. of 1972*, at 169–70 (Cong. Res. Serv. 1973)); *see*

review, what was deemed "demonstrated" technology turned on the sectoral boundaries drawn and the evidentiary burdens more than anything else.[127] BATEA standards could require "'a broader range of technological alternatives,' including techniques 'which exist in operation or which can be applied as a result of public and private research efforts.'"[128] But while EPA's search for solutions occasionally reached far afield,[129] its cryptic sectoral and temporal horizons and the averaging to be done remained sources of unrest even as the boundary drawing elicited not a single judicial rebuke.[130] Congress itself had named the first

---

also Hooker Chems. & Plastics Corp. v. Train, 537 F.2d 620, 632 (2d Cir. 1976); Kennecott Copper Corp. v. EPA, 612 F.2d 1232, 1242 (10th Cir. 1979); *cf.* American Frozen Food Inst. v. Train, 539 F.2d 107, 118–19 (D.C. Cir. 1976) (statutory factors for identifying "practicable" and "industrial category" including "the age of the plants, their size, the unit processes involved, and the cost of applying such controls" amount to a "limited cost-benefit analysis in order to maintain uniformity within a class and category of point sources").

[127] *See* La Pierre, supra note 67 at 805–29; Freeman, supra note 112 at 24; *cf.* Chem. Mfrs. Ass'n, 870 F.2d at 263 ("Congress did not intend the term [BADT] to limit consideration of treatment systems only to those widely in use in the industry. Instead, the present availability of a particular technology may be 'demonstrated' if even one plant utilizes the technology in question.").

[128] *Amer. Meat Inst.*, 536 F.2d at 462 (*quoting Legis. Hist.*, supra note 126 at 170); *cf.* Chem. Mfrs. Ass'n v. EPA, 870 F.2d 177, 226 (5th Cir. 1989) ("Congress intended these limitations to be based on the performance of the single best-performing plant in an industrial field."); *see also* American Iron & Steel Inst. v. EPA, 526 F.2d 1027, 1057 n.67 (3d Cir. 1975) (noting EPA was to be given the "capability and the mandate to press technology and economics" to achieve the pollution reductions attainable); CPC Int'l v. Train, 515 F.2d 1032, 1047 n.32 (8th Cir. 1975) (BATEA's "available control technology" is not confined only to technology that is "in actual routine use somewhere").

[129] *See* American Frozen Food Inst. v. Train, 539 F.2d 107, 132 (D.C. Cir. 1976) ("Technology in the modern world knows few boundaries—the United States–Canada boundary perhaps least of all."). On the searches EPA conducted, *see* WESLEY A. MAGAT ET AL., RULES IN THE MAKING: A STATISTICAL ANALYSIS OF REGULATORY AGENCY BEHAVIOR 31–44 (1986). EPA was repeatedly challenged for fashioning and using as a benchmark a "model plant" at this step. *See* Freeman, supra note 112 at 24.

[130] From among "several thousand" effluent limitations pertaining to roughly 40 industrial categories finalized by late 1977, La Pierre, supra note 67 at 808–09, the three dozen or so litigated to full judicial opinions concluded by then or in the years shortly following included *zero* instances where a court reversed EPA's decision to subcategorize or its refusal to do so.

industrial sectors for which BADT standards would be set.[131] But judicial deference to EPA's phased sectoral assessments eventually filled the gaps.[132]

Whether individual facilities' or whole categories of dischargers' changes to their operations were the issue, the focus remained on the incumbents.[133] Reviewing courts divided noticeably over whether BPT could require "internal alterations in production" as opposed to mere "end-of-pipe" add-ons,[134] but they agreed that if inter-sectoral technology transfers could work (to a reasonable approximation) within the target sector, such technology was cost-available within the meaning of BATEA and BADT.[135] As trade groups opposed EPA at every step,[136] arguing that

---

131 *See* Natural Resources Defense Council, Inc. v. EPA, 510 F.2d 692, 697 (D.C. Cir. 1975) (*citing* CWA § 306(b)(1)(A) listing 27 source categories to be prioritized for new source BADT standards).

132 *See, e.g.*, Citizens Coal Council v. EPA, 447 F.3d 879, 890–94 (6th Cir. 2006) (reversing earlier panel opinion and affording broad deference to EPA to subcategorize the coal mining sector according to age and condition of mines used); Amer. Petro. Inst. v. EPA, 661 F.2d 340, 354–55 (5th Cir. 1981).

133 *Cf.* United States Steel v. Train, 556 F.2d 822, 843–46 (7th Cir. 1977) (testing the cost-availability of facility's installation of recycling operation and finding no cost-prohibitive barriers thereto); BASF Wyandotte Corp. v. Costle, 598 F.2d 637, 656–58 (1st Cir. 1979); Amer. Petro. Inst. v. EPA, 661 F.2d 340, 346–57 (5th Cir. 1981). In *United States Steel*, for example, EPA hired US Steel's own process engineer to compare its plant to other, similar integrated steel mills and concluded that the re-engineering proposed was cost-available. *See* 556 F.2d at 845–46.

134 *See, e.g.*, FMC Corp. v. Train, 539 F.2d 973, 981 (4th Cir. 1976) (noting that "[i]n-process control measures may be required … if they are considered normal practice within the industry"); Tanners' Council of Amer., Inc. v. Train, 540 F.2d 1188, 1191 (4th Cir. 1976) ("[BPT] effluent standards are to rely primarily on end-of-manufacturing treatment facilities but may include control technologies within the process if these measures are considered normal practice within the industry."); American Petroleum Inst. v. EPA, 540 F.2d 1023, 1033–34 (10th Cir. 1976) (recognizing disagreement among courts).

135 *See* Natural Resources Defense Council, Inc. v. EPA, 808 F.3d 556, 572–74 (2d Cir. 2015) (*citing* Kennecott v. EPA, 780 F.2d 445, 453 (4th Cir. 1986), Hooker Chems. & Plastics Corp. v. Train, 537 F.2d 620, 636 (2d Cir. 1976)). EPA's finding that some such retrofit was cost-available to the target facilities was also demanded by some courts. *See, e.g.*, American Iron & Steel Inst. v. EPA, 568 F.2d 284, 299–300 (3d Cir. 1977); *American Iron & Steel Inst.*, 526 F.2d at 1047–48.

136 *See* La Pierre, supra note 67 at 806–29; William Funk, *The Exception that Approves the Rule: FDF Variances Under the Clean Water Act*, 13 B.C. ENVT'L AFFS. L. REV. 1 (1985).

the adoption/diffusion of various solutions in their sectors was cost-prohibitive,[137] and Congress intervened to focus attention on "toxic" pollutants,[138] the cost-achievability agenda entailed framing a sector and estimating how much abatement could be had without fundamentally altering or collapsing that sector. Just where the costs of compliance became *too* high, *i.e.*, not "achievable," remained the agency's decision to make.[139]

After *Entergy Corp. v. Riverkeeper, Inc.*,[140] the CWA's many references to "best" technologies probably all permit the weighing of compliance costs within some form of multivariate optimization as opposed to requiring a search for the most effective pollution abatement solution.[141] Yet *Entergy* gives little impetus to reading the Act's "best" technology

---

137 *See, e.g.*, R.S. Clark, *Impact of Environmental Regulations on Drilling-Fluid Technology*, J. PETRO. TECH. 806–08 (Sept. 1994) (describing the gradual substitution of water-based drilling fluids for more toxic and environmentally persistent predecessors); *cf.* Texas Oil & Gas Ass'n v. EPA, 161 F.3d 923, 930–33 (5th Cir. 1998) (reviewing prolonged and litigious history of discharge standards from oil/gas wells in coastal waters); Natural Resources Defense Council, Inc. v. EPA, 863 F.2d 1420, 1426–27 (9th Cir. 1988) (remanding EPA conclusion that it lacked needed evidence to require reinjection of produced water as "available technology" on the grounds that coastal operations in California and Alaska had proven reinjection was "technologically feasible" and the legislative history of CWA § 304 suggesting that "technologically feasible limitations" should be set as BATEA even without "precise cost figures").

138 *See* Hall, supra note 125 at 518.

139 *See* Patricia Ross McCubbin, *The Risk in Technology-Based Standards*, 16 DUKE ENVT'L. L. & POL'Y F. 1, 11–29 (2005); Freeman, supra note 112; ACKERMAN & HASSLER, supra note 1. For example, in its noted cluster rule for pulp and paper manufacturers, dioxin-reducing shifts in production—to chlorine-free bleaching processes—were resisted by the industry and its unions chiefly with projections that such shifts would close many more plants than a less stringent standard. *See* WILLIAM BOYD, THE SLAIN WOOD: PAPERMAKING AND ITS ENVIRONMENTAL CONSEQUENCES IN THE AMERICAN SOUTH 189–216 (2015). EPA's adoption of the less stringent standard was upheld against all challenges in *National Wildlife Fed'n v. EPA*, 286 F.3d 554 (D.C. Cir. 2002). Similar dynamics were afoot in the cooling water intakes rulemakings examined in Chapter 5.

140 556 U.S. 208 (2009).

141 *See Entergy*, 556 U.S. at 217–23 (holding that the term "best" technology does not necessarily mean the most efficient at producing some good no matter the cost); *cf.* Sierra Club v. Costle, 657 F.2d 298, 325–26 (D.C. Cir. 1981) (interpreting the several factors expressly named in CAA § 111(a)(1) as specifying the meaning of "best" technology).

mandates as mere efficiency maximizing.[142] EPA has long factored incumbents' particular costs into its CWA permitting and a shift from that norm seems both doubtful and unlikely to succeed in court if attempted.[143] This practice depends for its stringency on the quality of the underlying sample(s). But can it "crowd out" radical improvements by focusing the attention on incumbents and their extant solutions? Chapters 4 addresses that question directly. Let us briefly consider here, though, how industrial sectors' *geography* can skew an analysis of cost feasibility.

In its offshore subcategory of oil/gas drilling sector standards for "produced" water (the industry's highest-volume waste stream[144]), EPA confronted a competitive industry operating at or near marginal cost.[145] The range of treatment solutions reflected variations among operating

---

[142] *Cf. Entergy*, 556 U.S. at 237 (Stevens, J., dissenting) ("Unless costs are so high that the best technology is not 'available,' Congress has decided that they are outweighed by the benefits of minimizing adverse environmental impact."). The Court has made it abundantly clear that statutory factor balancing is not to be converted into anything else. *See, e.g.*, Citizens to Preserve Overton Park v. Volpe, 401 U.S. 402, 418–21 (1971); Motor Vehicle Mfrs. Ass'n v. State Farm Mut. Auto. Ins. Co. 463 U.S. 29, 43–44 (1983); Pension Benefit Guar. Corp. v. LTV Corp., 496 U.S. 633, 644–47 (1990); Massachusetts v. EPA, 549 U.S. 497, 528–35 (2007); Nat'l Ass'n of Homebuilders v. Defenders of Wildlife, 551 U.S. 644, 661–67 (2007). Moreover, as the majority in *Michigan v. EPA* made clear in construing a CAA provision that did not even mention the word "cost," the Supreme Court's notions of "cost" and weighing costs are far more elastic than orthodox benefit-cost analysis accepts. *See* Michigan v. EPA, 135 S. Ct. 2699, 2707–08 (2015).

[143] A convergence of doctrine, one stream known as the "major questions" canon neutralizing the ordinary deference paid to agency interpretations of law where some overtly political choice is afoot, *see, e.g.*, King v. Burwell, 135 S. Ct. 2480 (2015), and another the Supreme Court's preference for agencies' considering costs in risk regulation, *see, e.g.*, *Michigan*, 135 S. Ct. at 2707; EPA v. EME Homer City Gen., L.P. 134 S. Ct. 1584, 1606–07 (2014), suggests that such a move would come to searching scrutiny in court.

[144] Produced water emerges from "hydrocarbon-bearing strata with produced oil and gas" and can include "brines trapped with the oil and gas in the formation, waters injected into the reservoir to increase productivity," and a range of hazardous constituents like metals and radioactivity. Michael O. Waguespack, *Produced Waters in Coastal Louisiana*, 3 TUL. ENVTL. L.J. 7, 7 (1990).

[145] *See* NATIONAL COMMISSION ON THE BP DEEPWATER HORIZON OIL SPILL AND OFFSHORE DRILLING, REPORT TO THE PRESIDENT—DEEP WATER: THE GULF OIL DISASTER AND THE FUTURE OF OFFSHORE DRILLING 36–38 (2011).

capital, locations, and vintages.[146] So it had to evaluate how its standard would favor or disfavor the various production regions[147]—a precaution which years of litigation with the industry's different geographic segments likely prompted.[148] EPA found from its investigation that offshore operations had been molded both by the regulatory norms and the local circumstances of their adjacent states.[149] Although operations offshore of Alaska and California had achieved zero discharge in practice, they constituted but 33 out of 2,500 platforms identified for the 1993 rulemaking.[150] Thus, the Gulf of Mexico's challenging geology, coupled with an interrelated "coastal" subcategory's concurrent regulation, convinced EPA that a blanket reinjection requirement was unjustified.[151] For

---

146 *See* U.S. EPA, Oil and Gas Extraction Point Source Category; Offshore Subcategory Effluent Limitations Guidelines and New Source Performance Standards, 58 Fed. Reg. 12454, 12462–67 (1993). The technology it used to benchmark the standard, gas flotation for contaminant removal, had been used for many years and was in operation at more than a third of all operations surveyed. Id. at 12482.

147 *See* Offshore Guidelines, 58 Fed. Reg. at 12481–82. The move came after years of uncertainty over how to regulate oilfield wastes. *See* Waguespack, supra note 144 at 14 ("EPA could have recommended that many oilfield wastes, including produced water, be regulated under the Resource Conservation and Recovery Act (RCRA) requirements.").

148 *See* BP Exploration & Oil Co. v. U.S. EPA, 66 F.3d 784, 790–91 (6th Cir. 1995); *see also* Amer. Petro. Inst. v. EPA, 858 F.2d 261, 263–66 (5th Cir. 1988). EPA soon retraced these steps in its "coastal" subcategory rulemaking of 1996. *See* Texas Oil & Gas Ass'n v. EPA, 161 F.3d 923, 929–32 (5th Cir. 1998).

149 *See* Allison Wiedeman, *Regulation of Produced Water by the U.S. Environmental Protection Agency, in* PRODUCED WATER 2, 27, 34–41 (Mark Reed & Stale Johnsen eds., 1996); *cf.* Waguespack, supra note 144 at 16–21 (reporting data from coastal Louisiana production tending to show that produced water reinjection, though cost-available in Alaska, California, and other offshore locations, was infeasible in Louisiana wells because of legacy and other costs borne there).

150 *See BP Exploration*, 66 F.3d at 796; *cf.* Offshore Guidelines, 58 Fed. Reg. at 12482–483 (noting the energy requirements and air pollution associated with reinjection across much of the industry). For its "coastal" subcategory rulemaking in 1996, EPA noted that its regional office's general permit and state rules in Louisiana had required zero discharge of produced water—even as it refused to set zero discharge as the national BPT standard.

151 *See* Offshore Guidelines, 58 Fed. Reg. at 12482–83. The agency was somewhat equivocal, but not uncertain: "Although reinjection technology is feasible in some circumstances, some facilities cannot reinject produced water because of geologic conditions in specific locations. Also, the air emissions … and energy requirements … associated with this option at offshore facilities,

all could be told, the extent of Gulf production was aided by the adjacent states' refusal to require zero discharge, the consequent incremental improvement of gas flotation equipment, a concentration of market-serving vendors, and the offshore operations' relative integration with closer-in and onshore production.[152] Enhanced gas flotation had likely grown comparatively cheaper across the spectrum of applications because it had been so long preferred by the Gulf region while other, nominally more effective solutions—too costly in certain operating environments—remained relatively unimproved.[153]

By putting off the setting of *any* national standards on produced water for years, deferring to state and regional controls permit by permit, EPA headquarters may well have minimized the costs *it* imposed by its actions.[154] Whether that minimized *all* costs associated with produced water and the CWA is, however, a different question. EPA seemed to believe that requiring reinjection in all offshore areas would disadvantage and therefore diminish Gulf production and perhaps rejected it for that reason.[155] Legally, even a BPT mandate would have allowed EPA to

---

especially in light of the air emissions and energy requirements associated with potential future requirements for facilities in the coastal subcategory ... are unacceptably high." Id. (internal citations omitted).

[152] *Cf.* Offshore Guidelines, 58 Fed. Reg. at 12463–65 (describing the "engineering costs" of enhanced gas flotation and various uncertainties in the costs because of the prevalence of both extant gas flotation systems and of pipeline systems delivering produced water to onshore treatment facilities). By the early 1990s, gas flotation treatment technology for oilfield applications had improved significantly from its first use as BATEA in 1979, largely because of its widespread use throughout the Gulf. *See* id. at 12482–83, 12490–91; *see also* U.S. EPA, Final Effluent Limitations Guidelines and Standards for the Coastal Subcategory of the Oil and Gas Extraction Point Source Category, 61 Fed. Reg. 66086, 66099–100 (1996).

[153] A short time later, EPA found zero discharge (reinjection) for "coastal" operations "technically available, economically achievable," and thus to be BATEA for that subcategory—outside of Alaska's Cook Inlet. *See* Coastal Guidelines, 61 Fed. Reg. at 66100.

[154] *See* Coastal Guidelines, 61 Fed. Reg. at 66106 (counting regional permit standards as part of the "current regulatory requirements baseline"). That baseline had arisen through years of permit litigation. *See, e.g.*, Marathon Oil Co. v. EPA, 564 F.2d 1253, 1257–60 (9th Cir. 1977); Natural Resources Defense Council, Inc. v. U.S. EPA, 863 F.2d 1420, 1425 (9th Cir. 1988).

[155] *See* Offshore Guidelines, 58 Fed. Reg. at 12462–67, 12480–83, 12490–91. The very same considerations were dismissed from the "coastal" subcategory rulemaking three years later, excepting operations in Alaska's Cook Inlet, citing a

require a uniform solution like reinjection.[156] (An "average" is necessarily at least as good as half of its cohort.[157]) So its decisions on reinjection must have stemmed from what EPA believed was a geographic skew among incumbent operations, the threatened employment effects of ignoring that skew, or other practical challenges that could result.[158] The consequent decentralization of governance almost certainly raised *governmental* costs, fractured the industry's solutions to the environmental problems, and delayed the technical advances in produced water treatment that later ensued. Phasing solutions in can often minimize these latter costs if the phase-in is legal, public, and calculated to do so. But all of that is quite contingent and circumstantial.

2.4 THE CONSUMER PRODUCT SAFETY ACT (AND OTHERS): WHICH COSTS TO COUNT?

Unlike EPA, several agencies have been brought to their economic analyses in risk regulation less by a swarm of highly specific and interrelated statutory mandates than by an unbroken tradition of executive orders dating to the 1980s[159] or judicial constructions of their vague

---

modeled projection that few if any firms would fail as a result of a zero discharge limit there. *See* Coastal Guidelines, 61 Fed. Reg. at 66100–01.

[156] *Cf.* United States Steel Corp. v. Train, 556 F.2d 822, 843–46 (7th Cir. 1977) (finding that BPT for integrated steel mill included use of a "recycling" system observed at other mills, including some of permittee's mills).

[157] *See, e.g.*, Chemical Mfrs. Ass'n v. EPA, 870 F.2d 177, 203–64 (5th Cir. 1989); Citizens' Coal Council v. EPA, 447 F.3d 879, 898–900 (6th Cir. 2006); Trustees for Alaska v. EPA, 749 F.2d 549, 554–60 (9th Cir. 1984).

[158] *Compare* Coastal Guidelines, 61 Fed. Reg. at 66105–07 (finding only six facilities not currently regulated to the standard being set and analyzing the costs those facilities could incur as a result of the zero discharge requirement), *with* Offshore Guidelines, 58 Fed. Reg. at 12464 (finding that 37% of existing offshore platforms piped their produced water to onshore treatment facilities).

[159] These orders began in February 1981 with Executive Order 12291, which required "all agencies, to the extent permitted by law," to adhere to a list of requirements for promulgating rules—including the preparation of a "[r]egulatory [i]mpact [a]nalysis" for any "major" rules. *See* Executive Order 12291—Federal Regulation, 46 Fed. Reg. 13193, 13193–94 (1981). Each of these RIAs was to include "[a] description of the potential costs of the rule, including any adverse effects that cannot be quantified in monetary terms, and the identification of those likely to bear the costs." Id. at 13194 (§ 3(d)(3)). Also to be included was a "description of alternative approaches that could substantially achieve the same regulatory goal at lower cost, together with an analysis of this potential

statutory mandates. The Consumer Product Safety Act[160] (empowering the CPSC) and the Occupational Safety and Health Act (empowering the OSHA) are both representative of the (relatively) "independent" agencies in this experience. The CPSC is broadly empowered to regulate consumer goods, but it must first "consider" the "probable effect the rule will have on utility, cost, or availability of such products" as well as the available means to achieve the objective of the rule while "minimizing adverse effects on competition, manufacturing, and commercial practices."[161] In *Zen Magnets, LLC v. CPSC*,[162] the Tenth Circuit reduced all of this to a mandate to "balance the costs and benefits identified … to determine whether a safety standard is justified."[163] That was admittedly a short step from several prior holdings (in the Fifth Circuit) likening the consumer product statute to a kind of product liability balancing standard.[164] The

---

benefit and costs and a brief explanation of the legal reasons why such alternatives, if proposed, could not be adopted." Id. (§ 3(d)(4)). Executive Order 12866 followed up that focus by requiring any agency proposing a "major" rule to "identify and assess alternative forms of regulation" and "to the extent feasible, [to] specify performance objectives, rather than specifying the behavior or manner of compliance that regulated entities must adopt." Executive Order 12866—Regulatory Planning and Review, 58 Fed. Reg. 51735, 51736 (1993) (§ 1(b)(8)). The Clinton order was followed by a Bush order, *see* Executive Order 13422—Further Amendment to Executive Order 12866 on Regulatory Planning Review, 72 Fed. Reg. 2763 (2007), and Obama orders revoking the Bush order and further building on the Clinton order. *See* Executive Order 13563—Improving Regulation and Regulatory Review, 76 Fed. Reg. 3821 (2011); Executive Order 13610—Identifying and Reducing Regulatory Burdens, 77 Fed. Reg. 28469 (2012). The Trump Administration's "regulatory budget" orders, by contrast, initiated an as-yet untested and still closely guarded approach ostensibly requiring the cutting of regulatory costs for the imposition of any new costs.

160 Pub. L. No. 92-573, 86 Stat. 1207 (1972), *codified at* 15 U.S.C. §§ 2051–89.

161 15 U.S.C. § 2058(f)(1). CPSC must also determine that its rule is "reasonably necessary to eliminate or reduce an unreasonable risk of injury associated with such product" and find that issuing the rule is in the public interest. Id. at § 2058(f)(3)(A)–(B).

162 841 F.3d 1141 (10th Cir. 2016).

163 *Zen Magnets*, 841 F.3d at 1147 (citing 15 U.S.C. § 2058(f)(3)).

164 *See, e.g.*, Southland Mower Co. v. CPSC, 619 F.2d 499, 508–09 (5th Cir. 1980) ("The determination of whether an unreasonable risk of … injury exists involves 'a balancing test' like that familiar in tort law: The regulation may issue if the severity of the injury that may result from the product, factored by the likelihood of the injury, offsets the harm the regulation imposes upon manufacturers and consumers.").

Zen Magnets court found the rule at issue—banning certain high-powered magnet sets with small pieces for their risks to children[165]—insufficiently cost justified and vacated the rule.[166] The panel, which included then-Judge Neil Gorsuch, came to its conclusion in part by questioning the veracity of the agency's injury data[167] and in part from what it found to be a failure to evaluate the costs to consumers deprived of the magnets.[168] CPSC had weighed the rule's costs of compliance against what it considered to be the potential alternatives, *e.g.*, labeling, restrictions on point of sale, *etc.*, and had concluded that "a standard limiting the size and strength of magnets in a magnet set" was the only step likely to materially diminish the risk.[169] The court's objection that CPSC had not considered the consumers' lost "surplus" utility as between smaller and larger magnets (of like strength) was dictated not by statute but by that panel's interpretation of the relevant "costs." And that interpretation undoubtedly put the agency in an informational bind: CPSC had found no practical way of establishing that quantity.[170] Barred from taking its action, the agency was left to allow what amounted to excess lethal risk from toys—values that we have often agreed are only imperfectly monetizable.[171]

Similar troubles may be emerging in OSHA rulemakings turning on the "feasibility" of workplace hazard solutions. OSHA has generally regarded solutions limiting harmful chemical exposures which cost less

---

[165] The neodymium magnets at issue, if swallowed, presented unique risks to the gastrointestinal tract of the victim—some of which could be fatal. *See* Consumer Prod. Safety Comm'n, Final Rule: Safety Standards for Magnet Sets, 79 Fed. Reg. 59962, 59963 (2014).

[166] *Zen Magnets*, 841 F.3d at 1155.

[167] *See* id. at 1150–51 & n.12.

[168] *See* id. at 1153 ("Even though the task may be difficult, the [CPSC] is required to advance some explanation that allows a reviewing court to evaluate whether the cost of the lost utility is in fact outweighed by the benefits of the rule.").

[169] *See* Safety Standards for Magnet Sets, 79 Fed. Reg. at 59976.

[170] *Cf.* Safety Standards for Magnet Sets, 79 Fed. Reg. at 59964 (stating that CPSC staff had identified 25 firms marketing the magnet sets but that, to discover who was purchasing the magnet sets, the same staff had to scour online marketing platforms like Amazon.com).

[171] *See, e.g.*, ELIZABETH ANDERSON, VALUE IN ETHICS AND ECONOMICS 210–11 (1993) (arguing that some non-commodity values are "political goods" best secured through democratic institutions of voice, equity, and deliberation).

than 1 percent of firm revenues and 10 percent of firm profits as "feasible"[172] (the cost threshold its statute attaches to such standards[173]). OSHA's "feasibility" determinations have famously wavered on methodological basics,[174] though, leaving the courts to search for latent "arbitrariness" in each rulemaking.[175] Where the *Zen Magnets* court faulted CPSC for ignoring consumers' lost welfare in having to do without the exact product, OSHA's reviewing courts have tended to fault it (when they do) for failing to consider the affected industrial sectors in their *full* particularity.[176] Most problematic in this connection may be the projected employment effects, *i.e.*, expected job loss, from standards like OSHA's.[177] After all, even where projected job losses can be quantified,

---

[172] *See* Note—*OSHA's Feasibility Policy: The Implications of the "Infeasibility" of Respirators*, 129 HARV. L. REV. 2235, 2241 (2016).

[173] *See* United Steelworkers of Amer., AFL-CIO-CLC v. Marshall, 647 F.2d 1189, 1263–73 (D.C. Cir. 1980) (*quoting* 29 U.S.C. § 655(b)(5)); ASARCO, Inc. v. OSHA, 746, 483, 500 (9th Cir. 1984) (finding that "OSHA's methodology complie[d] with the guidelines for proving economic feasibility set out in *Steelworkers*" and upholding OSHA's findings as such).

[174] *See* Note—*OSHA's Feasibility Policy*, supra note 172; Jonathan S. Masur & Eric A. Posner, *Against Feasibility Analysis*, 77 U. CHI. L. REV. 657 (2010); Howard A. Latin, *The Feasibility of Occupational Health Standards: An Essay on Legal Decisionmaking Under Uncertainty*, 78 NW. U. L. REV. 583 (1983).

[175] *See, e.g.*, Forging Industry Ass'n v. Secretary of Labor, 773 F.2d 1436, 1453 (4th Cir. 1985) (upholding rule on grounds OSHA had demonstrated that the standard "poses no insurmountable burden to the continued viability of any of the affected industries"); National Grain and Feed Ass'n v. OSHA, 866 F.2d 717, 725–33 (5th Cir. 1989) (deferring to OSHA's interpretation of the Act freeing its "safety" standards from "feasibility" testing, suggesting that only certain "health" standards promulgated pursuant to § 6(b)(5) are covered by the test); Color Pigments Mfrs. Ass'n v. OSHA, 16 F.3d 1157, 1162–63 (11th Cir. 1994) (vacating OSHA rule on cadmium pigments for failure to demonstrate "technological" or "economic" feasibility in the "generic" rulemaking prepared).

[176] *See, e.g.*, American Iron & Steel Inst. v. OSHA, 939 F.2d 975, 1007–10 (D.C. Cir. 1991); AFL-CIO v. OSHA, 965 F.2d 962, 980–83 (11th Cir. 1992); *Color Pigments Mfrs.*, 16 F.3d at 1161–63.

[177] *See, e.g.*, Masur & Posner, supra note 174 at 695–97. Employment effects are difficult for *any* economic projection of expected costs. *See* Jonathan S. Masur & Eric A. Posner, *Regulation, Unemployment, and Cost-Benefit Analysis*, 98 VA. L. REV. 579 (2012). An employment effect will often include changes of uncertain sign and/or magnitude. *Cf.* Cary Coglianese & Christopher Carrigan, *The Jobs and Regulation Debate, in* DOES REGULATION KILL JOBS? 1 (Cary Coglianese *et al.* eds., 2013). "[W]hat matters is valuing the real welfare effects to workers as they are forced to transition to new jobs." Id. at 18.

why should the inquiry end there: The full stream of direct, indirect, and ancillary effects from the loss of a job might be quantifiable and significant.[178]

Weighing costs is an enterprise the conclusion of which turns first on whose costs should count. The ideal of "social" cost accounting at least implies that *everyone's* costs, however tangential or remote, should count. And that introduces an acutely Sisyphean prospect to the weighing of regulatory costs.[179] The executive orders requiring that cost-benefit evaluations be prepared for all "major" rulemakings, now bolstered by years of Office of Management and Budget (OMB) guidance and implementation in the historical record,[180] made some progress toward specifying which costs should count.[181] But just because a cost should count does not mean it can be counted. And if the volume of critical literature on agency "compliance" with OMB regulatory impact assessment is any indicator, a great deal of slack now separates what OMB has said was required by these executive orders and what is done.[182]

Finally, the courts have made equally clear that the reviewability of agency duties in court when the duties stem from these executive orders is subject to a dense web of doctrinal filters generally tilted toward

---

178 *See* Timothy J. Bartik, *Including Jobs in Benefit-Cost Analysis*, 4 ANN. REV. RES. ECON. 55 (2012); Masur & Posner, supra note 174 at 613–23.

179 *Cf.* Pizer and Kopp, supra note 88 at 1344 ("As pollution control moves away from end-of-pipe abatement and toward pollution prevention and process changes, it becomes increasingly difficult to identify the operating costs associated with environmental protection. Even worse, as we turn to research and new technology to provide cleaner alternatives to polluting activities, the cost of these research and development activities is virtually unknown.").

180 The central guidance document on the preparation of these "Regulatory Impact Analyses," OMB Circular A-4, states that "a good regulatory analysis should include … (1) a statement of the need for the proposed action, (2) an examination of alternative approaches, and (3) an evaluation of the benefits and costs—quantitative and qualitative—of the proposed action and the main alternatives identified … ." Office of Management and Budget, Circular A-4: Regulatory Analysis 2 (Sept. 17, 2003).

181 *See* Nestor M. Davidson & Ethan J. Lieb, *Regleprudence—at OIRA and Beyond*, 103 GEO. L.J. 259, 274–94 (2015).

182 *See* Nina Mendelson & Jonathan B. Wiener, *Responding to Agency Avoidance of OIRA*, 37 HARV. J.L. & PUB. POL'Y 447 (2014); Ethan Bueno De Mesquita & Matthew C. Stephenson, *Regulatory Quality Under Imperfect Oversight*, 101(3) AMER. POL. SCI. REV. 605 (2007).

finding these exercises of discretion unreviewable.[183] Chapter 6 explores one case study where OMB influence through these executive orders was manifest. Before coming to the case studies, though, we must understand the mechanisms of social cost avoidance and how the scales of a cost analysis can either emphasize or obscure these mechanisms.

---

183 The first filter is the fact that any executive order to subordinates within the executive branch is at least presumptively a matter of managerial presidential control. This makes judicial involvement especially likely to run afoul of inter-branch comity concerns. *Cf.* Chamber of Commerce v. Reich, 74 F.3d 1322, 1328–32 (D.C. Cir. 1996) (declining to conclude that presidential action is never subject to review for statutory review but noting the extreme deference that inter-branch concerns warrant in any such instance of review). A second filter is the reluctance courts express for "enforcing" executive orders unless they expressly state that their intent and effect is the creation of private rights, duties, *etc. See, e.g.*, Indep. Meat Packers Ass'n v. Butz, 526 F.2d 228, 234–36 (8th Cir. 1975); Gnotta v. United States, 415 F.2d 1271, 1275–78 (8th Cir. 1969). Finally, a third filter arises where statutory powers are exercised in executive orders that expressly declaim any intent to create private rights or duties. *See, e.g.*, Peter Raven-Hansen, *Making Agencies Follow Orders: Judicial Review of Agency Violations of Executive Order 12,291*, 1983 DUKE L.J. 285, 329–51 (struggling to find a path for litigants to "enforce" provisions of executive order that expressly declaimed any such private rights), *with* Robert V. Percival, *Who's In Charge? Does the President Have Directive Authority Over Agency Regulatory Decisions?*, 79 FORDHAM L. REV. 2487 (2011) (reviewing the history of "regulatory review" as ordered by OMB/OIRA and finding few judicial entanglements).

3. The economics of technological change and growth

One key to defining and predicting properly "social" costs—indeed, to understanding the estimative analyses available for quantifying and attributing the costs of regulation—is *scale*. Because individual costs of compliance are so often positional and/or balanced out by gains somewhere (or -when) else, *social* cost accounting invariably turns on the scales at which an assessment is made. We will confront three distinct kinds of scaling challenges in the case studies comprising Chapters 4, 5, and 6: temporal, factoral, and geographic. The *temporal* scale of an analysis is its nominal duration. Time's arrow of course enforces a methodological divide between the retrospective and prospective. Regardless, though, costs and cost avoidance can fundamentally transform as variables depending on what length of time is at issue. The *factoral* scale of an analysis concerns the indivisibilities, complementarities, natural capital, and returns to scale that are at work in econometric data like prices, revenues, outputs, inflation, and other standardized sets which can distort our perceptions thereof. Finally, the *geographic* scale of an analysis is its spatial extent and, in risk regulation particularly, the legal or political boundaries it spans. Often, the variability to be found in cost-of-compliance evaluations is that which stems from the variegated jurisdictions or spatial conditions involved. Each of these scales can determine the magnitude and sign of cost estimations in their own ways. This chapter suggests how.

3.1 INNOVATION: CALCULABLE PARAMETER OR THE TERMINUS OF ECONOMIC ANALYSIS?

Economic calculations have lately become a cultural inkblot: One's attitude toward them says a lot. Calculations can, of course, amplify our knowledge. But they can also distort or loosen our grasp of reality.[1] If the sum of the first n successive odd integers is n^2 then:

$$1 = 1^2$$

$$1 + 3 = 2^2$$

$$1 + 3 + 5 = 3^2$$

$$1 + 3 + 5 + 7 = 4^2$$

This Gaussian marvel is a property of the numbers, though.[2] Few (if any) economic calculations are quite like it. For economic calculations should not be about the *properties of numbers*; they should not be merely arithmetic.[3] Parameterized uncertainties in economic models, for example, should approximate "states of nature" and are typically found in state spaces of unknown complexity.[4] Models built from dozens or hundreds of such parameters, some consisting in nothing more than "insufficient reason,"[5] should really provide us *no* assurances.[6] Especially

---

[1] *See* THEODORE M. PORTER, TRUST IN NUMBERS: THE PURSUIT OF OBJECTIVITY IN SCIENCE AND PUBLIC LIFE 17–32 (1995). "Quantification is a powerful agency of standardization because it imposes order on hazy thinking, but this depends on the license it provides to ignore or reconfigure much of what is difficult or obscure." Id. at 85.

[2] *See* WILLIAM L. SCHAAF, CARL FRIEDRICH GAUSS: PRINCE OF MATHEMATICIANS 23–25 (1964).

[3] "As nineteenth-century statisticians liked to boast, their science averaged away everything contingent, accidental, inexplicable, or personal, and left only large-scale regularities." PORTER, supra note 1 at 86. Probabilities derived from some limit theorem or supposed central tendency exceeding the bounds of calculability are not about the numbers themselves, though. *See* Section 3.1.1.

[4] *Cf.* Martin L. Weitzman, *On Modeling and Interpreting the Economics of Climate Change*, 91(1) REV. ECON. & STATS. 1, 2 (2009) ("Modeling uncertain catastrophes presents some *very* strong challenges to economic analysis, the full implications of which have not yet been adequately confronted.").

[5] Bayesian probability assigns epistemic probabilities to $n > 1$ mutually exclusive, collectively exhaustive possibilities equal to $1/n$ as the simplest "non-informative" prior probability estimate. This is often called LaPlace's principle of "insufficient reason." *See* IAN HACKING, THE EMERGENCE OF PROBABILITY 126 (1975). Keynes labeled it the "principle of indifference." Id.

[6] *See* Weitzman, supra note 4 at 18 (concluding that, in the presence of "fat tailed uncertainty" where infinitely bad outcomes have unknown probability distributions, economic modelers do best to present nothing in the form of "accurate and objective … analysis").

for those using the tools of neoclassical economics in calculating expected costs, this bedrock separating practical approximations from fancy math underlies a vast interpretive landscape and also, most importantly, the correlative horizons by which unbiased economic analyses should be confined.

The mathematics of probability has figured uncomfortably in predictive economic modeling for most of the latter's existence.[7] Innovation, technical change, and their expected rapidity are the central drivers in that experience because they are essentially stochastic. Having to include variables like how people will innovate or behave strategically, typically as part of some idealized economic equilibration,[8] drains much of the confidence we would want out of the subject calculations.[9] And without that confidence most calculations' utilities diminish very quickly. What it costs us to build and run such models, we might say, is not justified by the expected benefit of doing so.[10]

---

[7] *See* Itzhak Gilboa *et al.*, *Probability and Uncertainty in Economic Modeling*, 22(3) J. ECON. PERSP. 173 (2008). The frictions perhaps stem clearest of all from the ambiguous logical and epistemic status of economics' general statements. Unlike the nomological statements in the physical sciences, economics' axioms' predictive failures cannot constitute the same kind of self-refutation—although they surely may give us reason to lose interest. *See* ALEXANDER ROSENBERG, MICROECONOMIC LAWS: A PHILOSOPHICAL ANALYSIS (1976); *cf.* Daniel Ellsberg, *Risk, Ambiguity and the Savage Axioms*, 75(4) Q.J. ECON. 643 (1961).

[8] As used herein, *equilibrium* refers to a balance of forces like supply and demand and the (occasionally counterintuitive) results of their equilibration as explicated by Jevons, Walras, Marshall, and other theorists in their tradition. *See* KENNETH J. ARROW & FRANK H. HAHN, GENERAL COMPETITIVE ANALYSIS 1–2 (1971). The field has always dealt rather uncomfortably with a variety of nonlinearities including complementarities, indivisibilities, dynamic feedbacks like income effects and changing expectations over time. *See* JOHN R. HICKS, VALUE AND CAPITAL 89–98, 130–40, 245–82 (2d ed. 1946).

[9] The vast literature on intellectual property law's supposed inducement of innovation (or lack thereof), replete with decades-old debates that are still unresolved, commends at least this much skepticism toward generalizations about economic incentives. For summaries, *see* John F. Duffy, *Rethinking the Prospect Theory of Patents*, 71 U. CHI. L. REV. 439 (2004); Brian D. Wright, *The Economics of Invention Incentives: Patents, Prizes and Research Contracts*, 83 AMER. ECON. REV. 691 (1983). On the conventional critique of cost estimations' limited confidence levels, *see* Winston Harrington *et al.*, *On the Accuracy of Regulatory Cost Estimates*, 19(2) J. POL'Y ANALYSIS 297 (2000).

[10] *See, e.g.*, Andrea Saltelli & Silvio Funtowicz, *When All Models Are Wrong*, 30(2) ISSUES SCI. & TECH. 79 (2014).

When economists' models of policy interventions include variables like the expected pace of technological change, they aim to predict how interrelated forces like supply and demand will respond to human strategies that can be self-compounding.[11] To do so for a single sector, *i.e.*, "partial" equilibrium, is a much simpler exercise than doing so for a wider economy (so-called "general" equilibrium).[12] But each of these endeavors has real limitations. The former ignores the interconnections of an economy's distinct sectors while the latter must rely on so many aggregates that it is typically the assumptions behind or the timing of the perturbations doing most of the work.[13] Too often in either, modelers must use hypothetical constants in the place of real data or functioning variables.[14] Too often, their so-called "convexities" of a transformation must be presumed where there is little reason to think the convexity holds under the posited conditions.[15] Whether the economic modeler takes a

---

[11] *Cf.* ROSENBERG, supra note 7 at 103–06 (distinguishing between economic explanations of phenomena dependent upon human reasoning and "causes" of the same phenomena not involving reasoning agents).

[12] *See* ARROW & HAHN, supra note 8. General equilibrium modeling can share several parallels with productivity growth modeling for such purposes, *see* CHARLES D. KOLSTAD, ENVIRONMENTAL ECONOMICS 271–72 (2000), which has contributed to "computable general equilibrium" (CGE) models' dominance in contemporary economics. *See* ROSS M. STARR, GENERAL EQUILIBRIUM THEORY: AN INTRODUCTION (2d ed. 2011).

[13] The modeling of a so-called "social cost of carbon" suggesting marginal, per-ton charges on GHG emissions involves the use of multiple (divergent) "computable general equilibrium" (CGE) models forecasting the feedbacks and interactivities of emissions, growth, climate damages, and population change in a single number which can then be discounted to net present value(s). If the number is, say, $42 per ton, an action that abated a million tons of GHGs would provide $42 million in benefits (or avoided costs). *See* NATIONAL ACADEMIES OF SCIENCE, ENGINEERING & MED., REPORT—VALUING CLIMATE DAMAGES: UPDATING THE SOCIAL COST OF CARBON DIOXIDE 2–3 (2017).

[14] *Cf.* Saltelli & Funtowicz, supra note 10 at 83 ("When after-the-fact sensitivity analysis reveals problematic or arguable assumptions, a stakeholder might reasonably ask: What were the motives behind the use of such implausible assumptions?").

[15] A convexity results from a linear progression. A non-convex set of, for example, prices would defeat equilibrium methods by supporting multiple independent equilibria in the same vector. A "non-convexity" in price, supply, demand, *etc.* confounds the Arrow-Debreu, Solow, Ramsey-Cass-Koopmans, and most other macroeconomic models. It also severely discounts most of the standard justifications for "market-oriented" regulatory tools like taxes and tradeable allowances. *See* David A. Starrett, *Fundamental Nonconvexities in the Theory of Externalities*, 4 J. ECON. THEORY 180 (1972).

bottom-up (partial equilibrium) or top-down (general equilibrium) approach to the prediction, technological innovation as a force can be made to seem either imperceptible and humdrum or colossal and all-important, depending on the assumptions.[16] It is, alternatively, just another parameter among vectors of them or a ghost in the machine.[17] The math can do nothing to change this basic nature of the relationship between technological change and economic growth.

For all the political struggle, the legislative delegations recounted in Chapter 2 arose from hopes of accelerating innovation without any (economic) plan or theory of how to do so.[18] And of all the economic analysis done by regulators since, where technical change of one kind or another stalks the calculations, none of the parameters has been more polarizing nor more determinative than it.[19] This chapter highlights the basic relationships in economic predictions so common in figuring regulatory costs. Chief among these is *innovation* and its role in economic thought more generally. The economics of induced innovation

---

[16] This has kept technical change at the forefront of efforts to model macroeconomic growth, *see* ELHANAN HELPMAN, THE MYSTERY OF ECONOMIC GROWTH 34–54 (2004), and environmental policies alike. *See* Daron Acemoglu *et al., The Environment and Directed Technical Change*, 102(1) AMER. ECON. REV. 131 (2012).

[17] *See* David Popp *et al., Energy, the Environment, and Technological Change, in* 2 HANDBOOK ON THE ECONOMICS OF INNOVATION 873, 877–80 (Bronwyn H. Hall & Nathan Rosenberg eds., 2010); Andreas Löschel, *Technological Change in Economic Models of Environmental Policy: A Survey*, 43 ECOL. ECON. 105 (2002). This has similarly remained true of productivity growth modeling. *See* Peter Howitt & Philippe Aghion, *Capital Accumulation and Innovation as Complementary Factors in Long-Run Growth*, 3(2) J. ECON. GROWTH 111 (1998).

[18] This is evident from the lack of any discoverable organization within that legislation as well as in the economic writings of the time. *Cf.* Hans P. Binswanger, *Induced Technical Change: Evolution of Thought, in* INDUCED INNOVATION: TECHNOLOGY, INSTITUTIONS, AND DEVELOPMENT 13, 41 (Hans P. Binswanger & Vernon W. Ruttan eds., 1978) (finding all models then available and reviewed therein incapable of predicting microeconomic or macroeconomic outcomes largely because of the unpredictability of technical change); J.H. DALES, POLLUTION, PROPERTY AND PRICES: AN ESSAY IN POLICY-MAKING AND ECONOMICS 102–03 (1968) (in classic popularizing account of market-oriented tools for pollution abatement, expressly excluding air pollution as too uncertain from technological change).

[19] *See* Adam B. Jaffe *et al., Technological Change and the Environment, in* HANDBOOK OF ENVIRONMENTAL ECONOMICS 461 (Karl-Göran Mäler & J.R. Vincent eds., 2003).

feature prominently in the predominant growth theories of today. Ultimately, we trace innovation and economic analysis to a single nexus in which cost-of-compliance predictions characteristically must operate and show that innovation's unhappy role is to be indispensable to economic calculations while at the same time rendering many of the outcomes we care most about essentially unpredictable.

3.1.1 The Microeconomics of Inducing Innovation

The economist John Hicks first hypothesized *induced innovation, i.e.*, that "a change in the relative prices of the factors of production is itself a spur to invention, and to invention of a particular kind—directed to economizing the use of a factor which has become relatively expensive."[20] Hicks juxtaposed labor and capital as macro-factors of production. But scarcity—or, really, production constraints—of any kind could in theory provide microeconomic inducements much as he posited for whole economies.[21] In this neoclassical vein, firms' production factors are fungible,[22] begging the very question of their costs as *social* costs.[23] Some production function made more costly by regulation could just as readily be cast as an upset thereof still to be transformed. If anything like competition obtains (putting aside the fictions of "perfect" competition), producers will minimize net aggregate costs: The business firm exists to minimize both exchange and production costs.[24] That is the impetus of

---

20 JOHN R. HICKS, THE THEORY OF WAGES 124–25 (1st ed. 1932).

21 *See* John R. Hicks, *Wages and Interest: The Dynamic Problem*, 45(179) ECON. J. 456, 462–68 (1935).

22 *See, e.g.*, Ronald H. Coase, *The Institutional Structure of Production*, 82 AMER. ECON. REV. 713, 713–15 (1992). Note, though, that production factors are often *not* perfectly divisible or substitutable (notwithstanding the orthodoxy). *See* Nicholas Georgescu-Roegen, *The Economics of Production*, 60 AMER. ECON. REV. 1, 8–9 (1970); *see* Section 3.2.

23 If the business firm (rather than individual persons) is the elemental agent of transformation functions in welfarism, comprising the ultimate repositories of technical knowledge for production, the relationship between individual and aggregate welfare becomes essentially impossible to express mathematically. *See* Sidney G. Winter, *On Coase, Competence, and the Corporation, in* THE NATURE OF THE FIRM: ORIGINS, EVOLUTION AND DEVELOPMENT 179, 184 (Oliver E. Williamson & Sidney G. Winter eds., 1993) (*quoting* J. DE V. GRAAF, THEORETICAL WELFARE ECONOMICS 16 (1957)).

24 *See* Ronald H. Coase, *The Nature of the Firm*, 4(16) ECONOMICA 386, 390–98 (1937); Armen A. Alchian & Harold Demsetz, *Production, Information Costs, and Economic Organization*, 62 AMER. ECON. REV. 777, 782–85 (1972); KENNETH J. ARROW, THE LIMITS OF ORGANIZATION 20–21 (1974); Eugene F.

economic integration. Only in that nexus's failure can policy interventions' relative efficiencies in spurring innovation diverge.[25] The decisive vector, easily forgotten in this neoclassical view, is *time*: Over time, cost avoidance and technological change exhibit a causal relationship—often to profound effect.[26] The best economic models, whatever their other commitments, are adapted to this condition.[27] When they are not, they suffer. For example, when some early models estimating the costs of

---

Fama & Michael C. Jensen, *Separation of Ownership and Control*, 36 J. L. & ECON. 301, 302 (1983); OLIVER E. WILLIAMSON, THE ECONOMIC INSTITUTIONS OF CAPITALISM (1985); Sanford J. Grossman & Oliver D. Hart, *The Costs and Benefits of Ownership: A Theory of Vertical and Lateral Integration*, 94(4) J. POL. ECON. 691, 692 (1986).

[25] *See* Starrett, supra note 15 at 189. Yet, for as long as "instrument choice" has been around it has been addressed to the microeconomic incentives to innovate. *Cf.* ALLEN V. KNEESE & CHARLES L. SHULTZE, POLLUTION, PRICES AND PUBLIC POLICY (1975) ("Over the long haul, perhaps the most important single criterion on which to judge environmental policies is the extent to which they spur new technology toward the efficient conservation of environmental quality.").

[26] This proposition is (intendedly) neutral as between orthodox and critical theories of growth, *i.e.*, the direction of that causality. *See, e.g.*, Howitt & Aghion, supra note 17 at 123–24 (presenting a "Schumpeterian" growth theory treating capital accumulation and innovation as equal forces in growth and allowing that capital "embodies" new technology); Robert M. Solow, *Technical Change and the Aggregate Production Function*, 39(3) REV. ECON. & STATS. 312, 316–17 (1957) (calculating an aggregate production function and a residual attributed to technical change).

[27] Within macroeconomics a line still divides those who seek to model for uncertainty in equilibration, *i.e.*, "dynamic efficiency," over time and those who regard that as operationally impossible, opting instead to describe "static" efficiencies within nominal sectors. *See* Andrew B. Abel *et al.*, *Assessing Dynamic Efficiency: Theory and Evidence*, 56(1) REV. ECON. STUDS. 1, 1–3 (1989); JOHN R. HICKS, METHODS OF DYNAMIC ECONOMICS 3 (1985) ("It is only too obvious that most traditional Welfare Economics—whether of the 'old' (Pigouvian) or of the 'new' variety—has in fact been static."); BURTON H. KLEIN, DYNAMIC ECONOMICS 12 (1977) ("The key difference between static and dynamic processes is that whereas the former involves types of change that can be predicted on the basis of initial conditions, the latter involves quite unpredictable changes in initial conditions."). But each has struggled with its own unverifiable assumptions and those "directly contradicted by observation—for example, perfect competition, perfect divisibility, linear-homogen[e]ous and continuously differentiable production functions, wholly impersonal market relations, exclusive role of prices in information flows and perfect knowledge of all relevant prices by all agents and perfect foresight." Nicholas Kaldor, *The Irrelevance of Equilibrium Economics*, 82 ECON. J. 1237, 1238 (1972).

GHG abatements converged to a common conclusion showing *delay* was the key to cost-minimizing action,[28] it emerged that those models did not allow for induced technical change from carbon-intensive to carbon-free energy sources.[29] That one change upended the consensus and spotlighted the way in which social cost minimization calculations are so often grounded in tendentious assumptions rather than mere arithmetic (appearances notwithstanding).

The Hicks hypothesis has proven remarkably resistant to empirical testing[30] even as it continues to dominate our talk of economic costs. Energy as a production factor is the case in point: It often exhibits significant price volatility with little or no detectable effect on production or average costs.[31] Electricity consumption in particular has had a notorious connection to economic growth—specifically growth in aggregate production.[32] But as the growth rate in US demand for electricity slowed while productivity continued to grow, the supposed linearity of

---

[28] *See, e.g.*, John P. Weyant, *Costs of Reducing Global Carbon Emissions*, 7 J. ECON. PERSP. 27, 34–42 (1993).

[29] *See* Michael Grubb *et al.*, *Induced Technical Change in Energy and Environment Modeling: Analytical Approaches and Policy Implications*, 27 ANN. REV. ENERGY ENVT. 271, 293 (2002) ("Some models (*e.g.*, Nordhaus) have just one aggregate energy-carbon sector with no opportunity for substitution toward non-carbon sources. Perhaps not surprisingly, these generate a modest response to induced technical change."). With the possibility of induced substitution of low- for high-carbon energy, the model results changed dramatically. *See, e.g.*, Lawrence H. Goulder & Stephen H. Schneider, *Induced Technological Change and the Attractiveness of CO_2 Abatement Policies*, 21 RES. & ENERGY ECON. 211 (1999).

[30] *See* Richard G. Newell *et al.*, *The Induced Innovation Hypothesis and Energy-Saving Technological Change*, 114(3) Q. J. ECON. 941, 942 (1999); Jaffe *et al.*, supra note 19 at 470–88.

[31] *See* Grubb *et al.*, supra note 29 at 277–82; *see also* Adam B. Jaffe & Robert N. Stavins, *Dynamic Incentives of Environmental Regulations: The Effects of Alternative Policy Instruments on Technology Diffusion*, 29 J. ENVTL. ECON. & MNGT. S-43, S-60 (1995). Such detection failures have long been attributed (variously) to complementarities, indivisibilities, returns to scale, and a variety of other nonlinearities. *See, e.g.*, Vernon W. Ruttan *et al.*, *Factor Productivity and Growth: A Historical Interpretation, in* Binswanger and Ruttan, supra note 18 at 44, 45–65.

[32] *Cf.* NATIONAL ACADEMY OF SCIENCES, ELECTRICITY IN ECONOMIC GROWTH 15 (1986) ("[E]lectricity use and gross national product have been … strongly correlated.").

that connection came under intense scrutiny.[33] What might be called "energy productivity" has grown faster than overall productivity in the US since the late 1980s (when the underlying data series began), "meaning that through some combination of directed technical change and factor substitution, the [US] is economizing on energy faster than it is economizing on other factors."[34] For regulators, this divergence of aggregate trends sharpens the double-edged sword of Hicks' hypothesis: The broad diffusion of (energy-conserving) technologies presents devilishly complex microeconomic possibilities.[35]

Although risk regulation need not entail *any* direct cost of compliance where the specific risk factor being regulated is substituted in due course,[36] even that law can have indirect or ripple effects.[37] Big enough ripples can change the sign of any estimate, forcing many analysts to conclude that the real determinants in cost-of-compliance estimation

---

[33] *See, e.g.*, Richard F. Hirsch & Jonathan G. Koomey, *Electricity Consumption and Economic Growth: A New Relationship with Significant Consequences?*, 28(9) ELEC. J. 72 (2015).

[34] Hunt Allcott & Michael Greenstone, *Is There an Energy Efficiency Gap?*, 26(1) J. ECON. PERSP. 3, 6 (2012).

[35] *See* Adam B. Jaffe & Robert N. Stavins, *The Energy Paradox and the Diffusion of Conservation Technology*, 16 RESOURCE & ENERGY ECON. 91 (1994).

[36] *See, e.g.*, Jaffe *et al.*, supra note 19 at 139 n.16 ("[I]f a firm chooses to close a plant because of a new regulation (rather than installing expensive control equipment), this would be counted as zero cost in typical compliance-cost estimates."). Of course a *supplier* might incur costs, although without knowing that supplier's circumstances, opportunities, *etc.*, counting it as pure cost is at least presumptuous. *Cf.* Sidney G. Winter, *Pursuing the Evolutionary Agenda in Economics and Management Research*, 41 CAMB. J. ECON. 721, 740–43 (2017) (noting that individual firm capabilities to adjust to supply and demand fluctuations vary greatly); *see also* David J. Teece *et al.*, *Dynamic Capabilities and Strategic Management*, 18(7) STRAT. MNGT. J. 509 (1997).

[37] *See* Hicks, supra note 21 at 466–68; *see also* Teece *et al.*, supra note 36 at 515–26. Although the Hicks hypothesis "has a long and somewhat tortured history in economics," Jaffe *et al.*, supra note 19 at 470, the efforts to confirm or refute it have been sustained, wide-ranging, and inconclusive. Id. at 474–79, 481–83. Energy is particularly vexing. Energy, like some other inputs, has varying elasticities of demand, complicating cost estimations tremendously. *See* id. at 483; Steve Sorrell & John Dimitropoulos, *The Rebound Effect: Microeconomic Definitions, Limitations and Extensions*, 65 ECOL. ECON. 636 (2008).

techniques—whatever the regulatory tool afoot—are how regulated parties will respond in the aggregate.[38] The problem is that such dynamics at the firm level have long been in mainstream economics' blind spot.[39] Technical change and its transition from autonomous function of time to ingenious algebraic axiom is work still to be done.[40] Somewhere between a tacit consensus that macroeconomic growth is the master end[41] and the microeconomics of firm behavior[42] lay the uncertainties, variabilities, and nonlinearities of induced technical change in a large, kinetic economy.[43]

---

[38] *See, e.g.*, E.J. MISHAN & EUSTON QUAH, COST-BENEFIT ANALYSIS 27–31 (5th ed. 2007); William A. Pizer & Raymond Kopp, *Calculating the Costs of Environmental Regulation, in* 3 HANDBOOK OF ENVIRONMENTAL ECONOMICS 1307, at 1323–29 (Karl-Göran Mäler & Jeffrey R. Vincent eds., 2005); *cf.* George Akerlof, *Behavioral Macroeconomics and Macroeconomic Behavior*, 92(3) AMER. ECON. REV. 411, 413–27 (2002) (reviewing a series of "micro-foundations" grounded in fact rather than theory which tend to overthrow conventional wisdom about market efficiency).

[39] *Cf.* Winter, supra note 36 at 724 ("In the economics discipline ... there is a strong methodological tradition that says that good theory does not have to be accurate (true) at a detailed level. ... [And] there is one large category of 'detail' that the mainstream considers ignorable—it comprises anything relating to the internal processes of business firms.").

[40] *Cf.* STARR, supra note 12 at 327 ("How informative is the general equilibrium theory about the results ... that the economy will actually realize? From one point of view, it is hardly informative at all.").

[41] *Cf.* HELPMAN, supra note 16 at 93 (concluding (tentatively) that inequality is bad because it slows growth); HICKS, supra note 27 at 156 (speculating that induced innovations economizing on labor, though they may have negative impacts on labor in the short run, are likely to benefit labor in the long run by following "a path which has greater expansionary potential").

[42] *Cf.* Winter, supra note 36 at 740–43 (tracing an example of a firm's "dynamic capability" to keep innovating along the same margin over time and thereby sustain a competitive advantage in producing products received by consumers as novel).

[43] *See* RICHARD G. LIPSEY ET AL., ECONOMIC TRANSFORMATIONS: GENERAL PURPOSE TECHNOLOGIES AND LONG TERM ECONOMIC GROWTH 34–35 (2005) ("Neoclassical theory treats competition as the *end state* of the competitive process. There is no ongoing process of rivalrous behavior. ... As a result, long-run equilibrium analysis of the competitive process is argued to be not just irrelevant but misleading because firms that are competing through innovations will cause technology to change endogenously long before any long-run tendency based on fixed technology and tastes is manifested in observed behavior."); Grubb *et al.*, supra note 29 at 295 (concluding that the incorporation of induced technical change in large-scale modeling is limited and problematic but that a consensus exists that technological development is a dynamic process); *cf.* KLEIN, supra note 27 at 89–139 ("An entrepreneurial discovering [*sic*] a way to

As Frank Knight is said to have observed, "every act of production is a speculation in the relative value of money and the good produced,"[44] and producers rarely solve their problems in pat or predictable fashion.[45]

The US agency with the most experience in this kind of modeling, the Environmental Protection Agency (EPA),[46] maintains general guidance on economic analysis which has at least acknowledged the dilemma since 2000: Estimating the costs resulting from any regulation entails estimating future technical change.[47] EPA's most recently updated guidance

---

produce a given output with fewer inputs changes initial conditions. And the change is quite unpredictable."); Akerlof, supra note 38 at 414 (noting the "pervasive empirical finding" of a wide spread of earnings for similar work and the "New Classical" explanations of wage rates above market-clearing prices).

[44] *See* PETER L. BERNSTEIN, AGAINST THE GODS: THE REMARKABLE STORY OF RISK 305 (1996). As Hicks was to argue later, "[p]roduction is itself a process; by its very nature it is a process of change." JOHN R. HICKS, CAPITAL AND GROWTH 6 (1965). He continued that "[t]he process is a process in time; time goes only one way. Past and future must be distinguished. Parameters that refer to the past, and those that refer to the future, each may enter into the determination of equilibrium values, but they will do so in different ways." Id. at 24. This foreshadowed a deeper "evolutionary" movement in explaining economic change from the bottom up. *See* Edith T. Penrose, *Biological Analogies in the Theory of the Firm*, 42 AMER. ECON. REV. 804 (1952); *see also* RICHARD R. NELSON & SIDNEY G. WINTER, AN EVOLUTIONARY THEORY OF ECONOMIC CHANGE (1982); EDITH T. PENROSE, THE THEORY OF THE GROWTH OF THE FIRM (3d ed. 1995).

[45] This makes modeling a whole economy of such producers at the very least more difficult. *See* William A. Pizer & David Popp, *Endogenizing Technological Change: Matching Empirical Evidence to Modeling Needs*, 30 ENERGY ECON. 2754 (2008); Patrick Söderholm & Thomas Sunqvist, *Empirical Challenges in the Use of Learning Curves for Assessing the Economic Prospects of Renewable Energy Technologies*, 32 RENEWABLE ENERGY 2559 (2007); Löschel, supra note 17. Despite Schumpeter's powerful criticisms of the excessive emphasis economists placed on static efficiency, the study of technological change as the source of growth arguably remains at the fringes of the economics profession. *See* LIPSEY ET AL., supra note 43 at 8–9.

[46] By some estimates, US EPA has more capacity for economic analysis than its nominal overseer, the Executive Office of the President's Office of Information and Regulatory Affairs (OIRA), and all other federal agencies combined. *See* Michael A. Livermore, *Cost-Benefit Analysis and Agency Independence*, 81 U. CHI. L. REV. 609, 625–39 (2014).

[47] *Cf.* U.S. EPA, GUIDELINES FOR PREPARING ECONOMIC ANALYSES 124–25 (2000) (acknowledging that "[b]enefit-cost models must predict what actions firms are likely to choose when attempting to comply with a new policy and what the compliance costs of those actions will be" but that those are likely to

observed that "[o]rganizations are able to learn with experience, which permits them to produce a given good or service at lower cost as their cumulative experience increases."[48] But it could say little more than that "default learning effects" should be developed and used widely.[49]

A series of executive orders and guidance implementing them from the OIRA have required such economic analyses from all executive agencies undertaking "major" rulemakings for the last 25 years.[50] This has generated a broad and deep record of estimating the costs of risk regulation.[51] Repeated attempts to show systemic biases from that record[52] have seldom trained the focus on variables like induced innovation or microeconomic change. Innovation and competition take time, usually long enough to avoid forcing economics' conventional wisdom under the microscope.[53] But if regulated parties can adjust their production in response to external constraints and the business firm itself is

---

overestimate costs because firms can substitute away from the burdened production factors).

[48] U.S. EPA, Guidelines for Preparing Economic Analyses 8–12 (2014 rev'd ed.).

[49] *See* id. at 8–12.

[50] *See* Livermore, supra note 46 at 614–18. Coverage of "major" rulemakings has varied. *See* Nicholas Bagley & Richard L. Revesz, *Centralized Oversight of the Regulatory State*, 106 Colum. L. Rev. 1260, 1268–82 (2006) (finding selective use of "regulatory impact analysis" (RIA) as implemented by OIRA). Current guidance requires cost-benefit analysis of any major rulemaking in RIAs and, where appropriate, cost-effectiveness analysis of available alternatives.

[51] *See* Cass R. Sunstein, *The Real World of Cost-Benefit Analysis: Thirty-Six Questions (And Almost As Many Answers)*, 114 Colum. L. Rev. 167 (2014); Jerry Ellig *et al.*, *Continuity, Change, and Priorities: The Quality and Use of Regulatory Analysis Across US Administrations*, 7 Reg. & Gov. 153, 155–56 (2013); Bagley & Revesz, supra note 50 at 1312–29.

[52] *See* Joseph E. Aldy, *Learning from Experience: An Assessment of the Retrospective Reviews of Agency Rules and the Evidence for Improving the Design and Implementation of Regulatory Policy*, Report to the Administrative Conf. of United States on Recommendation 2014-5 (2014); Harrington *et al.*, supra note 9 at 305–09; *see also* Thomas O. McGarity & Ruth Ruttenberg, *Counting the Cost of Health, Safety, and Environmental Regulation*, 80 Tex. L. Rev. 1997 (2002). Agencies appear biased against communicating cost estimate uncertainty as well as they do risk estimate uncertainty. *See* Adam M. Finkel, *The Cost of Nothing Trumps the Value of Everything: The Failure of Regulatory Economics to Keep Pace with Improvements in Quantitative Risk Analysis*, 4 Mich. J. Envt'l & Admin. L. 91 (2014).

[53] *See* Richard R. Nelson & Sidney G. Winter, *In Search of Useful Theory of Innovation*, 6 Res. Pol'y 36, 41–46 (1977).

fungible in both scale and scope, then the longer the time horizon of any estimative analysis, the more critical becomes *dynamic cost avoidance* by affected production.[54] Put strictly, formalizing the opportunity sets facing firms into some time-independent algebraic axiom remains beyond our grasp[55]—and will perhaps do so indefinitely.

From the earliest work on technology-based performance standards, the market for innovation which the standard itself influences (or creates) was a serious concern.[56] It has remained so since.[57] But professional economists have still not agreed how productivity and growth relate to technological change, *i.e.*, whether the latter accounts for the former or vice versa,[58] perhaps explaining why technological change is almost never present in the figuring of regulatory costs in practice. Consider a fictional industry sector, φ, comprised at the moment of three firms. Let us stipulate that production of φ generates externalities (some harmful, some not). One firm, *A*, is relatively diversified having three lines of business, φ, π, and ψ. Another firm, *B*, does only two of those businesses, φ and π. A third firm, *C*, is only in the business of φ. Now suppose that

---

54 *See* U.S. EPA, GUIDELINES FOR PREPARING ECONOMIC ANALYSES 2010 8–10 (rev'd ed. 2014) (hereafter "2010 EPA GUIDELINES"). Similar treatments of the issue date to EPA's 2000 guidelines—despite their supposedly exhaustive coverage. *Cf.* Michael A. Livermore, *Cost-Benefit Analysis and Agency Independence*, 81 U. CHI. L. REV. 609, 645 (2014) (noting that the "guidelines adopted by EPA in 2000 represented the first genuinely complete benefit-cost manual" and that "peer review played an important role" in their development); *see also* Timothy F. Malloy, *Regulating by Incentives: Myths, Models, and Micromarkets*, 80 TEX. L. REV. 531 (2002).

55 *Cf.* Nelson & Winter, supra note 53 at 46, 61–70 (arguing that the standard "production function" design in economic research into the causes of innovation is inherently limiting and that a better model would start from the premise that innovation is purposive but inherently stochastic and spread across market and non-market environments).

56 *See* Nicholas A. Ashford *et al.*, *Using Regulation to Change the Market for Innovation*, 9 HARV. ENVTL. L. REV. 419, 420–22 (1985); KNEESE & SCHULTZE, supra note 25, at 82 ("Any attempt to specify the costs of reducing air and water pollution is handicapped by the need to make some assumptions about technology.").

57 *Cf.* Finkel, supra note 52, at 119 ("[R]isks are elusive, but at least they are not capable of intentionally changing their size, whereas costs can increase or decrease strategically and perhaps even in response to being studied!").

58 *See* Richard G. Lipsey & Kenneth I. Carlaw, *Total Factor Productivity and the Measurement of Technological Change*, 37(4) CANAD. J. ECON. 1118, 1119–21 (2004).

at prevailing prices, *A*'s two profitable lines of business are π and ψ[59] and that it is losing money on φ; that *B*'s only profitable business is φ; and that *C* is breaking even. (In some sense, *B* is outcompeting *A* and *C* as to φ.)

If these firms comprise the sector and face some new constraint on an externality, that constraint will be an indeterminate cost vector wherever innovation and microeconomic change can occur.[60] Welfarism can insist that innovations allowing φ's production without the externality reduce "social" costs while regulation compensating those φ would otherwise burden merely *transfers* costs.[61] But such theoretical commitments do not account for cost-avoiding dynamics in real time.[62] Competitive interactions as they actually occur in real time remain the ultimate black box in economics and yet, ironically, the very thing commending capitalism

---

[59] If the φ market were in equilibrium *no* firm would be making a profit, but let us set aside such troublesome assumptions for the sake of argument.

[60] Again, assuming costs = C_i (a, z), where a is the vector of parameters describing the policy, z is the vector of parameters summarizing the current equilibrium and C_i (a, z) is the associated costs borne by agent i, summing costs across agents in production in response to final demand yields only one (static) measure of total costs. But if the constraint is to operate over time and producers' relative advantages and disadvantages can vary over the interval, either demand-side or supply-side forces may affect the allocation of inventive resources which determine final (total) costs and either of those may entail some degree of uncertainty. *See* Nelson & Winter, supra note 53 at 46–49.

[61] *See, e.g.*, PAUL A. SAMUELSON & WILLIAM D. NORDHAUS, ECONOMICS 126–30 (19th ed. 2009); MISHAN & QUAH, supra note 38 at 99–118; KOLSTAD, supra note 12 at 271–72. Of course, the most remarkable feature of this consensus might be the plasticity of economists' conception of *transfers*. *See* Karl W. Kapp, *Environmental Disruption and Social Costs: A Challenge to Economics*, 23 KYKLOS 833 (1970). For, even at common law, the "property" rules in question are not all "symmetrical" in the ways economists have long presumed. *See* Henry E. Smith, *Self-Help and the Nature of Property*, 1 J. L., ECON. & POL'Y 69 (2005).

[62] *Cf.* Coase, supra note 24 at 717–18 (observing that moving from a zero transaction cost world to the real world instantly highlights legal entitlements, transaction costs, organizations, and other distortions). Unfortunately, the classical theorists of marginal productivity either ignored this dynamic challenge or retreated into "aggregate production functions." *See* MARK BLAUG, ECONOMIC THEORY IN RETROSPECT 406–68 (5th ed. 1996).

itself.[63] Indeed, the orthodox assumptions of competition, *i.e.*, the ingenuity of minimizing own costs,[64] ignore many nonstandard but plausible prospects like increasing returns,[65] collusion between firms,[66] and raising rivals' costs,[67] each of which can complicate the calculus still further. Thus, even the most sophisticated economic modeling quickly runs aground of dynamic cost avoidance the longer the interval of time extends.

3.1.2 Economics or Engineering? To Predict Cost Avoidance

Competitive dynamics will determine the direction and pace of price changes, often because they determine the pace of technical change. Assume that a regulation adding constraints to φ production may (eventually) spur: (1) consolidation, *e.g.*, all sell out to *B*; (2) market contraction, *e.g.*, demand decreases from a price increase; (3) innovations reordering the production factors; (4) new entrants replacing (some of) the incumbents; or (5) permutations of the foregoing. Note first that *A*'s exit saves *A* its operating losses, *i.e.*, costs to its bottom line.[68] Second, compelling *A*, *B*, or *C* to buy a solution *D* owns will be to *D*'s profit.[69]

---

[63] *See* WILLIAMSON, supra note 24 at 1–12; NATHAN ROSENBERG, INSIDE THE BLACK BOX: TECHNOLOGY AND ECONOMICS 3–29 (1982).

[64] *See* ALFRED MARSHALL, 1 PRINCIPLES OF ECONOMICS 328–68 (1890) (explaining vertical integration as a capacity to minimize costs and maximize returns to scale); Coase, supra note 24 at 394–95; *cf.* ARTHUR C. PIGOU, THE ECONOMICS OF WELFARE 329–35 (5th ed. 1952) (so-called externalities are externalized just to enhance profitability); GEORGE J. STIGLER, THE ORGANIZATION OF INDUSTRY 5–16 (1968).

[65] *See* W. BRIAN ARTHUR, INCREASING RETURNS AND PATH DEPENDENCE IN THE ECONOMY (1994).

[66] *See* Herbert Hovenkamp, *Rationality in Law & Economics*, 60 GEO. WASH. L. REV. 293, 306–16, 319–24 (1992); Starrett, supra note 15 at 197; James M. Buchanan & William Craig Stubblebine, *Externality*, 29(116) ECONOMICA 371 (1962).

[67] *See* Steven C. Salop & David T. Scheffman, *Raising Rivals' Costs*, 73(2) AEA PAPERS & PROC. 267 (1983).

[68] It is especially telling that no standard has emerged to settle whether job losses are typically a social "cost" or an in-kind "benefit" to employers. *See* Ann E. Ferris & Al McGartland, *A Research Agenda for Improving the Treatment of Employment Impacts in Regulatory Impact Analysis, in* DOES REGULATION KILL JOBS? 170 (Cary Coglianese *et al.* eds., 2013).

[69] *See* Ashford *et al.*, supra note 56 at 427. The mystery of profit in the world of equilibrium economics—where it should not exist yet surely *is* what

Finally, a duty that *C* can fulfill at least cost could allow *C* to outcompete the others. So which of the foregoing will actually minimize all "costs" caused? Which is the more beneficial outcome to all concerned? Should the costs of producing φ be calculated as an average or a margin? When should we evaluate the average/marginal values and for what duration? How "competitive" is φ as a sector—can the incumbents pass added costs along to consumers as price increases? And supposing *A'*, *B'*, and *C'* are *types* of firms where profitability varies but, as a type, they are profitable in the aggregate, how should efficiencies be measured there? Table 3.1 aligns these comparisons with profitability designated ^{P}.

Table 3.1: Firms, Sectors, Businesses

Firm	**Line of Business (L.O.B.)**	**Firm Type {L.O.B.}**
A	φ, π^P, ψ^P	**A'** $\{\varphi, \pi^P, \psi^P\}$
B	φ^P, π	**B'** $\{\varphi^P, \pi, \psi\}$
C	Φ	**C'** $\{\varphi, \pi, \psi\}^P$

As a robust critical literature has revealed, what will induce innovation and its resultant efficiencies across the range of possibilities mentioned—what will *induce* innovation and not just *permit* it—is a richly varied empirical question with (at best) tentative answers.[70] The main trunk of that literature dwells on whether some type of "market-oriented" tool better induces innovation and, thus, net social cost

motivates real behavior—has long motivated heterodox critiques of microeconomic theory. *See* J. Fred Weston, *The Profit Concept and Theory: A Restatement*, 62 J. POL. ECON. 152, 153–54 (1954) (calling profit a "nonfunctional" component of the standard theory). Profits to be made should spur market entries, although the firms' costs are no more assurance than Pigouvian taxes can be that optimal market entries will occur in fact. *See* Dennis W. Carlton & Glenn C. Loury, *The Limitations of Pigouvian Taxes as a Long-Run Remedy for Externalities*, 95 Q. J. ECON. 141 (1980).

[70] *See* Cary Coglianese, *The Limits of Performance-Based Regulation*, 50 U. MICH. J.L. REF. 525, 541–53 (2017) (reviewing literature); Kenneth R. Richards, *Framing Environmental Policy Instrument Choice*, 10 DUKE ENVTL. L. & POL'Y 221 (2000); Gloria E. Helfand, *Standards versus Standards: The Effects of Different Pollution Restrictions*, 81(3) AMER. ECON. REV. 622 (1991).

minimization, relative to the simple command or "performance standard."[71] Regulatory reformers' so-called "price" and "quantity" instruments, generally acclaimed as simulating market signals,[72] share a long history of such comparisons under various assumptions and uncertainties.[73] If technological innovation is generally taken to be an increase in outputs without any corresponding increase in inputs, the conditions under which it may be induced become central to the vast majority of what economics can tell us about when or why to choose one of these tools.[74] In a word, if innovation is *endogenous*, it means that society can conceivably find ways to turn Hicks's hypothesis into better blueprints for tomorrow's capital stock, production, and economy. And, from the work done thus far, there seems to be some chance that *any* constraint can be innovation inducing, at least *a priori*.[75]

---

[71] *See* Nathaniel O. Keohane *et al.*, *The Choice of Regulatory Instruments in Environmental Policy*, 22 HARV. ENVT'L. L. REV. 313, 319–25, 347–62 (1998) (summarizing literature). In fact, neoclassical economics' attention to environmental policy has remained anchored to a caricature of performance standards and the canard that they cannot possibly be efficiency maximizing. But "performance" standards contrast with a "means" or "design" standard in that only the latter prescribes particularly how the regulated entity must behave/comply, instead of limiting its constraints to the externalities being corrected. *See* Coglianese, supra note 70 at 534.

[72] *See* Martin L. Weitzman, *Prices* vs. *Quantities*, 41(4) REV. ECON. STUDS. 477 (1973).

[73] *See, e.g.*, id. It can be demonstrated under certain idealized conditions that price and quantity instruments control pollution very similarly. *See* John Pezzey, *The Symmetry between Controlling Pollution by Price and Controlling It by Quantity*, 25(4) CANAD. J. ECON. 983 (1992). As for "performance standards," *i.e.*, a legal command setting some pollution abatement constraint, the *design* of the standard—how it constrains, who it advantages, *etc.*—accounts for much of the variation in outcomes. *See* Coglianese, supra note 70; Helfand, supra note 70 at 632–33.

[74] *Cf.* Pizer & Popp, supra note 45 at 2768 ("Technological change is at once the most important and least understood feature driving the future cost of climate change mitigation."); Löschel supra note 17 at 107 ("Virtually all studies of induced [technological change] in environmental economics have been theoretical."); Goulder & Schneider, supra note 29 at 212 ("[T]he current stock of policy evaluation tools tends to neglect a potentially important element that is relevant to both the benefits and costs of climate change policies. This element is *induced technological change*.") (emphasis in original).

[75] *See* Yoram Bauman *et al.*, *Does Technological Innovation Really Reduce Marginal Abatement Costs? Some Theory, Algebraic Evidence and Policy Implications*, 40 ENVTL. RES. ECON. 507 (2008); DAVID M. DRIESEN, THE ECONOMIC DYNAMICS OF ENVIRONMENTAL LAW 49–71 (2003); Daniel H. Cole &

Consider the common tools: *Rule 1* prohibiting pollution above a set mass per unit of output (the "performance" standard);[76] *Rule 2* taxing pollution by masses emitted (the "price" instrument);[77] and *Rule 3* issuing tradeable pollution allowances to the polluting firms (the "quantity" instrument).[78] For the sake of argument let us stipulate *B* as the least polluting incumbent. Any of these tools could conceivably put one, two, or all of the incumbents out of the φ business quickly or over time, changing the cost dynamics considerably.[79] (Even diversified firms will continue unprofitable business for only so long and start-up *E* could always out-innovate {*A,B,C* ...}.[80]) *Rule 3* has remained in focus because, assuming *B*'s willingness to sell, *A* and *C* might bid up a price for *B*'s excess allowances.[81] The price then becomes an incentive, and a

---

Peter Z. Grossman, *When Is Command-and-Control Efficient? Institutions, Technology, and the Comparative Efficiency of Alternative Regulatory Regimes for Environmental Protection*, 1999 WISC. L. REV. 887, 892–909; KOLSTAD, supra note 12 at 139–46; WILLIAM J. BAUMOL & WALLACE E. OATES, THE THEORY OF ENVIRONMENTAL POLICY 160–69 (2d ed. 1988); Wesley A. Magat, *The Effects of Environmental Regulation on Innovation*, 43(1) L. & CONTEMP. PROBS. 1 (1979). The related but distinct claim that regulatory costs tend to be *offset* by cost savings prompted in the process, *see* Michael E. Porter & Claas van der Linde, *Toward a New Conception of the Environment–Competitiveness Relationship*, 9(4) J. ECON. PERSP. 97, 100–05 (Fall 1995), is a different (empirical) question.

76 *See* Chapter 2, Section 2.2.1.

77 *See* William J. Baumol, *On Taxation and the Control of Externalities*, 62 AMER. ECON. REV. 307 (1972); BAUMOL & OATES, supra note 75 at 21–23.

78 *See* DALES, supra note 18 at 81–98.

79 Empirical questions of this sort—and they are empirical—have proven particularly hard to answer from practice. *See* Timothy F. Malloy, *Regulating by Incentives: Myths, Models, and Micromarkets*, 80 TEX. L. REV. 531, 541–51 (2002). Where Pigovian taxes can easily fail to match incentives with their underlying purpose(s), *see* Peter A. Diamond, *Consumption Externalities and Imperfect Corrective Pricing*, 4(2) BELL J. ECON. & MNGT. SCI. 526 (1973) (proof demonstrating that corrective taxes often fail to improve welfare given real variabilities), changing what had been a social norm to something more akin to a "price" can dramatically shift behaviors as well. *See, e.g.*, Uri Gneezy & Aldo Rustichini, *A Fine is a Price*, 29(1) J. LEGAL STUDS. 1 (2000).

80 *See* Anthony C. Fisher & Frederick M. Peterson, *The Environment in Economics: A Survey*, 14(1) J. ECON. LIT. 1, 15–16 (1976).

81 Dales' popularization of a tool like our *Rule 3* has dominated the literature on inducing innovation in regulation. *See* DANIEL H. COLE, POLLUTION & PROPERTY: COMPARING OWNERSHIP INSTITUTIONS FOR ENVIRONMENTAL PROTECTION 130–53 (2002). Yet Dales expressly excluded dynamics of the kind under discussion here from his analysis, acknowledging that under conditions of

powerful one depending on other variables involved. But why presume *B*'s willingness to sell to *A* or *C*?[82] The reality is that other influences might induce *A*, *C*, or someone else to innovate, too. *Rule 1* might even do so more directly.[83] In fact, any of the rules could, depending on omitted variables or contestable (but plausible) assumptions, prompt more search for new means of producing φ without the pollution.[84] What will occur in fact is characteristically enshrouded in doubt *ex ante*.[85]

What has emerged from the past four decades of theory and practice is that, without detailed study of particular firms and their modes of production, capital, labor forces, debts, and what has been called the

---

price and/or abatement uncertainty, the three tools' advantages and disadvantages were indeterminate. *See* Dales, supra note 18 at 102–03.

[82] *B* could envision doing better with *A* and *C* going defunct. *See* Walter S. Misiolek & Harold W. Elder, *Exclusionary Manipulation of Markets for Pollution Rights*, 16(2) J. ENVTL. ECON. & MNGT. 156 (1989). Or *B* might sell these rights to *A* or *C*'s neighbors. Finally, *B* might reserve these rights on the (mistaken) assumption that their value will increase over time. *See, e.g.*, Salop & Scheffman, supra note 67.

[83] Mediation of the need to innovate necessarily introduces some prospect for slack, frustration, *etc.* A legal command limiting the discretion/flexibility to operate can be the most direct, unmediated inducement to innovate. *See* Cole & Grossman, supra note 75 at 892–914.

[84] *See* DRIESEN, supra note 75 at 193–201. Whether the search ultimately benefits regulated incumbents, their vendor(s), or an upstart competitor, the cost outcome can be invariant—unless (as is often done) asymmetric assumptions are made about the different markets. *See, e.g.*, Magat, supra note 75 at 18 ("To the extent that a regulatory agency mandates the wide-spread adoption of a new technology developed by a firm, the agency creates a widely-expanded market for that firm's innovation. However, given the inherent difficulty in appropriating the benefits from new abatement technology … it is highly unlikely that this incentive to innovate could dominate the other incentives for abatement technology innovation.").

[85] In their defense of cost-benefit balancing in financial regulation, Posner and Weyl answer this indictment by acknowledging that *all regulations* "have complex causal effects" and, thus, that all forms of cost estimation are in the same boat, roughly speaking. *See* Eric A. Posner & E. Glen Weyl, *Cost-Benefit Analysis of Financial Regulations: A Response to Criticisms*, 124 YALE L.J. F. 246, 251 (2015). Although it may be true that all regulatory proposals' cost estimations should come not in point estimates but in the ranges that befit an uncertain enterprise, *see* Finkel, supra note 57 at 106–11, economists are not necessarily best positioned to give either.

firm's "dynamic capabilities,"[86] cost-of-compliance guesswork by econometrics is just that: *guesswork*.[87] The "engineering" investigations aiming to overcome the guesswork confront multitudes of variables—some hard, some soft—all in an effort to identify the costs of regulation that are more or less unavoidable. This monograph presents detailed case studies of three such efforts, the experiences they represent, and what we can learn from them as a sample. Our point of departure is this: The more explicit and disciplined the assumptions necessary to *a priori* "instrument choice" accounts have grown—now after decades of work—the more qualified and indeterminate those accounts have grown.

3.2 PRODUCTION AND PRODUCTIVITY AS MICRO- AND MACROECONOMIC GOODS

Popular myths, of course, often tint legislative intentions and expressions.[88] The global competition for mobile capital has been a political bugbear at least since the Soviet Union's collapse. Regulating risk without compromising "competitiveness" has been the leading trope in that struggle.[89] When the US Congress amended the Securities and Exchange Commission's authorizing legislation in 1996 it mandated that in any rulemakings governing the financial industry, even where SEC had first determined that a rulemaking was in the investing public's interest,

---

[86] *See* Section 3.3.

[87] *Cf.* DRIESEN, supra note 75 at 24 ("If pollution control expenditures produce non-environmental economic benefits that offset the cost to polluters and/or consumers (in addition to whatever environmental and public health benefits they produce), then it is hard to see why the costs are 'societal.'"); Porter & van der Linde, supra note 75 at 101 (dividing "innovation offsets" into product and process categories and exploring the variety of cost-saving innovations and productivity enhancements that can result from problem solving to surmount production constraints); Jamison E. Colburn, *Technology Based? Cost Factoring in US Environmental Standards*, 7 MICH. J. ENVTL. & ADMIN. L. 83 (2018).

[88] *Cf.* ZACHARY KARABELL, THE LEADING INDICATORS: A SHORT HISTORY OF THE NUMBERS THAT RULE OUR WORLD 73–90, 212–39 (2014) (tracing concentration of popular attention on the consumer price index, GDP, unemployment, and other aggregative indices after World War II and their propensities to mislead given the challenges of defining and measuring productivity).

[89] *See* Jaffe *et al.*, supra note 19 at 133 ("The conventional wisdom is that environmental regulations impose significant costs, slow productivity growth, and thereby hinder the ability of U.S. firms to compete in international markets.").

SEC must *also* weigh the proposal's expected effects on "efficiency, competition, and capital formation."[90] Now whether the 104th Congress used these terms in their economic sense is something of a mystery.[91] "Efficiency" was surely a terminological dodge.[92] But what of promoting "competition" or "capital formation"? The good of financial capital has been a polarizing subject of late.[93] Assuming Congress intended the term in its economic sense, the orthodox view remains that *too much* capital diminishes its own returns.[94] So capital formation as a goal is probably a means to some other end(s)—likely productivity or growth.[95] Did

---

[90] The National Securities Markets Improvement Act of 1996 added these so-called "ECCF" factors to four different Depression-era SEC-authorizing statutes. *See* James D. Cox & Benjamin J.C. Baucom, *The Emperor Has No Clothes: Confronting the D.C. Circuit's Usurpation of SEC Rulemaking Authority*, 90 TEX. L. REV. 1811, 1818–24 (2012). In 1999 Congress followed up by adding them to two further SEC-authorizing statutes. Id. at 181 n.62.

[91] *See* Cox & Baucom, supra note 90 at 1818–24 (tracing multiple cross-currents in the legislative history); *cf.* Business Roundtable v. SEC, 647 F.2d 1144, 1148 (D.C. Cir. 2011) (calling this mandate SEC's "unique obligation" "to apprise itself—and hence the public and Congress—of the economic consequences of a proposed regulation").

[92] *Cf.* ELIZABETH ANDERSON, VALUE IN ETHICS AND ECONOMICS 192 (1993) ("Markets do not produce efficient outcomes when market transactions impose welfare changes or "externalities" on third parties. They also fail to produce or protect sufficient quantities of public goods—goods which can be provided to one person only on condition that others have access to them as well.").

[93] *See, e.g.*, Paul Krugman, *Why We're in a New Gilded Age*, N.Y. REV. OF BOOKS, May 8, 2014 (*reviewing* THOMAS PIKETTY, CAPITAL IN THE TWENTY-FIRST CENTURY (2014)). Politics aside, measuring capital in an open economy presents formidable challenges. *Compare* Robert E. Hall, *The Stock Market and Capital Accumulation*, 91(5) AMER. ECON. REV. 1185 (2001) (contending that capitalization in the form of securities' prices is the proper measure of a firm's capital assets), *with* Franklin M. Fisher, *Aggregation Problem, in* 1 THE NEW PALGRAVE: A DICTIONARY OF ECONOMICS 53 (John Eatwell *et al.* eds., 1987) (arguing that treating capital stock as an aggregate and measuring it by its market value cannot yield a valid measurement). It becomes even harder to define and measure over time. *See* GEORGE J. STIGLER, THE THEORY OF PRICE 275 (3d ed. 1966) ("A capital good, because it yields services over an appreciable time period, inevitably involves the appraisal of future as well as present services.").

[94] *See, e.g.*, ROBERT M. SOLOW, GROWTH THEORY: AN EXPOSITION 59 (1969); HELPMAN, supra note 16 at 10–11.

[95] *Cf.* Cary Coglianese & Christopher Carrigan, *The Jobs and Regulation Debate, in* DOES REGULATION KILL JOBS? 1, 10–15 (Cary Coglianese *et al.* eds., 2013) (observing that politicians who campaign on regulatory issues care most about economic growth and employment). Solow prefaced his famous growth

Congress intend SEC to determine whether its policies would maximize *productivity*? Reviewing courts have thus far declined to hold that that is SEC's statutory duty—perhaps because the tools available to that end have proven so blunt and unreliable.[96]

Yet growth in economic sums like income or production remains a more or less dominant political end.[97] And productivity remains central to contemporary macro- and microeconomic work on growth.[98] Measuring the relative productivity of specific factors—labor, capital, *etc.*—or firms is how estimates are derived for various production constraints and their expected impact on realized returns like profits, wages, *etc.*[99] Modeling factor productivity has often been the means for suggesting

---

model with the caveat that he aimed to offer "crude but useful" insights from its results. *See* Robert M. Solow, *Technical Change and the Aggregate Production Function*, 39 REV. ECON. & STATS. 312, 312 (1957). His basic point, that there can be no growth without technical progress, was macroeconomic in nature—and not particularly helpful for deciding what technical progress to foster. *See* Robert E. Lucas, Jr., *On the Mechanics of Economic Development*, 22 J. MONETARY ECON. 3, 13–17 (1988).

[96] *See* ROBERT J. GORDON, THE RISE AND FALL OF AMERICAN GROWTH: THE U.S. STANDARD OF LIVING SINCE THE CIVIL WAR (2016). The D.C. Circuit has had ample opportunity to interpret these amendments as a "growth promotion" mandate but has kept to scrutinizing SEC analyses for their cost calculations. *See* Business Roundtable v. SEC, 647 F.3d 1144, 1149–56 (D.C. Cir. 2011); Amer. Equity Invest. Life Ins. Co. v. SEC, 613 F.3d 166, 177–79 (D.C. Cir. 2010); Chamber of Commerce of the U.S. v. SEC, 443 F.3d 890, 901–02 (D.C. Cir. 2006); Chamber of Commerce of the U.S. v. SEC, 412 F.3d 133, 138–45 (D.C. Cir. 2005).

[97] The "Washington consensus" grounding rising prosperity on free trade and expanding production and consumption, *see* Ruchir Sharma, *The Boom Was a Blip: Getting Used to Slow Growth*, 96(3) FOR. AFFS. 104, 109 (May/June 2017), has long had its doubters. *See, e.g.*, DOUGLAS E. BOOTH, HOOKED ON GROWTH: ECONOMIC ADDICTIONS AND THE ENVIRONMENT (2004); TIM JACKSON, PROSPERITY WITHOUT GROWTH: ECONOMICS FOR A FINITE PLANET (2009); GORDON, supra note 96 at 601–04. I adopt the standard assumptions here for the argument's sake.

[98] *See* LIPSEY ET AL., supra note 43 at 3–15.

[99] *See* Philippe Aghion & Peter Howitt, *Some Thoughts on Capital Accumulation, Innovation, and Growth*, 125/126 ANNALS ECON. & STATS. 57 (2017) (arguing that disentangling specific factors' causal relationships is necessary to estimating what causes growth). "Growth" accounting at the macro-level encounters some of the same difficulties that income accounting meets at a micro level. *See* DAN USHER, THE MEASUREMENT OF ECONOMIC GROWTH 3 (1980).

that regulatory constraints will be costly.[100] Entrepreneurs should rationally price "regulatory risk" into their plans, of course, but the magnitude of impacts from regulatory constraints can vary tremendously.[101] Macroeconomic accounts of production and productivity inevitably stem from the bottom up—particular firms and factors—and have long aimed to isolate technological change as an influence.[102] The annual changes are what we invoke in aggregate statistics like GDP, inflation, *etc.* These metrics, meant to track the changing magnitudes of an entire economy, are built up from "great masses" of year-over-year data recording values added and their differentials.[103] Yet the ultimate target—production—itself remains something of a dark art in what counts and why.[104]

---

[100] *See, e.g.*, Richard D. Morgenstern *et al.*, *The Cost of Environmental Protection*, 83(4) REV. ECON. & STATS. 732 (2001); Anthony J. Barbera & Virginia D. McConnell, *The Impact of Environmental Regulations on Industry Productivity: Direct and Indirect Effects*, 18(1) J. ENVT'L ECON. & MNGT. 50 (1990); Anthony J. Barbera & Virginia D. McConnell, *Effects of Pollution Control on Industry Productivity: A Factor Demand Approach*, 35(2) J. INDUS. ECON. 161 (1986).

[101] *Cf.* Morgenstern *et al.*, supra note 100 at 736 (concluding from modeled results that regulated parties' stated costs of compliance are, if anything, overstated); Barbera & McConnell, supra note 100 at 62 ("Whereas the direct effect unambiguously reduces [total factor productivity] by increasing costs with no commensurate increase in the manufactured output, the indirect effect could be positive, negative, or zero.").

[102] *See, e.g.*, JOSEPH SCHUMPETER, THE THEORY OF ECONOMIC DEVELOPMENT 63 (1911) (trans. 1934); SOLOW, supra note 95 at 33–38; USHER, supra note 99 at 259–92; LIPSEY ET AL., supra note 43 at 85–130; HELPMAN, supra note 16 at 19–33. "Total factor productivity" (TFP), a metric used by economists to gage the joint effectiveness of all inputs combined, originated as a measure of technological change with Solow. Measurable output growth that is not associated with any measurable growth in inputs might be, but is not necessarily interpreted as the returns to investing in new technologies, *i.e.*, supra-normal gains of technological change. This suggests two separate aspects of any TFP measurement: first, the returns to undertaking uncertainty (what might be called the costs of entrepreneurship), and, second, the effects of spillovers causing outputs to rise or inputs to fall without a corresponding change in the other. *See* Lipsey & Carlaw, supra note 58.

[103] *See* USHER, supra note 99 at 289–90. This grounding in aggregation enables theorists to posit any number of competing explanations for the measured differentials. *Cf.* Lipsey & Carlaw, supra note 58 at 1136 (arguing that total factor productivity residuals can be explained just as plausibly by the existence within TFP calculations of "omitted inputs" like natural resources).

[104] The interdependence of consumption and capital investment has been a pivotal part of macroeconomic theories of production for generations. A classic

Production is economics' principal source of *surplus*, *i.e.*, producer and consumer welfare gains.[105] Even analyses confined to a single sector (so-called "partial equilibrium") should proceed from measurable differences in surpluses.[106] Yet what separates economic production from other activities or outcomes rests in deeply discretionary judgments like what is not "personal," not "preparatory," not a "useful output," not a mere "transfer," not "consumption," *etc.*, all of which can and do expand and contract over time.[107] Indeed, the shifting boundaries take different positions in different economies at the *same* time.[108] What is production in London may not be production in New York. If it is something someone else can do it *might* be production as such. But of course that social, cultural, and technological frontier is always moving. Distinguishing economically productive from unproductive activities is not unlike deciding an activity's geographic locus when its participants are strewn across the planet. Production is perspectival.

The case of "financial intermediation services indirectly measured" (FISIM)—banking—illustrates. The bulk of what makes a bank *profitable*, *e.g.*, taking deposits and lending, providing secure liquidity, *etc.*, can be viewed either as producing *new* value or as wholly parasitic on the extant flows of financial capital, depending on some basic (but not very transparent) assumptions.[109] These assumptions remain opaque because they derive from and depend for their validity on other, contentious

account of their interrelations over time is Edmond Malinvaud, *Capital Accumulation and Efficient Allocation of Resources*, 21 ECONOMETRICA 233 (1953).

[105] *See* USHER supra note 99 at 1–11. Growth theories, orthodox and critical alike, abound in mainstream economics. But the role of production as the source of surplus remains secure. *See, e.g.*, MAURICE FITZGERALD SCOTT, A NEW VIEW OF ECONOMIC GROWTH 472–519 (1989); HELPMAN, supra note 16 at 19–33.

[106] *See, e.g.*, EDWARD M. GRAMLICH, A GUIDE TO BENEFIT-COST ANALYSIS 48–51 (2d ed. 1990); 2010 EPA GUIDELINES, supra note 54 at 8-3.

[107] *See* RICHARD J. NELL, PROSPERITY AND PUBLIC SPENDING: TRANSFORMATIONAL GROWTH AND THE ROLE OF PUBLIC SPENDING (1988); *see also* MICHAEL WARD, QUANTIFYING THE WORLD: UN IDEAS AND STATISTICS (2004). "Personal" activities often generate productive outputs but are not "production" because they cannot be done by anyone but that person. Parenting, for example, is personal where housework is productive. *See* MARGARET REID, ECONOMICS OF HOUSEHOLD PRODUCTION (1934).

[108] *See* WARD, supra note 107 at 23–62.

[109] *See generally* BRETT CHRISTOPHERS, BANKING ACROSS BOUNDARIES: PLACING FINANCE IN CAPITALISM (2013).

assumptions.[110] Likewise, the national accounting methods which cast capitalism's recent "financialization" and so much profit in banking as a *shift* in production (not pure rent taking[111]) pay no attention at all to the *causality* within that shift.[112] These same methods, so often behind cost-of-compliance estimations grounded in lost production, generally ignore known interactivities between metrics like factor productivity and capital accumulation.[113] Indeed, they generally ignore most "indirect" impacts completely.[114] And they ignore the prospects of *inducing* the technical changes driving so much of what they are supposedly tracking.[115] Ironically, though, it has been the economics literature about it that has *made* FISIM "productive" by tracking its increasing profitability over time.[116] Profits, that literature suggests, *must* indicate productivity.

Of course, *without* a production boundary it is impossible to measure the year-over-year changes in a whole economy behind summary national statistics like GDP.[117] So productivity is central to both macro- and

---

[110] *See* id. at 27–51. For example, disentangling saving from investment must precede any effort to identify year-over-year changes in wealth, which, itself, must be done before financial intermediation services can be judged "productive" or not. *See* USHER, supra note 99 at 65–97.

[111] The economic concept of a "rent" may itself be illustrative here. The orthodox concept, *i.e.*, payments to factors of production above what is required to keep them in the market, bears within it the *assumption* that competition necessarily pushes factor payments down to their marginal cost—an assumption that is often untenable. *See* JOSEPH E. STIGLITZ, THE PRICE OF INEQUALITY: HOW TODAY'S DIVIDED SOCIETY ENDANGERS OUR FUTURE 48–64 (2012).

[112] *See* CHRISTOPHERS, supra note 109 at 239–65.

[113] *See* HELPMAN, supra note 16 at 9–54; *cf.* SCOTT, supra note 16 at 306–07 (critiquing Simon Kuznets' *Economic Growth and Structure* (1966) for ignoring the causal relationships between the extensive growth of the economy and accumulation of capital from the Industrial Revolution to the twentieth century and the "enormous growth of knowledge" in the same period).

[114] *See, e.g.*, Barbera & McConnell, supra note 100 at 62.

[115] *But see* Binswanger, supra note 18 at 22 (recognizing innovation as a resource-using activity that leads to benefits over some future interval and, thus, as an "investment problem").

[116] *See, e.g.*, Robert G. King & Ross Levine, *Finance and Growth: Schumpeter Might Be Right*, 108(3) Q.J. ECON. 717 (1993); *cf.* CHRISTOPHERS, supra note 109 at 9 ("[E]conomics plays an active rather than purely passive role in the economy. Economists … and the economic ideas, models and measurements they produce, do not merely describe an "external" economic reality; they are always and everywhere part *of* the economy, shaping and reproducing it in the very moment that they attempt to capture it conceptually.").

[117] Without being able to track GDP changes, the "growth" agenda would surely have to change—perhaps by shifting to a more inclusive accounting of

microeconomic expertise today even as it remains a deeply troubled concept.[118] Were courts to require regulators like SEC to evaluate how their proposals might impact capital accumulation or capital's *productivity*, that would almost surely be judicial creep into matters for which judges are ill-suited.[119] Similar court/agency boundaries feature in the three case studies that follow. So much about economic analysis, if it were to be mandated, would be a setback not an advance in our grasp of regulation's costs. Section 3.3 proposes what, if anything, regulation should seek to gain from the economic analysis of social costs.

3.3 PRODUCTIVITY, INNOVATION, AND SOCIAL COSTS: FINDING A NEXUS

Despite the prevalence of its own risk regulation mandates and decades of experience ferreting out costs of compliance it believes are practically unavoidable, US EPA's general guidance on "economic analysis" offers little insight into the essential questions raised to this point. What might be called the *negotiability* of regulatory cost estimates—their tendencies to trade uncertainties for fully arithmetic, convertible quantities—may explain EPA's reticence.[120] The source literature for EPA's guidance

national wealth (as opposed to incomes). *See* Kenneth J. Arrow *et al., Sustainability and the Measurement of Wealth*, 17 ENVT. & DEV. ECON. 317 (2012).

[118] *Cf.* HELPMAN, supra note 16 at 26–28 (observing that high productivity induces capital accumulation and should be a reflection of high TFP but is not always so); Phillippe Aghion & Peter Howitt, *A Model of Growth through Creative Destruction*, 60(2) ECONOMETRICA 323 (1992) (presenting a model of endogenous growth in which vertical innovations generated by a competitive research sector depend on expectations of future innovations and the prospect of business-stealing from future research discouraging current research by threatening to take its rents).

[119] *See* ADRIAN VERMEULE, LAW'S ABNEGATION: FROM LAW'S EMPIRE TO THE ADMINISTRATIVE STATE 127–54 (2016) (reviewing various contexts where administrators must engage in "rationally arbitrary" decision making and seek progress only over time).

[120] *Cf.* Finkel, supra note 57 at 118–21 (describing a general problem, with EPA included, of a failure or refusal to report uncertainties in cost estimates); Porter & van der Linde, supra note 75 at 99 ("The possibility that regulation might act as a spur to innovation arises because the world does not fit the Panglossian belief that firms always make optimal choices."); Robert Cooter, *The Cost of Coase*, 11 J. LEGAL STUDS. 1, 20–24 (1982) (arguing that costs accrued from trading cannot be estimated accurately without first knowing the relevant parties' strategic positions).

naïvely treats costs of compliance as essentially static and, by definition, social.[121] As already discussed, however, regulatory costs of compliance are not necessarily social because (1) they are often avoidable; (2) they can diminish through trade; and (3) they often can be offset.[122] Furthermore, firms are known to have path-dependent, difficult-to-trade capital assets that can advantage them over their competitors when constraints change.[123] Thus, as Porter and colleagues have shown, a performance standard like our *Rule 1* above, paired with sufficient lead time, can prompt competitors to innovate in ways that minimize costs of factor substitution and/or productivity growth.[124] Innovations are so hard to

---

[121] *See* Pizer & Kopp, supra note 45 at 1311 ("The overwhelming focal point of the literature to date has been measurement of the direct compliance costs to firms."). EPA's separation of "partial" equilibrium (wherein sectoral compliance costs are proxies for social costs) from "general" equilibrium approaches (wherein distortions like regulation are eventually assimilated into a wider economic equilibrium) is unburdened by any indication of which is more likely *correct* in given circumstances. *See* 2010 EPA GUIDELINES, supra note 54 at 8-4. The source literature on which EPA relied noted that estimating technological change was the "most challenging" future work in estimating regulation's costs and that, though *much* more common, "partial" equilibrium analyses are generally inferior to "general" equilibrium analysis. *See* Pizer & Kopp, supra, at 1344. Pizer and Kopp dismiss the "engineering approach" described in the case studies of Chapters 4, 5 and 6 as "problematic when applied on a broad scale." Id. at 1312. Yet they admit that their "partial equilibrium analysis" is "wrong" when it misses "general equilibrium changes in output and prices and miss[es] potential welfare changes from altered production levels and distortions in other markets." Id. at 1326. But that is an especially wide remit for partial equilibrium's inadequacy.

[122] *See, e.g.*, Margaret R. Taylor *et al.*, *Regulation as the Mother of Innovation: The Case of SO_2 Control*, 27(2) LAW & POL'Y 348, 367–70 (2005); Amy Purvis & Joe Outlaw, *What We Know About Technological Innovation to Achieve Environmental Compliance: Policy Issues for an Industrializing Animal Agriculture Sector*, 77 AMER. J. AGRIC. ECON. 1237, 1241–42 (1995); Matthias Ruth, *Technology Change in US Iron and Steel Production: Implications for Material and Energy Use, and CO_2 Emissions*, 21(3) RESOURCES POL'Y 199, 205–08 (1995).

[123] *See* Teece *et al.*, supra note 36 at 513–15; George Baker *et al.*, *Relational Contracts and the Theory of the Firm*, 117(1) Q. J. ECON. 39 (2002).

[124] *See* Porter & van der Linde, supra note 75 at 100–05, 113–14. This "Porter Hypothesis" is not without its skeptics. *See, e.g.*, Karen Palmer *et al.*, *Tightening Environmental Standards: The Benefit-Cost or the No-Cost Paradigm?* 9(4) J. ECON. PERSP. 119 (1995). Many of them assume that "abatement" of the target externality takes the form of some costly end-of-pipe capital, *see,*

track precisely because they are so often embodied in new capital that has a changed role from what preceded it.[125] Production is constantly mutating in response to external signals of all kinds (sometimes even economists' signals![126]). If any more than the merest instant elapses within an estimative analysis, this kind of change must rationally be counted.[127]

Retrospective studies of so-called market-oriented regulatory tools like *Rules 2* and *3* above have occasionally reached this nexus. Some research has found radical gains made in factor switching while others find the very same outcomes less conclusive.[128] Although the Porter hypothesis is contestable and can only ever be confirmed or rejected case by case, that empirical work stands apart from the now orthodox view that "new technology for [externality] reduction is, from an analytical perspective, doubly underprovided by markets."[129] There are negative externalities which producers transfer, *e.g.*, pollution, and there are positive externalities for which they are under-compensated, *e.g.*, technological advances from which others benefit.[130] Thus, if innovation

---

e.g., id. at 123–25, while ignoring the variable dynamics of capital turnover in production.

[125] *See* Lipsey & Carlaw, supra note 58 at 1126 ("[Z]ero change in [total factor productivity] does not mean zero technological change. It means only that investing in R&D has had the same marginal effect on income as investing in existing technologies (investment with no technological change) and that there are no external effects that show up in current increases in output elsewhere in the economy without corresponding current increases in inputs.").

[126] *See* DONALD MACKENZIE, AN ENGINE, NOT A CAMERA: HOW FINANCIAL MODELS SHAPE MARKETS 12–18 (2008).

[127] *See* Cole & Grossman, supra note 75 at 914–45; DRIESEN, supra note 75 at 77–91; Paul Lanoie *et al., Environmental Regulation and Productivity: Testing the Porter Hypothesis*, 30 J. PROD. ANALYSIS 121, 128 (2008).

[128] *Compare* Taylor *et al.*, supra note 122 at 367–70 (finding a mixture of abatement technology maturation, fuel switching, and demand differentiation at the heart of Clean Air Act's SO_2 reductions), *with* Curtis Carlson *et al.*, *Sulfur Dioxide Control by Electric Utilities: What Are the Gains from Trade?*, 108 J. POL. ECON. 1292, 1319 (2000) (concluding that predicted gains from SO_2 allowance trading under the Clean Air Act never materialized because fuel switching was a much more attractive option than had been predicted).

[129] Adam B. Jaffe, Richard G. Newell & Robert M. Stavins, *A Tale of Two Market Failures: Technology and Environmental Policy*, 54 ECOL. ECON. 164, 168 (2005).

[130] Id. at 168–69.

itself is an *investment*[131]—not a costless investment but one that almost surely influences growth[132]—then it should be on economic par with other future wealth-enhancing choices.[133] And there is only one reason for regulators predicting the *social* costs of their actions to ignore its effects on productivity: Those effects are too often unpriced or otherwise impossible to track. But economists typically do ignore them—or offer multiple conflicting explanations of the same regression statistics.[134]

After decades of such work on the types of firms that invest most effectively in innovation the results remain inconclusive.[135] (The weight of the evidence suggests that soft variables like the precise skill sets of the personnel comprising firms or their partners are determinative.[136]) Intuitively, regulation can create demand-pull for externality-internalizing capital (like our firm *D* in Section 3.1.2) or other innovations and it can

---

[131] *Cf.* Maurice Scott, *A New Theory of Endogenous Economic Growth*, 8(4) OXFORD REV. ECON. POL'Y 29, 35 (1992) (defining "investment" as "the cost, in terms of consumption forgone, of changing … economic arrangements").

[132] *See generally* GORDON, supra note 96; *see also* HELPMAN, supra note 16 at 34–54; LIPSEY ET AL., supra note 43 at 85–93; Scott, supra note 131 at 34–39.

[133] *See, e.g.*, Partha Dasgupta, *Measuring the Wealth of Nations*, 6 ANN. REV. RESOURCE ECON. 17, 24 (2014) (observing that investments amount to deferred consumption). Dasgupta makes the normative case for the valuation of natural and human capital savings being valued as investments by resort to "shadow prices" on the grounds that they are vital to describing wealth and social well-being.

[134] *Cf.* Paul M. Romer, *The Origins of Endogenous Growth*, 8(1) J. ECON. PERSPS. 3, 10–11 (1994) (citing economists' perennial tendency to bemoan the indeterminacy of the available data while dismissing multiple forms of evidence, leading to the proliferation of plausible but inconsistent theories about a phenomenon like growth). Another problem at the core of this nexus is that "technological progress is often embodied in new capital goods, which makes it hard to separate the influence of capital accumulation from the influence of innovation." Philippe Aghion & Peter Howitt, *Some Thoughts on Capital Accumulation, Innovation, and Growth*, 125/126 ANNALS ECON. & STATS. 57, 71 (2017).

[135] *See* Wesley M. Cohen & Richard C. Levin, *Empirical Studies of Innovation and Market Structure, in* 2 HANDBOOK OF INDUSTRIAL STRUCTURE 1059 (Richard Schmalensee & R.D. Willig eds., 1989); Wesley M. Cohen, *Fifty Years of Empirical Studies of Innovative Activity and Performance, in* 1 HANDBOOK OF THE ECONOMICS OF INNOVATION 129 (Bronwyn H. Hall & Nathan Rosenberg eds., 2010).

[136] *See* David J. Teece, *Technological Innovation and the Theory of the Firm: The Role of Enterprise-Level Knowledge, Complementarities, and (Dynamic) Capabilities, in* 1 HANDBOOK OF THE ECONOMICS OF INNOVATION 679 (Bronwyn H. Hall & Nathan Rosenberg eds., 2010).

subsidize or incentivize investments ultimately embodied in new capital which improves upon rather than merely replicating its precedents. However, this regulation–innovation nexus consists in *at least* as many soft and confounding variables as have been mentioned above, all affecting the reliability of virtually any kind of "economic" analysis—whether of a partial or general, static or dynamic sort. Of course, economists remain convinced that corporate and legal forms powerfully shape incentives to innovate and are, likewise, shaped by them.[137] Microeconomic work on entitlement design,[138] contract design,[139] principal/agency relationships[140] and other means of allocating assets and liabilities has variously shown that firms are rent seekers, cost minimizers, and/or pools of capability providing evolution's raw material.[141] The Hicks hypothesis, despite the troubles in its empirical verifications, has never been controvertible in quite the same way. So this winds up at a paradox in predictive, estimative analyses of regulatory costs: We can agree that incentives and regulation matter and are not mutually indivisible but cannot agree on how, why, or to what degree particular entitlement designs matter.

The choices to be made in any such analysis are inevitably about scales: temporal, factoral, and geographic scales that define which "costs" are worth measuring, where and how to measure them, and what counts as variability or causality within those measurements. Ever since (if not before) Schumpeter's schematization of technological change into stages of production—invention, innovation, and diffusion—in his *The*

---

[137] *See* WILLIAMSON, supra note 24 at 279–90; Teece, supra note 136 at 701–09; Teece *et al.*, supra note 36 at 515–26.

[138] *See* YORAM BARZEL, ECONOMIC ANALYSIS OF PROPERTY RIGHTS 85–104 (2d ed. 1997).

[139] *See* WILLIAMSON, supra note 24; Grossman & Hart, supra note 24 at 700–16; Fama & Jensen, supra note 24.

[140] *See* Oliver Hart, *An Economist's Perspective on the Theory of the Firm*, 89 COLUM. L. REV. 1757 (1989); Michael C. Jensen & William H. Meckling, *Theory of the Firm: Managerial Behavior, Agency Costs and Ownership Structure*, 3 J. FINANCIAL ECON. 305 (1976).

[141] *See* Teece *et al.*, supra note 36; Winter, supra note 23 at 189–93; PENROSE, supra note 44.

Theory of Economic Development,[142] economists have investigated production, growth, and technical progress together.[143] The orthodox theories maintain that technical progress is independent of investment while theorists in Schumpeter's tradition have struggled to prove otherwise.[144] Not surprisingly, links between knowledge accumulation, innovation, and growth can be modeled,[145] but we still lack the generalized axioms by which to establish the unavoidable costs of particular performance expectations. We cannot formalize the opportunity sets our economic agents (firms) face unless the horizons in these analyses are tightened to practically nil. Which makes economic production and productivity rather uncertain metrics where regulation is concerned.

The case studies of Chapters 4, 5, and 6 offer a different kind of assessment. These case studies explore the multitude of reasons to care about regulatory costs, to tabulate—or attempt to tabulate—them carefully, and to sustain the exercise where improving the analysis is within reach.

---

142 *See* SCOTT, supra note 16 at 101–02 (*discussing* JOSEPH A. SCHUMPETER, THE THEORY OF ECONOMIC DEVELOPMENT: AND INQUIRY INTO PROFITS, CAPITAL, CREDIT, INTEREST, AND THE BUSINESS CYCLE (1934)).

143 *See* Benoît Godin, *In the Shadow of Schumpeter: W. Rupert Maclaurin and the Study of Technological Innovation*, 46(3) MINERVA 343, 350–55 (2008). Schumpeter's opus appeared in German in 1911 and was not translated into English until 1934. *See* SCOTT, supra note 16 at 101–02.

144 *See* SCOTT, supra note 16 at 101; Godin, supra note 143 at 355–56.

145 *See, e.g.*, Aghion & Howitt, supra note 134.

4. Auto emissions, compliance costs, and technological change, 1970–2017

Performance standards set by reference to available technology began in the US with auto emissions. It was the original "technology-forcing" showdown between government and an industry and may have originated the "job-killing regulation" bugbear so abominable today. California's efforts to quantify the automobile's effects on local air quality in the 1950s sparked one of our first sustained struggles between a major industrial sector and regulators aiming to spur its technological improvement from within.[1] By 1970, California had learned that the contours of industrial organization—as much as the chemistry or physics of pollution—were vital aspects of the agenda. Since then, public scrutiny of the Clean Air Act's (CAA) overall regulatory "costs" has been sustained at its own behest, due to its own requirement that we track the "costs of clean air."[2] But the cost figures informing that debate have pre-empted a deeper reckoning of the relevance of CAA cost estimates over time—either as those estimates are examined in retrospect or are

[1] That history is told in JAMES E. KRIER & EDMUND URSIN, POLLUTION AND POLICY: A CASE ESSAY ON CALIFORNIA AND FEDERAL EXPERIENCE WITH MOTOR VEHICLE AIR POLLUTION, 1940–1975 (1977). *See also* JACK DOYLE, TAKEN FOR A RIDE: DETROIT'S BIG THREE AND THE POLITICS OF POLLUTION 11–79 (2000).

[2] Section 812 of Title VIII of the 1990 amendments required a "comprehensive analysis of the [CAA's] impact ... on the public health, economy and environment" considering "the costs, benefits and other effects associated with compliance with each standard issue for," among others, "emissions from mobile sources." 42 U.S.C. § 7612(a). *See* U.S. EPA, THE BENEFITS AND COSTS OF THE CLEAN AIR ACT FROM 1990 TO 2020 1-1 (2011). It included a sweeping definition of "costs." *See* 42 U.S.C. § 7612(c) ("In describing the costs of a standard ... the Administrator shall consider the effects of such standard on employment, productivity, cost of living, economic growth, and the overall economy of the United States."); *see also* U.S. EPA, THE BENEFITS AND COSTS OF THE CLEAN AIR ACT 1990–2010: EPA REPORT TO CONGRESS (1999) (EPA-410-R-99-001).

used to inform ever-more sophisticated predictions of expected regulatory costs. This chapter examines the evolution of regulatory cost balancing in the setting of mobile source emissions standards since 1970. It ends with a note on late efforts to roll back controls that even manufacturers agreed only a few years ago could be attained at manageable cost.

4.1 A SEARCH FOR SOCIAL COSTS IN MOBILE SOURCE EMISSIONS CONTROLS

When the CAA took on its basic contours in 1970, Congress differentiated the "entitlements" to pollute[3] along two seminal axes: "mobile" versus "stationary" and "new" versus "existing" sources.[4] These two axes created serious challenges.[5] More stringent constraints for "new" sources, for example, can perversely add value to older, less efficient capital, distorting what may be an otherwise natural way to eliminate older, more polluting capital.[6] Distinguishing mobile from stationary sources assumes

---

[3] Pollution constraints may be understood as *entitlements to pollute* within the given strictures. *See* DANIEL H. COLE, POLLUTION AND PROPERTY: COMPARING OWNERSHIP INSTITUTIONS FOR ENVIRONMENTAL PROTECTION 3–4 (2002). But supra-compensatory constraints, *i.e.*, injunctions, regulatory prohibitions, *etc.*, introduce a dimension of imprecision (or cost) apart from simple allocative efficiencies. *See* Jules L. Coleman & Jody Kraus, *Rethinking the Theory of Legal Rights*, 95 YALE L.J. 1335, 1340–52 (1986).

[4] *See* Michael R. Barr, *Introduction to the Clean Air Act: History, Perspective, and Direction for the Future, in* THE CLEAN AIR ACT HANDBOOK 1, 3–12 (Julie R. Domike & Alex C. Zacaroli eds., 4th ed. 2016).

[5] Economically, these differentiations act as cost allocations, albeit to ambiguous effects. *See* COLE, supra note 3 at 14–18. Institutionally, by creating four principal categories (new and existing mobile, new and existing stationary), Congress divided the sum of all risks from ambient air pollution—whether acute or chronic, well known or deeply uncertain—into a series of bureaucratically separate programs targeting sources by vintage and primary economic function(s). This became a standard template in pollution control legislation in the 1970s despite economists' criticisms. *See* J. CLARENCE DAVIES & JAN MAZUREK, POLLUTION CONTROL IN THE UNITED STATES: EVALUATING THE SYSTEM 2–22, 269–83 (1998).

[6] An accessible account of this result in the coal-fired electricity generating sector is RICHARD L. REVESZ & JACK LIENKE, STRUGGLING FOR AIR: POWER PLANTS AND THE "WAR ON COAL" (2016). In theory, any gradation of stringency from existing to new sources will add (difficult-to-trade) value to older capital. *See* Robert N. Stavins, *Vintage-Differentiated Environmental Regulation*, 25 STAN. ENVTL. L.J. 29 (2006).

the two emissions streams are not fungible—an assumption that technology (in the form of electric cars) has now all but denied.[7] How to count the "costs" involved in the regulation of any of this was from the first an exercise in dynamic accounting involving an aggregate (if spatially patterned) risk, pollutants of local as well as (increasingly) global significance, and shifting regulatory institutions and norms.[8]

The mobile/stationary and new/existing divisions seemed intuitive enough in 1970.[9] The interstate competition for residents and capital commended cost-conscious approaches to the high-volume, "conventional" air pollutants like carbon monoxide (CO), particulates, sulfur oxides, nitrogen oxides (NO_x) and other ozone (O_3) precursors, *e.g.*, volatile organic compounds (VOCs).[10] By contrast, California's unique head-start regulating air pollution (which had reached crisis proportions there) in the face of a national market in cars and trucks seemed to demand a tailored approach for "mobile" sources of these pollutants.[11] And it had grown abundantly clear by March 1970 that control solutions' costs varied greatly source by source and place to place.[12] We might say that welfarist cost minimization was fused to the federalist structure of the Act in a deeply political—but also surprisingly robust—compromise.[13] This has made rule/entitlement design for mobile sources,

---

[7] *See* Section 4.5.

[8] Note that "conventional" pollutants (CO, NO_x, particulates, SO_2, and volatile organic compounds (VOCs)), toxic "hazardous air pollutants" (asbestos, metals, carcinogens, *etc.*) and GHGs (CO_2, methane (CH_4), *etc.*) all stem from new and existing, mobile and stationary sources alike. Even simple efficiency gains would, at least presumptively, reduce their emission in direct proportion.

[9] It would be decades before social scientists brought intuitive thinking like this into the disrepute which data-driven methods have cast it into today. *See* DUNCAN J. WATTS, EVERYTHING IS OBVIOUS 7–29 (2011); DANIEL KAHNEMAN, THINKING, FAST AND SLOW (2010).

[10] Regulators sensitive to the potential for regulated parties to *exit* their jurisdiction and/or invest elsewhere would, all else equal, prefer uniform common standards, or at least uniform common "floors." *See* Thomas W. Merrill, *Preemption in Environmental Law: Formalism, Federalism, Theory, and Default Rules, in* FEDERAL PREEMPTION: STATES' POWERS, NATIONAL INTERESTS 166, 167 (Richard A. Epstein & Michael S. Greve eds., 2007).

[11] *See, e.g.*, KRIER & URSIN, supra note 1 at 200–211; FRANK GRAD ET AL., THE AUTOMOBILE AND THE REGULATION OF ITS IMPACT ON THE ENVIRONMENT 393 n.12 (1975).

[12] *See* SECOND REPORT OF THE SEC. HEALTH, EDUC. & WELFARE, THE COST OF CLEAN AIR, S. Doc. 91-65 (March 1970) (hereafter "COST OF CLEAN AIR II").

[13] *See* RICHARD B. STEWART & JAMES E. KRIER, ENVIRONMENTAL LAW AND POLICY 406–41 (2d ed. 1978); KRIER & URSIN, supra note 1 at 102–118. It is

i.e., tailored to a durable consumer good uniquely capable of frustrating social cost accountants, into a long-run experiment testing the cost-benefit boundary and, indeed, economic methods over time.

As the principal risks of combustion engines' emissions have shifted from localized, well-known health threats into the truly global menace of GHG concentrations and planetary climate disruption, the CAA's differentiations of mobile/stationary and new/existing emissions have only added to our practical political problems, at times putting the Act's different aspects at cross purposes with one another and transforming the very notion of social costs into a cipher lacking steady foundations. Tracing that evolution from the beginnings of cost-conscious mobile source controls on conventional pollutants to today's efficiency standards targeting GHG abatements reveals just how dramatically changes in the scale of cost accountings can affect their relevance and meaning.

4.1.1 The Automotive Sector: A Technology–Growth Intersection

The spark combustion engine is what some would call a "general purpose technology."[14] With its broad diffusion came economic impacts disproportionate to the value of the capital itself.[15] Its low relative cost, high power-to-weight ratio, and complementarities with other factors yielded profits, growth, and social change across so much of the economy and

---

worth noting that some of California's tailpipe and crankcase emissions controls had become *de facto* national standards because the automobile manufacturers preferred to market common units. Id. at 177–95.

[14] *See* Timothy F. Bresnahan & Manuel Tratjenberg, *General Purpose Technologies: "Engines of Growth"?*, 65 J. ECONOMETRICS 83, 84 (1995). Though diesel engines are often lumped together with spark engines, they differ in several substantial respects. *See* Thorsten Raatz & Hermann Grieshaber, *Basic Principles of the Diesel Engine, in* DIESEL ENGINE MANAGEMENT: SYSTEMS AND COMPONENTS 18 (Konrad Rei fed., 2014). For our purposes, we may regard it as a derivative, though.

[15] *See* VACLAV SMIL, CREATING THE TWENTIETH CENTURY: TECHNICAL INNOVATIONS OF 1867–1914 AND THEIR LASTING IMPACT (2005). Questions surrounding the utility of the "general purpose technology" (GPT) concept itself still linger. *See* Richard G. Lipsey *et al.*, *What Requires Explanation?, in* GENERAL PURPOSE TECHNOLOGIES AND ECONOMIC GROWTH 15, 48 (Elhanan Helpman ed., 1998). But combustion piston engines have unequivocally demonstrated important complementarities with other factors and have long been the principal power source for the automobile—itself an outsized segment of the North American (and many European) economies.

society that it became the stuff of social science legend.[16] Yet its externalities and dependence on public goods have been equally outsized.[17] Fossil fuel combustion generates a catalogue of wastes that are both chronically and acutely hazardous to human health[18]—threats which renewable, "biofuel" alternatives can reduce only marginally.[19] Public goods like roads and bridges are growing progressively costlier to build, to maintain, and to reconcile with environmental quality.[20] Finally,

---

[16] *See, e.g.*, Lipsey *et al.*, supra note 15 at 28; Craig N. Oren, *Getting Commuters Out of their Cars: What Went Wrong?*, 17 STAN. ENVTL. L.J. 141 (1998). The direction and pace of growth as influenced by GPTs like the spark combustion engine is of long-standing theoretical debate. *See* NATHAN ROSENBERG, INSIDE THE BLACK BOX: TECHNOLOGY AND ECONOMICS 14–15 (1982).

[17] *See, e.g.*, Ian W.H. Parry *et al.*, *Automobile Externalities and Policies*, 45(2) J. ECON. LIT. 373, 373–84 (2007); Kenneth F. Dunker & Basile G. Rabbat, *Why America's Bridges Are Crumbling*, 268(3) SCIENTIFIC AMER. 66, 70–72 (1993) (noting a large and growing backlog of deferred maintenance on American bridges).

[18] The mix of toxins in mobile source emissions has changed dramatically since 1970, due in part to CAA controls. *See, e.g.*, NATIONAL RESEARCH COUNCIL, AIR QUALITY MANAGEMENT IN THE UNITED STATES 155–61 (2004) (hereafter NRC, "AIR QUALITY MNGT.") (reviewing experiences with lead, methyl tertiary butyl ether, and other toxics).

[19] *See* Parry *et al.*, supra note 17 at 391–92. On the challenges of accounting for pollution abatements in switches from petroleum to biofuels, *see* John M. DeCicco, *Biofuel's Carbon Balance: Doubts, Certainties and Implications*, 121 CLIMATIC CH. 801 (2013).

[20] NRC, AIR QUALITY MNGT., supra note 18 at 162–65; Dunker & Rabbat, supra note 17; Richard Arnott & Kenneth Small, *The Economics of Traffic Congestion*, 82(5) AMER. SCIENTIST 446 (1994) (presenting multiple proofs that expansion of driving infrastructure only increases driver demand); Bent Flyvbjerg *et al.*, *How Common and How Large Are Cost Overruns in Transport Infrastructure Projects?*, 23(1) TRANSP. REVS. 71 (2003) (presenting longitudinal study of cost increases in major infrastructure projects in Europe, North America and elsewhere and concluding that cost overruns are the norm). The formal modeling done to estimate new or enhanced roads' impacts on local and regional environmental quality has remained infamously inaccurate. *See* Morten Skou Nicolaisen & Petter Næss, *Roads to Nowhere: The Accuracy of Travel Demand Forecasts for Do-Nothing Alternatives*, 37 TRANSP. POL'Y 57 (2015); RICHARD T.T. FORMAN ET AL., ROAD ECOLOGY: SCIENCE AND SOLUTIONS 63–72 (2003). Finally, changing climate baselines are increasing the risk that design/build optimizations in this infrastructure are deeply mistaken. *See* B. Shane Underwood *et al.*, *Increased Costs to US Pavement Infrastructure from Future Temperature Rise*, 7 NATURE CLIM. CH. 704 (2017).

tailpipe emissions of CO_2 and other GHGs are a significant and growing contributor globally to climate disruption.[21]

As will become clear, economists' static partial equilibrium analyses of the social costs of combustion engines have proven to be of little practical value in assessing the good and bad of curbing these emissions. The more pervasive it became, the greater the automobile's "consumption externalities" grew.[22] Its very ubiquity today induces continued investment in further innovation and diffusion.[23] Inertia of this kind can impede aggregate shifts to socially desired alternatives,[24] something many argue is currently afoot in global transport markets.[25] Of course, such network effects can be self-limiting, *i.e.*, congestion,[26] and may dampen the

---

[21] *See* Parry *et al.*, supra note 17 at 376–77; U.S. EPA, Endangerment and Cause or Contribute Findings for Greenhouse Gases under Section 202(a) of the Clean Air Act, 74 Fed. Reg. 66496, 66499–50 (2009).

[22] For some products, the utility a user derives from consumption increases (or decreases) with the number of other agents consuming that good. *See* Michael L. Katz & Carl Shapiro, *Network Externalities, Competition, and Compatibility*, 75(3) AMER. ECON. REV. 424, 424 (1985). With automobiles, for example, certain roads, gas stations, repair shops, *etc.*, comprise such "consumption externalities." Id. at 425.

[23] Some of this may even be attributable to the standardization achieved in automobiles as a result of CAA mobile source controls! *See* Herman R.J. Vollebergh & Edwin van der Werf, *The Role of Standards in Eco-Innovation: Lessons for Policymakers*, 8(2) REV. ENVTL. ECON. & POL'Y 230, 235–39 (2014). These "returns to scale" have had a pronounced impact on the technology and capitalization of fossil fuel production. *See* Thomas Covert, Michael Greenstone & Christopher R. Knittel, *Will We Ever Stop Using Fossil Fuels?*, 30(1) J. ECON. PERSPS. 117, 131–36 (2016). Finally, predictions about the US transport sector have often failed to anticipate transformative technological change—like the rise of electric vehicles, a renewably powered grid, autonomous vehicles, ride sharing, *etc. See, e.g.*, Andrew P. Morriss, *The Next Generation of Mobile Source Regulation*, 17 N.Y.U. ENVTL. L.J. 325, 339 (2008) ("The future of the market for personal transportation services looks remarkably like the present.").

[24] *See, e.g.*, Joseph Farrell & Garth Saloner, *Standardization, Compatibility and Innovation*, 16(1) RAND J. ECON. 70 (1985).

[25] *See, e.g.*, Eftichios S. Sartzetakis & Panagiotis Tsigaris, *Environmental Externalities in the Presence of Network Effects: Adoption of Low Emission Technologies in the Automobile Market*, 28(3) J. REG. ECON. 309 (2005).

[26] *See* Alan A. Walters, *The Theory and Measurement of Private and Social Costs of Highway Congestion*, 29(4) ECONOMETRICA 676 (1961).

inertia. But that turns as much or more on the distortions at work in a contemporary political system as it does on markets or available technology.[27]

Since 1977 CAA § 202(a)(3) has required US EPA to pursue "the greatest degree of emission reduction achievable" while weighing "cost, energy, and safety factors."[28] Did this particular optimization lock in a "static" view of the unavoidable costs and trade-offs?[29] Did it protect the incumbent firms from competition? As discussed in Chapter 2, Section 2.2.1, CAA mobile source controls got off to a rough start. The 1970 legislative mandate was to cut tailpipe emissions of VOCs, CO, and NO_x[30] from "light-duty" vehicles by 90 percent by model year 1975–76 *unless* EPA made a finding that the technology to achieve those cuts was not "available."[31] Two years later when EPA refused to budge and the American auto manufacturers sued, a reviewing court was thrust into a now-familiar dilemma as the litigation revealed what divided the parties.[32] Emissions chemistry, the dynamics of large-scale manufacturing, and shifting automobile markets dominated the case.[33] The automakers

---

[27] *See* STAN LUGER, CORPORATE POWER, AMERICAN DEMOCRACY AND THE AUTOMOBILE INDUSTRY (2000); KRIER & URSIN, supra note 1 at 199–247; Oren, supra note 16.

[28] 42 U.S.C. § 7521(a)(3)(A). This mix of factors stemmed from the 1977 amendments—after EPA's initial encounter with car makers over the 1970 amendments' mandated emissions cuts. It is indicative of other, related CAA provisions on the control of mobile source emissions.

[29] Driesen argued that the "assumption of identity between polluter and societal economic interests produces a static approach to economic considerations," DAVID M. DRIESEN, THE ECONOMIC DYNAMICS OF ENVIRONMENTAL LAW 23 (2003), something he concluded could only be remedied through what he deemed a more "dynamic" understanding of economic costs. Id. at 24–25 (arguing that a cost to one producer which advantages other producers with less harmful alternatives may be fully offset by societal efficiency gains over time).

[30] *See* R. SHEP MELNICK, REGULATION AND THE COURTS: THE CASE OF THE CLEAN AIR ACT 28–29 (1983) (noting this was the part of the Act that got the "most attention in Congress and the press"); NRC, AIR QUALITY MNGT., supra note 18 at 133–41.

[31] *See* GRAD ET AL., supra note 11 at 325–68. The symbolic politics of the 90% figure were part of the presidential race between Nixon and several of his rivals in the Senate. *See* LUGER, supra note 27 at 87–88. The judicial contest over the agency's implementation of the Act ignored these origins. *See* International Harvester Co. v. Ruckelshaus, 478 F.2d 615, 641–50 (D.C. Cir. 1973).

[32] *See* DOYLE, supra note 1 at 85–88; KRIER & URSIN, supra note 1 at 234–36.

[33] *See Int'l Harvester*, 478 F.2d at 633–47.

had turned this intersection to their advantage ever since California had first sought to push emissions technology in 1964.[34] Six months later the court sided with the manufacturers and remanded EPA's decision to it as arbitrary—or at least unexplained.[35] The court was noticeably swayed by a National Academy of Sciences panel report that had, in February 1973, referred to the American firms' "bolt-on" technologies as "most disadvantageous with respect to first cost, fuel economy, maintainability, and durability."[36] The 1970 gambit of "forcing" manufacturers to innovate[37] seemed to have failed.[38]

After the remand, the American firms' cooperation against dramatic CAA emissions cuts continued to flourish for a time,[39] becoming a monument to the strategic perils of targeting a consolidated industry with

---

[34] *See* KRIER & URSIN, supra note 1 at 148–69; DOYLE, supra note 1 at 83–85 (reviewing EPA hearings).

[35] *See Int'l Harvester*, 478 F.2d at 648; GRAD ET AL., supra note 11 at 355–60. A "basic dilemma" that would confront *any* reviewing court was the intricacy of the technologies and their interactivity with other factors, combined with the generalist judges' own lack of expertise. *See* MELNICK, supra note 30 at 53–70. That did not deter the *International Harvester* panel from setting aside EPA's refusal to delay the 1975 mandate, though.

[36] *See* LUGER, supra note 27 at 88. "By selecting the catalytic converter, with its inherent problems, the industry virtually guaranteed that pollution policy would be an ongoing political battle." Id. *Cf. Int'l Harvester*, 478 F.2d at 627–28, 648–49 (noting a remand to EPA in December 1972 to consider the National Academy's report and using report to question EPA conclusions, cataloguing the number of instances EPA's methods were "at variance" with Academy's); *see also* John B. Heywood, *Future Emission Control Technology, in* GRAD ET AL., supra note 11 at 279, 281.

[37] In retrospect, given the industry's primitive structure, from late 1970 to Model Year (MY) '75 left only about two years' lead time for research and development, *see* LUGER, supra note 27 at 88, which probably shows Congress expected some sort of creative "breakthrough" to follow from the CAA mandate. *See* id. ("[Senator] Muskie admitted that the targets were technologically unreachable at the time, but he believed that tight deadlines would force the industry to develop the needed technology."). That breakthrough took longer than expected.

[38] *Cf.* Heywood, supra note 36 at 283–96 (reviewing the state of the art in catalysis and exhaust gas recirculation and finding that several basic obstacles had remained insuperable for the MY '75 target).

[39] *See* David Gerard & Lester B. Lave, *Implementing Technology-Forcing Policies: The 1970 Clean Air Act Amendments and the Introduction of Advanced Automotive Emissions Controls in the United States*, 72 TECH. FORECASTING & SOC. CHANGE 761 (2005).

technology-based performance standards.[40] Who can know better about the "available" technology than the small handful of large, integrated firms producing the good themselves?[41] Organized labor and mass panic were mobilized over the unemployment that might ensue in the event one of the firms, *e.g.*, Chrysler, failed to meet the standard.[42] The only hard estimates in circulation were projections of what the three American firms would do and how their solutions might fare on a durable consumer good designed to last a decade or more while facing increasingly capable (foreign) competition.[43] Troubles continued to plague those firms' equipment throughout the decade.[44] As their solutions kept coming up short, though, it became clear that consumers would bear at least some of the costs of failure.[45] And although it paled beside the ordeal of trying to

---

[40] *See* MELNICK, supra note 30 at 35–38; GRAD ET AL., supra note 11 at 350–68; DOYLE, supra note 1. A narrative of the natural advantages enjoyed by such quasi-cartels and the havoc they can wreak in contexts like the CAA's mobile source controls—through impact litigation, *etc.*—is reviewed in MELNICK, supra note 30. At least one economic model of this confederating was proposed. *See* Dennis A. Yao, *Strategic Responses to Automobile Emissions Control: A Game-Theoretic Analysis*, 15(4) J. ENVTL. ECON. & MNGT. 419 (1988). A similar narrative about certain stationary sources is told in BRUCE ACKERMAN & WILLIAM T. HASSLER, CLEAN COAL/DIRTY AIR (1983). *See also* Craig N. Oren, *Detail and Delegation: A Study in Statutory Specificity*, 15 COLUM. J. ENVTL. L. 143 (1990).

[41] Hicks formulated his hypothesis in terms of factor pricing. But the performance standard EPA derived from studying the manufacturers' solutions for the 1970 mandate was to be enforced by a cost-prohibitive fine per noncompliant vehicle sold—rendering returns to all inputs mutually dependent on success in the abatement factor. Finally, whatever gains might be realized from the induced innovation could be fully, partially, or not at all captured depending on outside influences, *e.g.*, information sharing. This would make measuring the financial viability of any given performance standard dependent upon information only the manufacturers possess.

[42] *See* David Vogel, *A Case Study of Clean Air Legislation 1967–81, in* THE IMPACT OF THE MODERN CORPORATION 345 (Betty Bock *et al.* eds., 1984); DOYLE, supra note 1 at 109–11.

[43] *See* Heywood, supra note 36 at 283–319; NRC, AIR QUALITY MNGT., supra note 18 at 148–62.

[44] *See* Heywood, supra note 36 at 283–300; 309–19; NRC, AIR QUALITY MNGT., supra note 18 at 136–48. In-use equipment maintenance/reliability turned out to be a much more persistent challenge than was expected. Id. at 149.

[45] *See* GRAD ET AL., supra note 11 at 418–21. A massive Chrysler recall for defective CO controls affected an estimated 208,000+ vehicles in 1978. *See Chrysler Corp.*, 631 F.2d at 867. That was after an 825,000+ vehicle recall for defective CO sensors in 1973. *See* DOYLE, supra note 1 at 156–61.

deter driving with "transportation control plans,"[46] the contests over these standards churned on uneasily for another decade.[47]

The 1973 court-ordered delay was the first of several.[48] But the sectoral confederacy that triumphed in that first round of the struggle soon lost its footing.[49] Business interest in solving the emissions problem quickened.[50] Even in 1970, the catalytic conversion technology GM and Ford were developing was understood; adapting it to the automobile was the hold-up.[51] Targeted efforts by EPA and others pushed the innovation and diffusion processes, eventually overcoming the back-pressure.[52] By the time of the second round, fuel economy standards, the industry had diversified and a confederacy of manufacturers never materialized.[53]

---

[46] *See* MELNICK, supra note 30 at 299–342; South Terminal Corp. v. EPA, 504 F.2d 646 (1st Cir. 1974); Texas v. EPA, 499 F.2d 289 (5th Cir. 1974); Brown v. EPA, 521 F.2d 827 (9th Cir. 1975); Maryland v. EPA, 530 F.2d 215 (4th Cir. 1975); District of Columbia v. Train, 521 F.2d 971 (D.C. Cir. 1975).

[47] *See* NRC, AIR QUALITY MNGT., supra note 18 at 137 ("The CAA Amendments of 1977 extended the emission standards deadlines for [CO] and [VOCs] until 1983 and 1980, respectively. The amendments also extended the deadlines for NO_x to 1982 and changed the standard from a 90% to a 75% reduction.").

[48] *See* Chrysler Corp. v. U.S. EPA, 631 F.2d 865,867 n.3 (D.C. Cir. 1980).

[49] *See* GRAD ET AL. supra note 11 at 355–64, 369–79; *see also* NRC, AIR QUALITY MNGT., supra note 18 at 167–68 ("The history of vehicle emission controls is one of long-term success, albeit success that came more slowly than policy-makers intended. Delays were due in part to opposition from the automotive industry facing the challenge in a cost-effective manner. ... Actual costs of the improvements have often proved to be less than anticipated. Lower costs were realized as production experience was acquired, economics of scale were achieved, and the desire to meet a mass market had fueled substantial competition.") (internal citations omitted).

[50] *See* DOYLE, supra note 1 at 64–66. Even in an oligopolistic market the incentive to innovate and raise a rival's costs through a technology-based performance standard can be material. *See* Steven C. Hackett, *Pollution-Controlling Innovation in Oligopolistic Industries: Some Comparisons between Patent Races and Research*, 29 J. ENVT'L ECON. & MNGT. 339, 341 (1995).

[51] *See* Gerard & Lave, supra note 39 at 767–71. Though the automakers had been experimenting with catalytic converters since 1959, the variable powering of combustion engines and down-sizing to automobile scale proved formidable challenges. Id.

[52] *See* Gerard & Lave, supra note 39 at 772.

[53] *See* LUGER, supra note 27 at 176–78; Gerard & Lave, supra note 39 at 773–75; *cf.* SANYA CARLEY ET AL., A MACROECONOMIC STUDY OF FEDERAL AND STATE AUTOMOTIVE REGULATIONS 53–63 (2017) (reviewing the diversification of

Indeed, by 2012, US regulators had agreed to require a doubling of sales-weighted average fuel economy by 2025[54]—a move the manufacturers, by and large, supported[55]—and emissions control technology was fast progressing through the electronic age. Combined corporate average fuel economy (CAFE)/tailpipe GHG standards were projected by the National Academies to add from \$526 to \$705 of cumulative direct manufacturing cost to a representative midsize, spark combustion auto in MY 2017–25.[56] But what were the social costs of reaching that point where such extraordinary progress in emissions control would add more than 3 percent to the sticker price of an average car?

4.2 COST-AVAILABILITY AND PARTIAL EQUILIBRIUM: INNOVATION IN FOCUS

As the technological questions mounted in the 1970s, EPA remained at a disadvantage.[57] Congress, it bears recalling, had intervened twice after 1970 with statutory amendments slackening the expectations on the automakers[58] but reaffirming EPA's authority to adopt performance

---

supply chains, manufacturing locations, and relative values added by different factors).

[54] *See* Environmental Protection Agency & Dept. of Transp., National Highway Traffic Safety Admin., Final Rule—Light-Duty Vehicle Greenhouse Gas Emission Standards and Corporate Average Fuel Economy Standards, 75 Fed. Reg. 25324 (2010) (hereafter "Final Phase I Tailpipe Rule").

[55] *See* National Research Council, Cost, Effectiveness and Deployment of Fuel Economy Technologies for Light-Duty Vehicles vii (2015) (hereafter NRC, "Cost Effectiveness Report").

[56] *See* id. at 82.

[57] *See* Doyle, supra note 1 at 99–148. Formal modeling of such predicaments confirms the limited options available. *See* Partha Dasgupta, Peter Hammond, & Eric Maskin, *On Imperfect Information and Optimal Pollution Control*, 47 Rev. Econ. Studs. 857 (1980). "If firms argue that meeting a standard is impossible, and regulators have no foundation to contradict them, it is unlikely that regulatory pressure will persuade the firms to make R&D outlays. Therefore, regulators must establish credibility by limiting or erasing any information advantages for the firms. As a practical matter, regulators might limit the asymmetry by targeting a specific technology, or by setting less ambitious performance targets … ." Gerard & Lave, supra note 39 at 764.

[58] On Congress's extension of the 1975 suspension that EPA granted following the remand in *Int'l Harvester*, *see* D. Bruce La Pierre, *Technology-Forcing and Federal Environmental Standards*, 62 Iowa L. Rev. 771, 795–96 & n.128 (1977). On the automakers' role therein, *see* Doyle, supra note 1 at

standards on emissions as achievable.[59] For much of that search, the available solutions bundled the approaches for more than one pollutant.[60] And this multidimensional "achievability" guided by particular technologies has been the statutory benchmark for auto emissions constraints and fuel economy ever since.[61] What quickly became standard was a practical focus on the actual equipment, solution, or principle in question, *i.e.*, installation, operation, durability, *etc.*—the "cost-as-designed, built

---

115–48, and David P. Currie, *The Mobile-Source Provisions of the Clean Air Act*, 48 U. CHI. L. REV. 811, 819–24 (1979); *see also* GRAD ET AL., supra note 11 at 360–64.

[59] At least one legal scholar, Arnold Reitze, has tracked mobile source controls along this see-saw since the 1977 amendments. *See* Arnold W. Reitze, Jr., *Controlling Automotive Air Pollution Through Inspection and Maintenance Programs*, 47 GEO. WASH. L. REV. 705 (1979); Arnold W. Reitze, Jr., *The Regulation of Fuels and Fuel Additives under Section 211 of the Clean Air Act*, 29 TULSA L. REV. 485 (1994) (hereafter "Reitze 1994"); Arnold W. Reitze, Jr., *Federalism and the Inspection and Maintenance Program under the Clean Air Act*, 27 PAC. L.J. 1461 (1996); Arnold W. Reitze, Jr., *Mobile Source Air Pollution Control*, 6 ENVTL. LAW. 309, 318–27 (2000) (hereafter "Reitze 2000"); Arnold W. Reitze, Jr., *The CAA Motor Vehicle Inspection and Maintenance Program: Is It Cost Effective?*, 47 ENVTL. L. RPTR. 10877 (2017) (hereafter "Reitze 2017").

[60] The O_3 precursor (hydrocarbons or VOCs) targets were set by the 1977 amendments, but EPA's general statutory delegation otherwise was to control emissions to the degree technologically achievable. *See* Natural Resources Defense Council, Inc. v. U.S. EPA, 655 F.2d 318, 322 (D.C. Cir. 1981) ("The requirement that emission standards be technologically achievable highlights the need for the EPA's power to divide the broad spectrum of motor vehicles into classes or categories."). This again turned on the definition of a "light duty vehicle," id. at 326, 338–40, and to the interaction of regulatory standards with market forces. *See* id. at 329–36.

[61] *See* Alec C. Zacaroli, *Regulation of Mobile Sources: Motor Vehicles, Nonroad Engines, and Aircraft, in* THE CLEAN AIR ACT HANDBOOK 371, 374–402 (Julie R. Domike & Alex C. Zacaroli eds., 4th ed. 2016); *see also* Currie, supra note 58; Reitze 2000, supra note 59 at 333–38. When Congress lifted the ban on increasing CAFE standards in the 2007 Energy Independence and Security Act, Pub. L. No. 110-140, the Secretary of Transportation was empowered to set the standards "to a level that the Secretary decides is the maximum feasible average fuel economy level for that model year." 49 U.S.C. § 32902(c). By then, "feasibility" standards were quite familiar in the court (the D.C. Circuit) vested with exclusive original jurisdiction over challenges to EPA CAA actions with nationwide effect. It was even willing to opine on the expected veracity of obligated parties' contentions versus those of their equipment vendors. *See* National Petrochem. & Refiners Ass'n v. EPA, 287 F.3d 1130, 1136–37 (D.C. Cir. 2002) (*citing* George J. Stigler, *The Economic Theory of Regulation*, 2 BELL J. ECON. & MNGT. 3 (1971)).

and operated."[62] Gradually, this focus reinforced two clear patterns: (1) insufficient research/development (R&D) expenditures from domestic automakers (perhaps content to rely on their political or legal leverage), and (2) diversified investment, some public and some private, in capabilities to address collectively the technological hurdles which had hardened in the sector's experiences.[63]

Of course, combined, these two patterns question any simple sector-bound accounting of CAA regulation's costs. And it is important to recall that this collectivized search for technological solutions to auto emissions literally began from the three American firms'—GM, Ford, and Chrysler—collusion against California regulators.[64] Environmental groups have routinely charged EPA with a kind of complicity in that collusion.[65] And American manufacturers have just as long answered that EPA is actually too rigid and unrealistic.[66] As early as 1975 it was clearly *possible* to meet the CAA's ambitious goal of cutting 90 percent of the conventional pollutants from tailpipes. The uncertainties came down to making the needed investments in innovation and diffusion.[67] EPA has

---

[62] *See NRDC*, 655 F.2d at 331–36; Natural Resources Defense Council v. Thomas, 805 F.2d 410, 428–34 (D.C. Cir. 1986); Natural Resources Defense Council v. Reilly, 983 F.2d 259, 261–66, 268–73 (D.C. Cir. 1993); Husqvarna AB v. EPA, 254 F.3d 195, 197–99 (D.C. Cir. 2001); *Nat'l Petrochem.*, 287 F.3d at 1135–42; Bluewater Network v. EPA, 370 F.3d 1, 6–11, 19–23 (D.C. Cir. 2004).

[63] *See* DOYLE, supra note 1 at 452–45; Gerard & Lave, supra note 39 at 774–76. Both trends attracted modelers' attention at the time. *See* Yao, supra note 40 at 433–34; Hackett, supra note 50 at 354.

[64] *See* DOYLE, supra note 1 at 29–49; KRIER & URSIN, supra note 1 at 176; LUGER, supra note 27 at 84–86. After a decade of experience with the consent decree that settled US Justice Department antitrust charges against the big three, it was unclear just how "competitive" their emissions control R&D had been in the 1970s. *See* Bennett H. Goldstein & Howell H. Howard, *Antitrust Law and the Control of Auto Pollution: Rethinking the Alliance between Competition and Technical Progress*, 10 ENVT'L L. 517 (1980).

[65] *See, e.g.*, JOHN H. ADAMS ET AL., A FORCE FOR NATURE: THE STORY OF NRDC AND THE FIGHT TO SAVE OUR PLANET 179–83 (2010).

[66] CAA § 202(a) cases have often taken this form, *see, e.g., Thomas*, 805 F.2d at 414; Natural Resources Defense Council v. Reilly, 983 F.2d 259 (D.C. Cir. 1993); Natural Resources Defense Council, Inc. v. EPA, 22 F.3d 1125 (D.C. Cir. 1994), as have several of the fuels cases under CAA § 211 and others. *See, e.g.*, Bluewater Network v. EPA, 372 F.3d 404 (D.C. Cir. 2004) (reviewing EPA's marine diesel engine standards under CAA § 213(a)).

[67] *See* GRAD ET AL., supra note 11 at 421–31. Estimating the own "costs" of changing a product line, especially one as path dependent and demand elastic as

routinely found itself in this strategic position since—in court and elsewhere—of having to decide what is/not "feasible" given some pace of expected shift(s) in production.[68] The American firms (at first) clearly chose to "invest" in litigation challenging EPA as much or more than they did in innovation.[69] As the struggle wore on, however, with various neutrals like the National Academies adding their own contributions and several battles involving California regulators as well,[70] abundant public information on the technological and economic bases of feasibility judgments was, thus, amassed.[71]

Take, for example, the setting of NO_x and particulate standards for diesel engines MY '84–85 and after.[72] Daimler and Volkswagen were already heavily invested in diesel powertrains even then,[73] making this into a cross-border case of standards, competition, and innovation.[74] In

---

automobiles, is theoretically possible—but has thus far resisted even the most careful empirical efforts. *See* Adam B. Jaffe *et al.*, *Technological Change and the Environment, in* 1 HANDBOOK OF ENVIRONMENTAL ECONOMICS 461, 505 (Karl Göran-Mäler & Jeffrey R. Vincent eds., 2003).

[68] *See, e.g.*, 655 F.2d at 334; *see also Thomas*, 805 F.2d at 425.

[69] *See* MELNICK, supra note 30 at 193–238. It would seem perverse to attribute such production costs to the standards, though. The big three American auto firms implemented a similar investment strategy regarding NHTSA safety standard 208, much to their own cost advantage. *See* JERRY L. MASHAW & DAVID HARFST, THE STRUGGLE FOR AUTO SAFETY (1990).

[70] *See, e.g.*, American Motors Corp. v. Blum, 603 F.2d 978 (D.C. Cir. 1979) (necessary "lead time" for more stringent California NO_x standards); Ford Motor Co. v. EPA, 606 F.3d 1293, 1300–03 (D.C. Cir. 1979) (geographic scope of a California waived car in post-1977 amendments standards); Motor & Equip. Mfrs. Ass'n, Inc. v. EPA, 627 F.2d 1095 (D.C. Cir. 1979) (potential scope of EPA's power to waive pre-emption of California standards); Engine Mfrs. Ass'n v. EPA, 88 F.3d 1075 (D.C. Cir. 1996) (scope of California's jurisdiction to regulate "non-new" non-road sources); Motor & Equip. Mfrs. Ass'n, Inc. v. Nichols, 142 F.3d 449, 454–56 (D.C. Cir. 1998) (California's requirement of "on-board diagnostic" devices two years before EPA's).

[71] *See, e.g.*, Motor & Equip. Mfrs. Ass'n v. Nichols, 142 F.3d 449 (D.C. Cir. 1998); Motor & Equip. Mfrs. Ass'n v. EPA, 627 F.2d 1095 (D.C. Cir. 1979); Ford Motor Co. v. EPA, 606 F.2d 1293 (D.C. Cir. 1979).

[72] *See* Natural Resources Defense Council, Inc. v. EPA, 655 F.2d 318, 328–44 (D.C. Cir. 1981).

[73] *See* DOYLE, supra note 1 at 93. GM's experience with diesel powertrains in large trucks had given it to consider developing a large car diesel powertrain, id. at 190, although that never came to fruition.

[74] *Cf.* Vollebergh & van der Werf, supra note 23 at 242 (arguing that the presence of standards beyond national borders can change the domestic policy perspective significantly).

the court's opinion, achievability came down to the role of lead times and expected technical improvements made in actual production.[75] Factual questions surrounding those technical judgments occupied much of the court case. This time, however, the court found all of EPA's judgments "reasonable," pointedly observing that "EPA is not obliged to provide detailed solutions to every engineering problem posed in the perfection of the [equipment]."[76] Reviewing courts have generally accepted that this "reasonableness" can include subordinating emissions reductions to considerations like manufacturer costs or identifiable consumer preferences (or vice versa) as EPA sees fit.[77] The depth of the court's assessment was its own signal, though, tracing a path through the rhetoric[78] in order to forecast how product lines and market forces could conceivably align.[79]

---

[75] *See NRDC*, 655 F.2d at 333–40. "[T]he agency conclude[d] that it is merely a question of time before the [equipment] is perfected. 'The improvements that are necessary are engineering problems, and are more a function of the resources allocated to the problem than any scientific or technical breakthrough.'" Id. at 333. Affording a long lead time to achieve dramatic improvements has been a core CAA strategy. *See, e.g.*, U.S. EPA, Final Rule—Control of Air Pollution from New Motor Vehicles: Heavy-Duty Engine and Vehicle Standards and Highway Diesel Fuel Sulfur Control Requirements, 66 Fed. Reg. 5002 (2001) (phasing in combined fuel and tailpipe emissions restrictions from 2007–30 for 95% reductions in NO_x from diesel drivetrains in trucks and buses).

[76] 655 F.2d at 333; *see also* NRDC v. Thomas, 805 F.2d 410, 432 (D.C. Cir. 1986) ("Our task stops with an assessment of the reasonableness of the agency's decision given the evidence it had before it."). The court continued that "[i]n the absence of theoretical objections to the technology, the agency need only identify the major steps necessary for development of the device, and give plausible reasons for its belief that the industry will be able to solve those problems in the time remaining." 655 F.2d at 333.

[77] *See* 655 F.2d at 331; *see also Thomas*, 805 F.2d at 419–25. The *Thomas* court was emphatic that EPA had selected an engine configuration as its benchmark by appropriately balancing its emissions performance "against several other factors such as cost, noise, energy and safety." Id. at 421. The fuel economy cases embracing this approach include *Center for Auto Safety v. NHTSA*, 793 F.2d 1322, 1338–40 (D.C. Cir. 1986), *Public Citizen v. NHTSA*, 848 F.2d 256, 265 (D.C. Cir. 1988), and *Center for Biological Diversity v. NHTSA*, 538 F.3d 1172, 1194–98 (9th Cir. 2008).

[78] The panel made no dismissive references to "the driving preferences of hot rodders," as had Judge Leventhal in *International Harvester. See* International Harvester v. Ruckelshaus, 478 F.2d 615, 640 (D.C. Cir. 1973).

[79] *See* 655 F.2d at 344 ("[A] reviewing court's role is to make sure that the agency has acted responsibly in formulating a reasoned prediction."). One panel member sided with the manufacturers. *See* id. at 345–46 (Robb, concurring in part and dissenting in part). EPA faced similar scrutiny in Clean Water Act

That same signal would be sent in subsequent auto, fuel, and fuel economy standard settings alike.[80]

For these feasibility judgments, EPA staff consisted mainly of engineers working opposite industry engineers throughout the development of the actual catalytic devices and techniques which eventually tamed VOCs, CO, and NO_x.[81] The 1990 CAA amendments further entrenched this approach with a slate of new feasibility/achievability standards focused on ground-level O_3, particulates, NO_x, and SO_2.[82] Contemporary estimates put the expected cost of compliance with those demands at between $170 and $600 per car,[83] a price increase perhaps big enough to keep older, more polluting cars on the road longer.[84] Still, this persistent focus on the technical challenges of catalytic conversion systems and

---

standard-setting cases at the time. *See* La Pierre, supra note 58 at 772–73, 794–805 (distinguishing between basic, intermediate, and major innovations in pollution control and how each factored into performance standard-setting of the time).

[80] *See* National Ass'n Clean Air Agencies v. EPA, 489 F.3d 1221, 1230–32 (D.C. Cir. 2007) (upholding EPA's balancing of cost, safety, and other factors in setting aircraft engine standards); Blue Water Network v. U.S. EPA, 370 F.2d 1, 19–23 (D.C. Cir. 2004) (upholding EPA's balancing of cost and feasibility in setting performance standard for snowmobile engines); Sierra Club v. EPA, 325 F.3d 374, 377–83 (D.C. Cir. 2003) (upholding EPA's balancing of various toxic emissions reductions on "achievability" concerns); Small Refiner Lead Phase-Down Task Force v. U.S. EPA, 705 F.2d 506, 524–37 (D.C. Cir. 1983) (accepting EPA's balancing of costs and benefits by a feasibility standard as not arbitrary or capricious); Union Oil Co. Cal. v. U.S EPA, 821 F.2d 678, 684–85 (D.C. Cir. 1987) (accepting EPA's treatment of lead restrictions in California fuels as reasonable balancing of costs and benefits); Geo. E. Warren Corp. v. U.S. EPA, 159 F.3d 616, 626–29 (D.C. Cir. 1998) (upholding fuel import restrictions as not arbitrary imposition of importer-specific performance duties).

[81] *See* Gerard & Lave, supra note 39 at 768, 775; Tim Palucka, *Doing the Impossible*, 19(3) INVENTION & TECH. MAG. (Winter 2004). Ceramics engineers from Corning, Inc. (funded in part by the US government) eventually solved the interrelated puzzles of three-way catalysis, id., winning the National Medal of Technology in 2005 for their efforts.

[82] *See* Henry A. Waxman *et al.*, *Cars, Fuels and Clean Air: A Review of Title II of the Clean Air Act Amendments of 1990*, 21 ENVT'L. L. 1947 (1991); GARY BRYNER, BLUE SKIES, GREEN POLITICS: THE CLEAN AIR ACT OF 1990 AND ITS IMPLEMENTATION (2d ed. 1995); *cf.* LUGER, supra note 27 at 161 ("The ability of the auto industry officials to influence the outcome of clean air legislation represented the low point of their power during this period.").

[83] *See* LUGER, supra note 27 at 162.

[84] The price elasticity of demand for *new* cars has long confounded cost-benefit analyses of mobile source controls for if it is high, any added cost to

their alternatives would eventually open new fronts in regulatory cost evaluation—the combination of cars and fuels to develop together.[85] For, as EPA noted in 1990, "[o]ne problem with using regression equations based on a small number of data points to extrapolate costs is the potential for under- or over-estimating future costs for relatively immature pollution control programs."[86] To assess a whole market and its gradual transformation by shifts in what is being produced and how really must put the power of technological change to alter cost landscapes in focus.[87]

4.3 COSTING A TRANSITION: WHEN COMPETITIVE PRESSURES MINIMIZE COSTS

In a questionable retrospective analysis prepared in 1990, EPA concluded that the annualized capital and operating costs of its mobile source controls had increased steadily from $1.3 billion in 1972 to $7.5 billion in 1987.[88] Shaped in part by the small number of firms to be studied, EPA's counting exercise took virtually no account of what economists call "learning by doing"—or increasing returns to scale in production.[89]

---

the price of a new car becomes a kind of price support for used cars as substitute goods. *See* CARLEY ET AL., supra note 53 at 17–18. *See* Section 4.4.

[85] *See* BRYNER, supra note 82; ADAMS ET AL., supra note 65 at 180–83 (describing a relational breakthrough between Natural Resources Defense Council, EPA and diesel engine industry executives working to create the low-sulfur diesel technology that later materialized in the 2000s).

[86] U.S. EPA, ENVIRONMENTAL INVESTMENTS: THE COST OF A CLEAN ENVIRONMENT § 1.3.2.1 (1990) (EPA-230-11-90-083) (hereafter EPA, "COST OF CLEAN").

[87] Economists consider such an assessment one of endogenous technological change (invariably contributing to some general equilibrium). *See* William A. Pizer & David Popp, *Endogenizing Technological Change: Matching Empirical Evidence to Modeling Needs*, 30 ENERGY ECON. 2754, 2768 (2008); Michael Grubb *et al.*, *Induced Technical Change in Energy and Environmental Modeling: Analytical Approaches and Policy Implications*, 27 ANN. REV. ENERGY & ENVT. 271, 277–82 (2002).

[88] *See* COST OF CLEAN, supra note 86 at § 3.1.2 (in constant 1986 dollars). Included in that figure were EPA's own (budgeted) expenditures and regulated firms' estimated capital and operating costs due to mobile source controls. EPA expected those annualized costs to rise to $11 billion in 1995 and to $14 billion by 2000. Id.

[89] The automobile sector, in particular, has long been a textbook example of these increasing returns. *See* NRC, COST EFFECTIVENESS REPORT, supra note 55

This was particularly noteworthy given the auto industry's well-known returns to scale.[90] EPA paid no attention to the changing complexion of the sector—at a moment when foreign manufacturers' fleets and factories were besetting the American market[91] and it was well known that the necessary technologies were arising from expensive models and trickling down to higher-volume models.[92] Though perhaps uneven, the competitive pressures at work were surely important. By 2002, the big three's collective profit margin was at 1.4 percent while Toyota, Honda, BMW and Nissan all averaged 10 percent or more.[93] As the sector's diversification continued, the search for emissions solutions did too. Of course, firms' internal accounting methods of the day varied (often dramatically),

---

at 249–51. EPA later fashioned what it called "learning curve adjustments" for downwardly adjusting per unit, "total annualized cost" estimates for the equipment required by its standards for 2000, 2010 and 2020. *See* EPA, BENEFITS AND COSTS, supra note 2 at 3-5–3-6. But it made clear the thin-to-nonexistent empirical basis for the values in those adjustments, id. at 3-6, and also noted that it had subtracted vehicle owners' fuel savings from the very same "direct compliance cost" totals! *See* id. at 3-6.

[90] The industry was arguably the original in this regard. *Cf.* ROBERT J. GORDON, THE RISE AND FALL OF AMERICAN GROWTH: THE U.S. STANDARD OF LIVING SINCE THE CIVIL WAR 152–57 (2016) (noting the "genius of Henry Ford" in pioneering the assembly line production model that allowed sustained price decreases coincident with quality increases).

[91] *See* MICHELINE MAYNARD, THE END OF DETROIT: HOW THE BIG THREE LOST THEIR GRIP ON THE AMERICAN CAR MARKET (2003). On one hand, a small number of incumbents to study can lower study costs. But it will also invest more importance in any given firm's experiences (or bluffing). *See, e.g.*, James W. Coleman, *How Cheap is Corporate Talk? Comparing Companies' Comments on Regulations with their Securities Disclosures*, 40 HARV. ENVTL. L. REV. 47, 55–56 (2016) ("Regulators concerned by Lee Iacocca's prophesies of doom in 1970 would have been reassured if they had read Ford Motor Company's contemporaneous Form 10-K disclosures."). In all events, cost estimations confined to the sector's own costs will ignore other, less direct effects and related causes. *See* William A. Pizer & Raymond Kopp, *Calculating the Costs of Environmental Regulation, in* 3 HANDBOOK OF ENVIRONMENTAL ECONOMICS 1307, at 1326 (Karl-Göran Mäler & Jeffrey R. Vincent eds., 2005) ("Costs to the firm measured in a partial equilibrium analysis ignore general equilibrium changes in output and prices and miss potential welfare changes from altered production levels and distortions in other markets.").

[92] *See, e.g.*, Matthew Wald, *Muscle, Muscle Everywhere*, N.Y. TIMES, May 19, 1999, at A18 ("Behind the trend in engine innovations are several refinements, most of which began in high-end cars and are working their way down to the 'econobox' end of the market.").

[93] MAYNARD, supra note 91 at 234.

no doubt variously accounting for R&D costs either as marginal or as average/fixed costs depending on that firm's timing of entry into the market.[94] Yet as to these varied experiences of own costs of compliance, EPA's aggregative statistics were completely aloof.

The folly of EPA's approach eventually became unmistakable in the search for better fuel economy through combustion enhancements like variable valve timing, multi-valve engines, direct injection, turbochargers, 6+ speed transmissions, continuously variable transmissions, microchip-controlled cylinder deactivation systems, and other advances which grew increasingly robust as more firms implemented their own solutions.[95] The 1990 amendments' uniform "Tier I" standards fed into EPA's more stringent "Tier II" standards, which the amendments authorized when "needed," when the technology was "available," and where the resultant reductions would be "cost effective."[96] By the turn of the century, with the standards grounded in three-way catalytic technology,[97] a consumer's overall costs of owning and operating a vehicle were thought to have barely risen since the early 1970s.[98] Much of that had to do with dynamics beyond the auto sector and, in any event, would remain invisible to any purely "partial" equilibrium accounting (no matter how dynamic).[99] Yet the more EPA studied the many solutions for reducing conventional emissions, the more it came to view combustion engine

---

[94] On the turbulence in intra-firm cost accounting around that time, *see* Robin Cooper & Robert S. Kaplan, *How Cost Accounting Distorts Product Costs*, 69(10) MNGT. ACCOUNT. 20 (1988); Robin Cooper & Robert S. Kaplan, *Measure Costs Right: Make the Right Decision*, HARV. BUS. REV. 96 (Sept.–Oct. 1988).

[95] *See* CARLEY ET AL., supra note 53 at 33–34; NRC, AIR QUALITY MNGT., supra note 18 at 137–42.

[96] *See* 42 U.S.C. § 7521(i)(3)(C); *see also* Zacaroli, supra note 61 at 380–81. In addition to further cuts in NO_x and VOCs, the Tier II rules promulgated in 2000 also capped all fuels' sulfur contents. NRC, AIR QUALITY MNGT., supra note 18 at 141. Tier II's uniform controls, fully implemented as of MY' 09, set a uniform NO_x ceiling of 0.07 grams per vehicle mile as well as a host of other, differentiated CO, PM and other pollutant ceilings.

[97] *See* Gerard & Lave, supra note 39 at 773–75.

[98] *See* NATIONAL RESEARCH COUNCIL, EFFECTIVENESS AND IMPACT OF CORPORATE AVERAGE FUEL ECONOMY (CAFE) STANDARDS 18 (2002) (hereafter NRC, "CAFE STANDARDS").

[99] *Cf.* ROSS M. STARR, GENERAL EQUILIBRIUM THEORY: AN INTRODUCTION 3–4, 203–05 (2d ed. 2011) (arguing that expansions and contractions of the sort in automobile markets must be accounted for with general "axiomatic methods").

transport as one system of many interrelated parts—expanding both its accounting and the potentials for cost avoidance.[100]

4.4 FUELS: END OF THE ROAD FOR AGGREGATIVE, PARTIAL EQUILIBRIUM ESTIMATES

The Atlantic Richfield Company (ARCO) initially reformulated gasoline for Southern California in 1989, cutting tailpipe emissions of VOCs, NO_x, SO_2, and CO while inadvertently opening a new regulatory front.[101] Refiners had by then almost eliminated lead from gasoline (a cheap octane booster) as required by the 1977 amendments.[102] EPA was, thus, familiar with refining.[103] But ARCO's innovation prompted a push in Congress to target the conventional pollutant cuts to be found by reformulating *all* fuels,[104] especially given the more volatile lead-free gas

---

[100] Different engine configurations, fuels, and weight classes created differently peaked challenges as between CO, particulates, VOCs, and NO_x and eventually entailed tight regulation of fuels as well. *See* Jonathan S. Martel *et al.*, *Regulation of Fuels and Fuel Additives, in* THE CLEAN AIR ACT HANDBOOK 415 (Julie R. Domike & Alec C. Zacaroli eds., 4th ed. 2016). It is clear in hindsight that, barring the governance of consumer demand, fuels, and other determinants of mobile source pollution, EPA's use of performance standards for (at least) the reduction of conventional air pollutants from automobiles was, if not futile, deeply constrained. *See* NRC, AIR QUALITY MNGT., supra note 18 at 172–73. On the systematic information asymmetries between automobile buyers and sellers, *see* Parry *et al.*, supra note 17 at 389–90; *cf.* DOYLE, supra note 1 at 115–48, 223–38 (describing Ford, Chrysler and GM's orientation to stratified production lines targeting different income brackets wholly divorced from cost-of-production pricing, which aligned them against fuels as the root cause of air pollution); NRC, AIR QUALITY MNGT., supra note 18 at 153–62.

[101] *See* Reitze 1994, supra note 59 at 487–91; J.G. Calvert *et al.*, *Achieving Acceptable Air Quality: Some Reflections on Controlling Vehicle Emissions*, 261 SCIENCE 37, 42 (1993) (noting how the reduction of sulfur content in fuels lowered SO_2 emissions and enabled much more effective catalytic reductions of VOCs, CO and NO_x).

[102] *See* Martel *et al.*, supra note 100 at 418–24.

[103] The elimination of lead from fuels involved a complex scheme of restrictions differentiated by the refiner's size, market share, vintage of capital, and other factors. *See* Small Refiners Lead Phase-Down Taskforce v. EPA, 705 F.2d 506 (D.C. Cir.1983).

[104] *See* Waxman *et al.*, supra note 82 at 1949–52.

then being sold.[105] The 1990 amendments did so directly.[106] By then, the reformulation of refined fuels to reduce sulfur content—a necessary step toward three-way catalytic technology—was projected to shift emission abatement costs significantly.[107] And alternative, "renewable" fuels and the costs of inducing a shift to their production and consumption would be another step.[108] This combined regulation of powertrains and fuels cut a permanent divide in the analysis of mobile source emissions abatement and its "social costs." Suddenly, it was the production and refining of fossil fuels (and the alternatives) as well as the engineering of vehicle fleets that comprised the baseline against which regulatory interventions' costs were to be estimated. The addition of fuel economy to the slate of considerations soon followed suit—yielding an inclusive effort to minimize all costs of transport in a car-dependent America.[109]

In retrospect, the long drive to improve catalytic technology reduced aggregate emissions of VOCs, particulates, CO, and NO_x from 1975 to 1985 despite a 34 percent jump in vehicle miles traveled (VMTs) over

---

105 Id. at 1972–2011. Octane boosters like lead were incompatible with 1970s catalytic technology, leading EPA to ban its addition to gasoline (albeit with a phase-in favoring small refiners in deference to their claims of high cost of compliance). *See* Thomas O. McGarity, *Radical Technology-Forcing in Environmental Regulation*, 27 Loy. L.A. L. Rev. 943 (1994).

106 *See* Waxman *et al.*, supra note 82 at 156–62 (describing Tier I and Tier II phase-in schedules and expected cuts in conventional pollution emitted per mile).

107 *See* Martel *et al.*, supra note 100 at 453–56. Sulfur content restrictions were tightened repeatedly to aid the equipment controlling NO_x and particulates. *See* National Petrochem. & Refiners Ass'n v. EPA, 287 F.3d 1130, 1142–46 (D.C. Cir. 2002).

108 *See* Deepayan Debnath *et al., Complement or Substitute: Ethanol's Uncertain Relationship with Gasoline Under Alternative Petroleum Price and Policy Scenarios*, 191 Applied Energy 385, 386 (2017).

109 With 200 million+ vehicles on 4 million+ miles of road and a "suburbanization" not likely to be reversed, the situation confronted in the 1990 amendments led some (erroneously) to suppose that induced ride sharing might be a least-cost means of reducing tailpipe emissions. *See* Oren, supra note 40. Experience with (irrational) consumer decision making and other confounding influences has guided regulatory efforts to the equipment ever since. *See* NRC, Cost Effectiveness Report, supra note 55 at 15–16.

the same period.[110] Those trends continued, augmented by sulfur restrictions on reformulated fuels, cutting SO_2 emissions in the process.[111] Refiners no doubt developed their own cost-saving solutions in turn.[112] And at just about that time, mainstream economics was coming to grips with the potentially vast effects of increasing returns.[113] Network effects can overthrow much of conventional economic reasoning.[114] Increasing returns to scale in production can create any number of nonlinearities stemming from the "dependence of the level of technology on the experience of production."[115] And that is both a micro- and macroeconomic problem. For example, had technological innovation in fuel economy taken the place of innovation in engine power outputs over that era, fuel economy might have increased by as much as 60% from 1980 to 2006.[116] Likewise, had the American firms come sooner to the manufacturing and marketing of attractive small cars, emissions and fuel economy breakthroughs may well have come much cheaper than they did.[117]

In hindsight, the interval from 1985 to the present records a technological "leap forward" as three-way catalytic solutions minimizing conventional pollutants matured and then matured again in the shift to computerized injection and combustion control and the gradual redesign

---

[110] Gerard & Lave, supra note 39 at 763. Gerard and Lave were quick to add that the accelerated progress with catalyst technologies came at a steep cost to the manufacturers. Id. at 763–64.

[111] *See* NRC, AIR QUALITY MNGT., supra note 18 at 134 (Table 4-1) (reporting that Tier II requirements required roughly 99% reduction below previous control levels for light-duty vehicles); Zacaroli, supra note 61 at 379–86; Martel *et al.*, supra note 100 at 453–71.

[112] *See* Thomas O. McGarity & Ruth Ruttenberg, *Counting the Cost of Health, Safety, and Environmental Regulation*, 80 TEX. L. REV. 1997. 2024 (2002).

[113] *See* W. Brian Arthur, *Positive Feedbacks in the Economy*, 262(2) SCI. AMER. 92, 92–94 (1990).

[114] *See* W. BRIAN ARTHUR, INCREASING RETURNS AND PATH DEPENDENCE IN THE ECONOMY (1994).

[115] *See* ROBERT M. SOLOW, LEARNING FROM "LEARNING BY DOING": LESSONS FOR ECONOMIC GROWTH 3 (1997).

[116] *See* Christopher R. Knittel, *Automobiles on Steroids: Product Attribute Trade-Offs and Technological Progress in the Automobile Sector*, 101(7) AMER. ECON REV. 3368 (2011).

[117] *See* MAYNARD, supra note 91 at 77–88 (describing GM and Toyota's joint venture and American personnel being coached in the "Toyota Production System" for manufacturing plant in Fremont, California); DOYLE, supra note 1 at 178, 450–55 (same).

of the automobile.[118] What were the *social* costs of that transition? Automobiles became substantially better products in that leap forward. So sweeping a retrospective surely prompts some reference to *what might have been* without the CAA constraints (or if the constraints had been different). The costs surely must be measured where they were felt.[119] But costs leading to qualitatively better products are notoriously difficult to pin down. And what of the fact that the government's study costs substituted for at least some R&D costs the sector would have borne? Was that a mere subsidy? Should the government's study costs have been divided per vehicle sold in the interval or by VMT? Government over that same interval, it bears mentioning, was also working to *deter driving, i.e.*, depress demand.[120] Furthermore, California and other states would surely have kept regulating ambitiously had there been no CAA.[121] Public investments in catalysis and combustion R&D were substantial

---

[118] *See* Gerard & Lave, supra note 39 at 773 (noting the progression from simple oxidizing catalytic converters of the 1970s which were much less effective than three-way catalysts used with the help of computer-controlled combustion chambers and precise air–fuel ratios and that, without the breakthrough in electronics, the latter would not have happened); Currie, supra note 58 at 904; NRC, CAFE STANDARDS, supra note 98 at 15–20; *see also* CARLEY ET AL., supra note 53 at 20–24 (tracking the technological adaptations to GHG-constraining auto emissions standards).

[119] In its required reports on recorded and expected costs from CAA programs, EPA held as much—creating "counterfactual 'without-CAAA'" baseline scenarios against which the 1990 amendments' programs were compared and using "computable general equilibrium" (CGE) modeling. *See* U.S. EPA, THE BENEFITS AND COSTS OF THE CLEAN AIR ACT FROM 1990–2020 (Final Report, rev. A) (April 2011) (hereafter EPA, "BENEFITS AND COSTS"), at 3-2.

[120] *Cf.* David C. Mowery & Nathan Rosenberg, *Technical Change in the Commercial Aircraft Industry, 1925–1975, in* ROSENBERG, supra note 16 at 163, 170–73 (tracing significant effect on private R&D spending in response to military procurement policies affecting both supply and demand of innovation and commercial aviation's costs).

[121] *See* McGarity & Ruttenberg, supra note 112, at 2021 ("Had Congress not written the 1970 [CAA] amendments, state and local governments would have encountered strong demands from their constituents for stronger air pollution controls."); *cf.* Pac. Merchant Shipping Ass'n v. Goodstene, 517 F.3d 1108 (9th Cir. 2008) (affirming holding below that California's marine vessel rules prohibiting the use of auxiliary diesel engines within 24 miles of shore were pre-empted by the CAA); Engine Mfrs. Ass'n v. South Coast Air Qual. Mngt. Dist., 541 U.S. 246 (2004) (holding that CAA pre-empted California's public transit fleet purchasing rules). Some of the supposedly costliest mobile source controls comprising EPA's aggregate estimates were local ambient air quality-based constraints. *See* EPA, BENEFITS AND COSTS, supra note 119 at 3–7.

and surely would have continued at some level.[122] Finally, the electronics sector has profited handily from the computerization of the automobile, which started with emissions and powertrains.[123] And all of this is to ignore the fact that the automobile sector itself changed profoundly during the interval through capital turnovers, offshoring, contraction, and growth.[124]

When progressively more stringent performance standards drive production and varied product lines to evolve, estimating the costs of the transition from among the separable but interrelated elements of that production is really more an exercise in mapping adaptation than anything else.[125] For that task, static estimative techniques will surely fail.[126] In retrospective studies and modeling alike, each of the influences

---

[122] *See* URSIN & KRIER supra note 1 at 95–118; Jaffe *et al.*, supra note 67 at 170; *cf.* Kinga Skalska *et al.*, *Trends in NO_x Abatement: A Review*, 408 SCI. TOTAL ENVT. 3976, 3985–88 (2010) (detailing public research into NO_x abatement in autos worldwide).

[123] One member of the team leading the auto bailouts in 2009–10 was told by Ford representatives that the value of electronics, software, and intellectual property rights accounts for about 30% of an average vehicle's price today. *See* Austan D. Goolsbee & Alan B. Krueger, *A Retrospective Look at Rescuing General Motors and Chrysler*, 29(2) J. ECON. PERSP. 3, 19 (2015).

[124] *See* Knittel, supra note 116 at 3369; DOYLE, supra note 1 at 217–394, 439–60; LUGER, supra note 27 at 104–81; NRC, CAFE STANDARDS, supra note 98 at 13–20.

[125] *Cf.* Timothy F. Bresnahan & Dennis A. Yao, *The Nonpecuniary Costs of Automobile Emissions Standards*, 16(4) RAND J. ECON. 437 (1985) (concluding that technological progress in assimilating emissions control technology into the products lowered the costs drivers experienced over time, even as those same emissions standards tightened).

[126] Tracking proper "costs" econometrically across so robust a space and so much turbulence would entail data EPA simply did not (and perhaps could not) amass. *Cf.* Richard G. Newell *et al.*, *The Induced Innovation Hypothesis and Energy-Saving Technological Change*, 114(3) Q.J. ECON. 941, 970 (1999) (using microeconomic data sets to associate some—but not all—innovation over time with various inducements and concluding that product differentiation in a much smaller market was in some way related to technological advances); Paul L. Joskow & Nancy L. Rose, *The Effects of Technological Change, Experience, and Environmental Regulation on the Construction Cost of Coal-Burning Generating Units*, 16(1) RAND J. ECON. 1 (1985) (finding substantial returns-to-scale and learning-by-doing, varied across product lines and production teams, in the evolution of coal-burning steam-electric generating unit production as regulatory constraints came into effect).

mentioned above can skew cost figures dramatically[127] and that ought to make a mere tabulation of *ex ante* estimates from old regulatory impact assessments (RIAs) unacceptable.[128] But what might a more dynamic evaluation be or mean?

4.5 ESTIMATING SOCIAL COSTS IN A TECHNOLOGY TRANSITION

Any analyst would be forgiven for cursing the quest to measure the role of emissions constraints in transitioning Americans to electric powertrains. Such a substitution of one risk vector (centralized electricity generation) for another (the combustion engine) has occupied economists for decades.[129] A major source of contention is whether any sort of "lock-in effect" is advantaging combustion technology and whether it is worth correcting in terms of social costs.[130] It is relatively uncontroversial to posit that vehicle attributes and technological change intersect with consumer demand and emissions constraints, perhaps to dramatic effect.[131] Yet the methods ostensibly able to predict a direction of forces like increasing returns in such large-scale technological transitions keep showing that small differences in, for example, worker skills, input prices, indivisible factors of production (on the production side), or rational expectations of continued adoptions (on the consumption side)

---

[127] *Cf.* Winston Harrington *et al.*, *On the Accuracy of Regulatory Cost Estimates*, 19(2) J. POL'Y ANALYSIS & MNGT. 297, 309–11 (2002); McGarity & Ruttenberg, supra note 121 at 2025–27, 2041–51; Lisa Heinzerling, *Regulatory Costs of Mythic Proportions*, 107 YALE L.J. 1981 (1998).

[128] EPA's estimates—just over $29 billion in annualized costs by 2020 as between on-road and non-road engine and fuel controls—were aggregated from the component programs' RIAs. *See* EPA, BENEFITS AND COSTS, supra note 2 at Table 3-2.

[129] *See* NRC, CAFE STANDARDS, supra note 98 at 10–11; NRC, COST EFFECTIVENESS REPORT, supra note 55 at 20–21; Howard Gruenspecht, *Zero Emission Vehicles: A Dirty Little Secret*, RESOURCES (Winter 2001) at 7.

[130] As a market failure, welfarists would presumably find it worth correcting because the current dominance of combustion-driven powertrains is less the result of efficiency than of timing. *See* ARTHUR, supra note 114 at 13–15. Typically, these effects stem from falling unit costs in increasing outputs, learning effects, coordination effects where "going along" with others confers benefits or self-reinforcing expectations from prevalence are afoot. *See* id. at 112.

[131] *See* Knittel, supra note 116 at 3368–69.

can be of enormous consequence.[132] As product attributes were traded off along the model/price curve following the 1990 CAA amendments, it is evident that manufacturers were able to fund technological advances of fleet-wide significance through their pricier models first.[133] And that is exactly the kind of dynamic spill-over in R&D[134] that challenges the measurement of factor inputs over long periods, whether as a means of estimating so-called "total factor productivity"[135] or as a means of estimating costs of compliance.

It is also relatively uncontroversial to posit that growing demand can mask—or offset—even a stringent production constraint's expected consequences,[136] including employment effects.[137] But with so much about new car markets dependent on macroeconomic trends and so many consumer choices possible, calculating how much cost will be borne by manufacturers, how much by retailers, and how much by consumers is as much psychology (or voodoo) as economics. Once the hypothesis was successfully modeled showing that stringent controls on new vehicles could have the indirect effect of inflating secondary markets for *used* vehicles (with those avoiding purchasing new units

---

[132] *See, e.g.*, Daron Acemoglu *et al.*, *Transition to Clean Technology*, 124(1) J. POL. ECON. 52 (2016); STARR, supra note 99 at 4, 328–30; Adam B. Jaffe & Robert N. Stavins, *The Energy Paradox and the Diffusion of Conservation Technology*, 16(2) RES. & ENERGY ECON. 91 (1994); ARTHUR, supra note 114 at 13–28, 111–29; *cf.* Michael Kremer, *The O-Ring Theory of Economic Development*, 108(3) Q.J. ECON. 551 (1993) (showing that wages and outputs rise sharply in unison and that because of the imperfect observability of skill leading to imperfect pairings of high-skilled workers, various "spillovers" are to be expected, further entrenching the advantages of having high-skilled workers).

[133] *See* Knittel, supra note 116 at 3397. This is consistent with similar findings on home appliances and energy efficiency advances. *See* Richard G. Newell *et al.*, *The Induced Innovation Hypothesis and Energy-Saving Technological Change*, 114(3) Q. J. ECON. 941 (1999).

[134] *See, e.g.*, Robert D. Mohr, *Technical Change, External Economies, and the Porter Hypothesis*, 43 J. ENVTL. ECON. & MNGT. 158 (2002).

[135] *See* Richard G. Lipsey & Kenneth I. Carlaw, *Total Factor Productivity and the Measurement of Technological Change*, 37(4) CANAD. J. ECON. 1118, 1119–21 (2004).

[136] *Cf.* Antoine Dechezleprêtre & Misato Sato, *The Impacts of Environmental Regulations on Competitiveness*, 11(2) REV. ENVTL. ECON. & POL'Y. 183, 191–200 (2017) (disaggregating studies on impacts and separating particular impacts by category, magnitude, and sign).

[137] *See, e.g.*, Wayne B. Gray & Ronald J. Shadbegian, *Do the Job Effects of Regulation Differ with the Competitive Environment?*, *in* DOES REGULATION KILL JOBS? 51, 66 (Cary Coglianese *et al.*, eds., 2013).

beset by emissions price premiums[138]), the means–ends rationality of efficiency constraints went under a permanent cloud of suspicion.[139] It made growth in auto travel out as the root cause of whatever problem(s) emissions constituted.[140]

In this vein, the merger of fuel economy and tailpipe constraints eventually accentuated how even dynamic "general equilibrium" techniques can fail to yield informative estimates of the social costs of regulatory actions. An evolution in fuel economy set by CAFE rules[141] administered by the National Highway Traffic Safety Administration (NHTSA)[142] overlapped the revolution in catalytic and electronic combustion controls.[143] From 1975 to 1984, the fuel economy of cars and light trucks improved about 66 percent (from 15.8 miles per gallon (mpg) to 26.3 mpg) and 50 percent (13.7 mpg to 20.5 mpg), respectively.[144]

---

138 *See* Howard K. Gruenspecht, *Differentiated Regulation: The Case of Auto Emissions Standards*, 72(2) AMER. ECON. REV. 328 (1982). This so-called "Gruenspecht effect" focused on the scrapping of used autos over their being sold in a secondary market. Id. at 328–29. The model showed that stringent emissions controls on new sources could cause perverse outcomes through this leakage out of the regulated market, id. at 330–31, a claim that later entangled GHG abatement efforts as well. *See* Howard Gruenspecht, *Zero Emission Vehicles: A Dirty Little Secret*, RESOURCES 142:7 (Winter 2001).

139 Fuel economy standards reduce consumption only if drivers do not simply drive more. *See, e.g.*, David Austin & Terry Dinan, *Clearing the Air: The Costs and Consequences of Higher CAFE Standards and Increased Gasoline Taxes*, 50(3) J. ENVT'L ECON. & MNGT. 562, 563 (2005). Of course, driving more because of the reduced costs of doing so can be consumption, production, or something else—depending on the assumptions taken.

140 *See* Waxman *et al.*, supra note 82 at 1953–67; Oren, supra note 40 at 150–74.

141 *See* NRC, CAFE STANDARDS, supra note 98 at 1–5; CARLEY ET AL., supra note 53 at 20.

142 Estimating fuel demand elasticities from price or other factors has been notoriously treacherous work. *Cf.* Carol Dahl & Thomas Sterner, *Analyzing Gasoline Demand Elasticities: A Survey*, 13 ENERGY ECON. 203 (1991) (offering a meta-analysis of disparate study results). Because market signals have been an unreliable inducement to fuel efficiency, most economists have agreed that some kind of mileage requirement, *e.g.*, CAFE, is a necessary inducement to auto fuel economy. *See* NRC, CAFE STANDARDS, supra note 98 at 9–11.

143 Throughout the development of catalytic conversion systems, substantial fuel economy penalties were common. Besides being an engineering challenge, it has also been a substantial political wedge. *See* DOYLE, supra note 1 at 99–125.

144 *See* NRC, CAFE STANDARDS, supra note 98 at 76. The NRC committee was convinced that vehicle "downsizing accounted for about 25 percent of the

The more these standards were studied, however, the more ambiguous their exact welfare effects grew.[145] Most of those first-generation gains are believed to have come from simple down-weighting of vehicle fleets, which the auto industry eventually convinced NHTSA was lethal to drivers.[146] A majority of the National Academies' committee studying first-generation CAFE concluded that "the downsizing and weight reduction that occurred ... most likely produced between 1,000 and 2,600 crash fatalities and between 13,000 and 26,000 serious injuries in 1993."[147] But two dissenters boldly disagreed, observing that "[t]he relationship between fuel economy and highway safety is complex, ambiguous, poorly understood, and not measurable by any known means at the present time."[148] Then, attacking the majority's economics, the dissenters made a key *distributional* point: All else equal, down-weighting the *heaviest* vehicles in the fleet could be expected to decrease total fatalities while improving fuel economy.[149] In short, a *more specific* performance standard would have improved fuel economy without the excess fatalities.[150]

---

improvement in fuel economy of cars and 10 percent of the improvement of light trucks between 1975 and 1984." Id.

145 *See* Carolyn Fischer, Winston Harrington & Ian W.H. Parry, *Should Automobile Fuel Economy Standards Be Tightened?*, 28(4) ENERGY J. 1 (2007). Fischer and colleagues determined that the evidence on CAFE's efficiency was inconclusive given how varied the effects would be across different scenarios. *See* id. at 22–25.

146 *See* NRC, CAFE STANDARDS, supra note 98 at 77.

147 NRC, CAFE STANDARDS, supra note 98 at 77. The NRC majority's conclusion paralleled NHTSA's conclusions in 1991 regarding vehicle down-weighting from 1970 to 1982. *See* NAT'L HWY. TRAFFIC SAFETY ADMIN., FINAL REGULATORY IMPACT ANALYSIS: CORPORATE AVERAGE FUEL ECONOMY FOR MY 2012–MY 2016 PASSENGER CARS AND LIGHT TRUCKS 437 (2010) (hereafter NHTSA, "CAFE RIA"). Of course, these estimates paled in comparison to what the majority conceded the nationally uniform 55 mph speed limit had accomplished in avoided mortalities. Id.

148 *See* NRC, CAFE STANDARDS, supra note 98 at 117 (App. A—*Dissent on Safety Issues: Fuel Economy and Highway Safety*).

149 *See* id. at 117–19; *see also* Parry *et al.*, supra note 17 at 383.

150 Still, fleet manufacturers' own costs (assuming uniform constraints and homogeneous firms) would presumably be at least whatever value was lost from a residual claimant's stranded capital devoted to producing the heaviest vehicles. But to weigh these as social costs without also counting the "costs" borne by someone killed in a collision with one of those vehicles (through no fault of their own) could only follow from a particularly warped approach to "social" costs, though. *See* Coleman & Kraus, supra note 3 at 1343–52, 1356–65.

Then a modeling study emerged suggesting that the social cost of reducing fuel demand by 7 percent with binding CAFE constraints was about $4 billion—far more costly than a simple fuel tax aimed at deterring driving.[151] Of course, if improved efficiency induces more consumption it will also induce still more investment in the production supporting it.[152] In this regard, light-duty vehicle purchasers were burdened, pure and simple: CAFE (which voters and survey respondents consistently supported by wide margins[153]) traded mileage for the sort of vehicle attributes which consumers should supposedly prefer (horsepower, torque, price, *etc.*).[154] The mere prospect of Pigovian taxes again obscured the socialized value of technological advance as cost avoidance.

So NHTSA began work on a second generation CAFE standard with Congress watching closely.[155] By this time, simple vehicle shrinkage and down-weighting strategies were being replaced by the advent of advanced high-strength steels, aluminum, and carbon fiber materials science.[156] Yet the resulting 2006 rule was still invalidated as arbitrary and contrary to law in a legal challenge, *Center for Biological Diversity v. NHTSA (CBD).*[157] But the *CBD* court faulted NHTSA's monetization of costs for a lack of impartiality and, thus, for being means–ends

---

[151] *See* Andrew N. Kleit, *Impacts of Long-Range Increases in the Fuel Economy (CAFE) Standard*, 42(2) ECON. INQUIRY 279 (2004); *see also* David Austin & Terry Dinan, *Clearing the Air: The Costs and Consequences of Higher CAFE Standards and Increased Gasoline Taxes*, 50 J. ENVTL. ECON. & MNGT. 562 (2005).

[152] *Cf.* Fischer, Harrington & Parry, supra note 145 at 3–4 (noting that the welfare justification for stronger fuel efficiency standards may turn on the alternative values in enhancing other vehicle attributes from the technologies used to improve fuel economy).

[153] *See* NRC, COST EFFECTIVENESS REPORT, supra note 55 at 316–17.

[154] *See* Knittel, supra note 116 at 3398.

[155] The legislation that would become the Energy Independence and Security Act (EISA) of 2007, Pub. L. No. 110-140, 121 Stat. 1492 (2007), was introduced shortly after the National Academies' 2002 report. *See* Kleit, supra note 151 at 280.

[156] *See* Final Phase II Tailpipe Rule, 77 Fed. Reg. at 62740–68.

[157] 538 F.3d 1172 (9th Cir. 2008). The *CBD* court was particularly concerned with NHTSA's statutory mandate to set the CAFE standards at the "maximum feasible" level, balancing technological feasibility, economic practicability, *etc. See* id. at 1205; id. at 1194 ("Here, 'maximum feasible' standards are to be determined in light of technological feasibility, economic practicability, the effect of other motor vehicle standards, and the need of the nation to conserve energy.").

irrational.[158] NHTSA had estimated (certain) costs of a more stringent CAFE standard *without* any commensurate evaluation of its *benefits*—like the benefits from averted GHG emissions.[159] This faulting of NHTSA's economic analysis for its partiality was, in one sense, a familiar outcome.[160] But it was no less surprising in its familiarity. For how could NHTSA have calculated the social costs of something as complex and dynamic as different versions of fleet-wide fuel efficiency mandates?

By 2008, Congress had mandated that NHTSA move to a second-generation CAFE[161] and the Obama Administration was poised to respond.[162] The agency interpreted the *CBD* holding as a call to monetize the social costs of GHG emissions in calibrating the stringency of its CAFE standards.[163] Following up on the remand, the Great Recession, the GM and Chrysler bailouts, and a "cash for clunker" scrappage program, the moment to debut an aggregated social cost of carbon (SCC) arrived.[164] Derived from a trio of computable general equilibrium (CGE) growth models,[165] its authors claimed that this SCC would "measure

---

158 *See CBD*, 538 F.3d at 1194–1203.

159 *CBD*, 538 F.3d at 1198–1200.

160 *See, e.g.*, Michigan v. EPA, 135 S. Ct. 2699, 2707–12 (2015); Zen Magnets, LLC v. CPSC, 841 F.3d 1141, 1152–55 (10th Cir. 2016); Business Roundtable v. SEC, 647 F.2d 1144, 1148–53 (D.C. Cir. 2011); New Mexico Cattlegrowers Ass'n v. U.S. Fish & Wildlife Serv., 248 F.3d 1277, 1282–85 (10th 2001); Ass'n of Oil Pipe Lines v. FERC, 281 F.3d 239, 241–48 (D.C. Cir. 2002); Corrosion Proof Fittings v. EPA, 947 F.2d 1201, 1214–23 (5th Cir. 1991).

161 The EISA of 2007 required automakers to achieve certain minimum fleet-wide averages by 2020 and empowered NHTSA to require the "maximum feasible average fuel economy" for the vehicle fleets as well. *See* Pub. L. No. 110-140 at § 102(b)(2)(B), *codified at* 49 U.S.C. § 32902(c).

162 *See* Final Phase I Tailpipe Rule, 75 Fed. Reg. at 25326 (describing President Obama's May 2009 national fuel efficiency policy directive).

163 *See* Dept. of Transp., National Highway Traffic Safety Admin., Final Rule—Average Fuel Economy Standards, Passenger Cars and Light Trucks; Model Years 2011–2015, 73 Fed. Reg. 24352 (2008). This then carried over into the unified NHTSA/EPA rule. *See* Final Phase I Tailpipe Rule, 75 Fed. Reg. at 25342–46.

164 *See* Michael Greenstone *et al.*, *Developing a Social Cost of Carbon for US Regulatory Analysis: A Methodology and Interpretation*, 7 Rev. Envtl. Econ. & Pol'y 23 (2013).

165 *See* Greenstone *et al.*, supra note 164 at 25 (explaining that the CGE models used were linked to general circulation climate models, allowing them to

incremental policy benefits relative to a baseline or range of baselines."[166] Paired with sophisticated tools meant to track both direct and indirect manufacturing costs—less any returns to scale in production—incurred as a result of the standards,[167] this SCC figure seemed to be welfarism triumphant.[168] But from that triumph, welfarism's oldest challengers—newly reinvigorated—stepped up.[169]

After CAA § 202(a) jurisdiction over GHGs was established in *Massachusetts v. EPA*[170] and after the subsequent "endangerment" finding under CAA § 202(a),[171] NHTSA and EPA had to fashion combined fuel economy/GHG tailpipe standards that would operate fleet wide and phase in during 2012–25.[172] Both were statutorily empowered to balance technological feasibility, cost, manufacturer capabilities, and other factors with little to constrain them in prevailing doctrine.[173] The computational work they did—if not the confidence it instilled—was notable.[174] The

---

"translate emissions into changes in atmospheric GHG concentrations, atmospheric concentrations into changes in temperature, and changes in temperature into economic damages").

166 William Pizer *et al., Using and Improving the Social Cost of Carbon*, 346 SCIENCE 1189, 1189 (2014).

167 *See* NRC, COST EFFECTIVENESS REPORT, supra note 55 at 245–60.

168 *See* Pizer *et al.*, supra note 166 at 1190.

169 In particular, it has deep troubles with uncertainty and demographic change, *see* Partha Dasgupta, *Three Conceptions of Intergenerational Justice, in* RAMSEY'S LEGACY 149 (Hallvard Lillehammer & D.H. Mellor eds., 2005), or what in Chapter 2, Section 2.1.1 was dubbed Broome's multidimensionality of goods.

170 549 U.S. 497, 525 (2007).

171 *See* U.S. EPA, Final Rule—Endangerment and Cause or Contribute Findings for Greenhouse Gases under Section 202(a) of the Clean Air Act, 74 Fed. Reg. 66496, 66500–02 (2009) (concluding that an "endangerment" finding under the Act can precede the requirements put on the auto sector pursuant to CAA § 202 for the six principal GHGs emitted).

172 *See* Final Phase I Tailpipe Rule, 75 Fed. Reg. at 25326–28 (describing unified "National Program" consisting of EPA and California rules authorized by CAA §§ 202 and 209 and NHTSA rules authorized by Energy Policy and Conservation Act of 1975 as amended).

173 On EPA's authority under CAA § 202(a), *see* Natural Resources Defense Council, Inc. v. EPA, 655 F.2d 318, 322–28 (D.C. Cir. 1981), and International Harvester v. Ruckelshaus, 478 F.2d 615, 640 (D.C. Cir. 1973). On NHTSA's authority under the Energy Policy and Conservation Act, *see* Center for Auto Safety v. NHTSA, 793 F.2d 1322, 1338–41 (D.C. Cir. 1986).

174 *See* Robert S. Pindyck, *The Use and Abuse of Models for Climate Policy*, 11(1) REV. ENVTL. ECON. & POL'Y 100, 105 (2017) (calling the modeling a "veneer of scientific legitimacy"). The "discounted utility" theory of future costs

so-called "rebound effect" of drivers driving more with more efficient cars was factored into the savings estimates.[175] In shifting to a "footprint"-based CAFE standard allowing each manufacturer's obligations to vary with its vehicles' sizes and sales volumes,[176] the agencies blunted any argument that their standards would merely cause down-weighting while at the same time limiting the effects GHG/efficiency could have on consumer choice or competitive advantages.[177] And yet the GHG/CAFE standards would still advantage the use of electric drivetrains.[178]

Importantly, though, the agencies demonstrated how the manufacturers would recoup their costs of compliance through vehicle price hikes while the consumers buying them would make back the price differential in

---

and benefits must assume that the overall value ("global utility") of the sequence of outcomes being modeled is equal to the sum of the utilities in each period. That "independence" assumption is deeply problematic, though, *see* Shane Frederick *et al.*, *Time Discounting and Time Preference: A Critical Review*, 40 J. Econ. Lit. 351 (2002), as was discussed in Chapter 2, Section 2.1.1.

[175] *See* Final Phase I Tailpipe Rule, 75 Fed. Reg. at 25516–17 (using a 10% estimate for the "rebound effect" of drivers driving more, but noting that a "dynamic" estimate of future rebound effect would be around 5%).

[176] EISA amended the Energy Policy and Conservation Act to expressly require a "vehicle attribute" CAFE standard. *See* Final Phase I Tailpipe Rule, 75 Fed. Reg. at 25601 (*citing* 49 U.S.C. § 32902(a)(3)(A)).

[177] *See* NRC, Cost Effectiveness Report, supra note 55 at 337–38. "A strong motivation for a [size-]based standard is that its cost tends to fall more evenly on all manufacturers, allowing the domestic companies who produce a larger-sized fleet to meet a less-stringent fleetwide average standard than, for example, the Asian companies." Id. at 338. *Cf.* Final Phase I Tailpipe Rule, 75 Fed. Reg. at 25401 (explaining the "temporary lead-time allowance" flexibility EPA was including with the fleet-wide rules for manufacturers with annual sales > 400,000 vehicles).

[178] NHTSA's MY 2012–16 standards required an estimated 4.3% average annual increase in mpg, Final Phase I Tailpipe Rule, 75 Fed. Reg. at 25669, and the second phase for MY 2017–25 effectively doubled that. *See* Environmental Protection Agency & National Highway Traffic Safety Admin., Final Rule—2017 and Later Model Year Light-Duty Vehicle Greenhouse Gas Emissions and Corporate Average Fuel Economy Standards, 77 Fed. Reg. 62624, 62630 (2012) (hereafter "Final Phase II Tailpipe Rule"). This was understood as a significant inducement to electric powertrains, id. at 62632 n.23, and included within the rule were specially enhanced incentives for "advanced vehicle technologies" in electrified powertrains. Id. at 62650–52.

other savings—principally averted fuel costs.[179] And they estimated that that first phase of second-generation CAFE would add about $1,000 to the average MY' 16 vehicle, result in $130–$180 in savings from that vehicle, and subtract about 16 metric tons of GHG emissions over its lifetime.[180] In short, the original equipment manufacturers (OEM) of the auto sector were expected simply to pass the standards' costs along to consumers, who, in turn, were expected to reap offsetting benefits. Of course, if part of the reason society has so long tracked regulatory costs in this sector is out of fairness to these OEMs, then a corps of them so remarkably resilient to change surely proves more about the socialization of costs than any telescopic emphasis on particular equipment or technical challenges could show.

Nonetheless, the welfare implications of these GHG/CAFE standards blurred in the interaction of changing product qualities, industry variability, and externalized costs over time.[181] The CGE models were made to estimate marginal damages per ton, globally, *i.e.*, to all affected persons in the aggregate for all time.[182] To calculate such damages into a distant future forces the use of controversial "discount rates" aiming to convert

---

[179] *See* Final Phase I Tailpipe Rule, 75 Fed. Reg. at 25328 (CAA § 202(a) standards); *cf.* id. at 25634 (CAFE standard projected to add about $396 to average MY 2012 light duty vehicle, rising to $903 in MY 2016).

[180] *See* Final Phase I Tailpipe Rule, 75 Fed. Reg. at 25328–29.

[181] Surely without a common fuel economy standard automakers would be unwilling to invest in long-term R&D into fuel economy technologies. *See* Adam B. Jaffe & Robert N. Stavins, *The Energy Paradox and Diffusion of Conservation Technology*, 16 RESOURCE & ENERGY ECON. 91 (1994); *cf.* NRC, COST EFFECTIVENESS REPORT, supra note 55 at 318 ("The Agencies point out that consumer valuation of fuel efficiency can change more rapidly than the industry is able to change its product offerings."). And surely a corporate fleet as a whole will affect the likely safety effects of downsizing or down-weighting particular vehicle types. *Cf.* NHTSA, CAFE RIA, supra note 147 at 442 (reporting studies done subsequent to NRC's 2002 report confirming that down-weighting heavier vehicles implicated no safety trade-off). But peripheral developments like computerized safety and combustion controls progressed markedly from the 1970s to the present, as well, *see* CARLEY ET AL., supra note 53, complicating immensely any attempt to estimate overall "social" costs from EPA's or NHTSA's regulations.

[182] *See* Greenstone *et al.*, supra note 164 at 34–35; Arden Rowell, *Foreign Impacts and Climate Change*, 39 HARV. ENVTL. L. REV. 371, 375–91 (2015). Professor Rowell argued that incorporating foreign losses into the setting of CAFE was contrary to EISA's animating purpose of reducing US oil consumption, id. at 419, although that presumes that "the need" of the US to conserve energy was somehow bound to particular reasons for doing so.

costs into present-day currencies.[183] Modeling like this ignores challenging distributional issues[184] while simply aggregating the many interactions between emissions/damage and the economic outcomes which the models are supposedly predicting.[185]

In truth, the social cost of a marginal ton of GHG emissions can be derived for present decision making only if the outcomes of present—and many future—decisions are already known.[186] (The CGE models have been, in a sense, telling us what we tell them to tell us.[187]) Even putting the vast uncertainty of climate sensitivities aside, human ingenuity and adaptive markets make predictions of this kind essentially circular. Especially in the case of climate change, as emissions and damages mount, people will surely adapt. Ironically, indeed, no sooner had SCC

---

[183] *See* Pindyck, supra note 174 at 108.

[184] *See* John Broome, *Cost-Benefit Analysis and Population*, 29 J. LEGAL STUDS. 953, 969 (2000) (arguing that global warming's population-altering effects confuse attempts to derive inter-temporal cost-benefit figures); Dasgupta, supra note 169 (demonstrating how intergenerational distributions interact with intragenerational distributions to defeat linear calculation of just savings or welfare maximization over prolonged intervals).

[185] *See* Greenstone *et al.*, supra note 164 at 30–34; *cf.* Pindyck, supra note 174 at 108 (arguing that the models themselves are "almost a distraction" because virtually all of what controls the variance therein is the selection of discount rates and the estimations of climate sensitivities). On the impossibility of modeling future climate sensitivities, *see* Martin L. Weitzman, *On Modeling and Interpreting the Economics of Catastrophic Climate Change*, 91(1) REV. ECON. & STATS. 1 (2009); Gerard H. Roe & Marcia B. Baker, *Why Is Climate Sensitivity So Unpredictable?*, 318 SCIENCE 629 (2007).

[186] *See* Martin L. Weitzman, *Fat-Tailed Uncertainty in the Economics of Catastrophic Climate Change*, 5(2) REV. ECON. & POL'Y 275, 280–85 (2011) (noting a seeming "immunity" of "standard benefit-cost analysis" to five separate sources of "structural uncertainty," most especially how to discount the distant future and how to predict unpredictable catastrophes).

[187] *See* Richard A. Rosen & Edeltraud Guenther, *The Economics of Mitigating Climate Change: What Can We Know?*, 91 TECH. FORECASTING & SOC. CHANGE 93, 96–104 (2015) (showing that each of the major modeling teams' input assumptions, reference or "base case" emissions scenarios, and sectoral coverages are essentially arbitrary reflections of the teams' biases and beliefs). There is even a persuasive argument to be made that, with more than one catastrophe like climate disruption to be averted into a distant future, net benefit maximization in the face of any single potential catastrophe individually will not end up being means–ends rational. *See* Ian W.R. Martin & Robert S. Pindyck, *Averting Catastrophes: The Strange Economics of Scylla and Charybdis*, 105(10) AMER. ECON. REV. 2947 (2015).

estimates begun informing regulatory cost-benefit analyses[188] than the attention turned to those critics insisting that induced (societal) *cost avoidance* as climate change intensified was a needed correction to the models.[189]

To be clear, the agencies had also invested amply in developing techniques to estimate both direct and indirect costs of fuel efficiency/GHG abatement technologies like reducing rolling resistance, enhancing aerodynamics, reducing lubricant friction, regenerative breaking, and advanced powertrains.[190] The indirect costs of these technologies varied, not least because the internal firm accounting and firm dynamics varied.[191] Demand-pull would surely be at work. For example, the costs of battery sourcing/manufacturing and other technologies vital to the shift to electric powertrains was projected to decline significantly over time.[192] But by MY 2013, 19 different brands offered 41 different hybrid electric models, including four wheel drives, pickups, and the $120,000+ Lexus LS 600h L.[193] So-called "learning by doing" or increasing returns from scaled production featured prominently in the manufacturing cost estimates behind the program's second phase, set for MY 2017–25.[194] And it was this second, more ambitious phase that drew the scrutiny of an incoming Trump Administration.

---

[188] *See* Rowell, supra note 182 at 402–19. It remains an open question just how informative any US agency took the SCC numbers to be before President Trump disbanded the working group. *See* Robert W. Hahn & Robert A. Ritz, *Does the Social Cost of Carbon Matter? Evidence from US Policy*, 44 J. LEGAL STUDS. 229 (2015) (concluding that the SCC figures rarely tipped a regulatory balance one way or the other).

[189] *See, e.g.*, Jason Scott Johnston, *The Social Cost of Carbon: How Is It Derived and How Is It Used to Justify America's Climate Policy*, REGULATION MAG. 36, 40–43 (Spring 2016) (insisting on the importance of human adaptation to sea level rise and lost agricultural production); M. Burke *et al.*, *Opportunities for Advances in Climate Change Economics*, 352 SCIENCE 292, 292–93 (2016).

[190] *See* NRC, COST EFFECTIVENESS REPORT, supra note 55 at 245–60.

[191] *See* Alex Rogozhin *et al.*, *Using Indirect Cost Multipliers to Estimate the Total Cost of Adding New Technology in the Automobile Industry*, 124 INT. J. PROD. ECON. 360, 363–64 (2010).

[192] *See* NRC, COST EFFECTIVENESS REPORT, supra note 55 at 259–60, 266–74, 323–24.

[193] *See* id. at 323.

[194] *See* id. at 249–51; Final Phase II Tailpipe Rule, 77 Fed. Reg. at 62711–12.

4.5.1 Tailoring, Lead Times, and Flexibility-minimizing Costs: Never Enough?

The engineering cost projections done to back up the combined GHG/fuel efficiency standards bridged major confounding influences in cost-of-compliance figuring, leading EPA and NHTSA—and, for a time, their political principals—to conclude the rules' costs were justified.[195] It undoubtedly reflected a certain urgency in reducing GHG emissions.[196] But it may now be just another casualty of the 2016 presidential election. In a frenzied dash to protect Phase II GHG/CAFE, the Obama EPA cobbled together a so-called "mid-term evaluation" just after that election,[197] one the Trump Administration blocked from being published in the *Federal Register*.[198] The Trump Administration's notice requested comment on whether the GHG rules remained "appropriate" in light of changes after 2012,[199] which quickly led to a finding that they were no longer appropriate[200] and reportedly the Administration's effort to freeze

---

[195] *See* Final Phase I Tailpipe Rule, 75 Fed. Reg. at 25444–68 (explaining EPA's finding of "feasibility" on final CO_2 standards); id. at 25605–07 (explaining NHTSA's finding on "technological feasibility" and "economic practicability").

[196] *Cf.* U.S. EPA, Final Rule—Endangerment and Cause or Contribute Findings for Greenhouse Gases under Section 202(a) of the Clean Air Act, 74 Fed. Reg. 66496, 66524 (2009) (finding that "the public health of current generations is endangered and that the threat to public health for both current and future generations will likely mount over time as [GHGs] continue to accumulate in the atmosphere and result in ever greater rates of climate change").

[197] *See* U.S. EPA, Final Determination on the Appropriateness of the Model Year 2022–2025 Light-Duty Vehicle Greenhouse Gas Emissions Standards under the Midterm Evaluation ((Jan. 2017) (EPA-420-R-17-001), *available at* https://nepis.epa.gov/Exe/ZyPDF.cgi?Dockey=P100QQ91.pdf (hereafter U.S. EPA, "Final Mid-Term Evaluation").

[198] The new administration eventually announced that the "finalization" was in error and that Phase II was under review. *See* National Highway Traffic Safety Admin. & Environmental Protect. Agency, Request for Comment on Reconsideration of the Final Determination of the Mid-Term Evaluation of Greenhouse Gas Emissions Standards for Model Year 2022–2025 Light Duty Vehicles; Request for Comment on 2021 Greenhouse Gas Emissions Standards, 82 Fed. Reg. 39551 (2017).

[199] *See* 82 Fed. Reg. at 39553.

[200] *See* U.S. EPA, Mid-Term Evaluation of Greenhouse Gas Emissions Standards for Model Year 2022–2025 Light Duty Vehicles: Notice of Withdrawal, 83 Fed. Reg. 16077, 16079 (2018).

the standards at 2021 levels, flattening Phase II's most ambitious efficiency ramps.[201]

As of this writing it is unclear how the agencies could walk back findings on their standards' feasibility when the available information still showed that: (1) each OEM had a range of options for meeting the MY 2022–25 standards at *lower than predicted* per-vehicle costs; (2) gas price projections still show that consumers would save money from averted fuel and other costs; and (3) OEMs had performed better than expected in balancing fuel economy against other consumer preferences in the standards' early interval.[202]

Of course, regulatory costs have often changed significances (and even signs) over the course of a presidential transition. What is relatively clear here in retrospect is that the automotive sector's competitive search to meet both consumer demand and the second-generation combined GHG/CAFE requirements drove significant technological innovation in lighter, stronger materials, aerodynamics, computerization, and hybrid- to fully-electric powertrains. The agencies' extended engagement with the regulatory costs attending that transition evidences equal parts concern and respect for the manufacturers and confidence in the power of innovation to maximize cost avoidance over a long run.

---

[201] *See* Evan Halper, *Trump and California Are Set to Collide Head-on Over Fuel Standards*, L.A. TIMES, April 27, 2018, *available at* http://www.latimes.com/politics/la-na-pol-mileage-20180427-story.html.

[202] *See* U.S. EPA, Final Mid-Term Evaluation, supra note 197 at 17–28.

5. The costs of generality: cooling water withdrawals in retrospect

If auto emissions are a case of cost-of-compliance evaluations growing immensely in scale and complexity as production evolved, a case study of cooling water withdrawals provides a punctuated contrast. Like auto emissions, high-volume cooling water withdrawals represent a long-lived, multidimensional environmental and legal challenge. The withdrawal of trillions of gallons of water annually from US rivers, coasts, and estuaries—fatally crushing billions of organisms at the intake and throughout some industrial process flow—has been a mountain of unpriced natural capital in American industry for more than a century.[1]

In 2014 as EPA finalized a set of remade rules governing intakes designed to withdraw 2 million gallons per day or more (≥ 2 MGD), it had focused on some 1,065 such facilities, from metal fabrication and electric power plants to oil refineries to steel and paper mills.[2] The agency maintained that this volume threshold covered "99.8 percent of total water withdrawals by utilities and other industrial sources ... which includes 70 percent of manufacturing facilities and 87 percent of electric generators."[3] EPA figured its intakes rule would cost covered electricity producers $203.7 million annually (or about $400,000 per facility), covered manufacturers another $67.7 million annually (about $100,000 per facility), and $1 million in annual state and federal administrative

[1] Whether we take this to be an externality or a public good is beside the point. The point is that users became reliant upon it at essentially no cost to themselves but at untold costs dispersed to many others in the aggregate.

[2] *See* EPA, National Pollutant Discharge Elimination System—Final Regulations to Establish Requirements for Cooling Water Intake Structures at Existing Facilities and Amend Requirements at Phase I Facilities, 79 Fed. Reg. 48300, 48308 (2014) (hereafter "Final CWIS Rule"). Most of the manufacturing sites included withdrew the majority of their water for their own on-site electricity production. Like its predecessors, the 2014 rule limited its applicability to those facilities using at least 25% of the withdrawal for cooling purposes. Id. at 48305.

[3] Final CWIS Rule, 79 Fed. Reg. at 48308.

costs.[4] It estimated that between 123 and 159 entities owned in-scope facilities and that 91–94 percent of them would incur annualized costs of > 1 percent of revenues.[5] It also figured that of 500 in-scope manufacturing facilities, 496 would incur costs of ≤ 1 percent of revenues, and four would incur costs of 1–3 percent.[6]

None of these calculations or the reasoning framing them explained the relevance EPA attached to its cost estimates, though. EPA's discussion was unfocused, filled with tangential defenses of questionable assumptions and cross-references to immense peripheral analyses (both economic and technical).[7] In the end, after a dozen lengthy rulemaking notices, three carefully reasoned opinions from the Courts of Appeal[8] and an opinion from the US Supreme Court granting the agency what seemed to be a wide discretion,[9] the proper role of the costs of compliance in EPA's control of cooling water withdrawals remained enshrouded in mystery.[10] This chapter's conclusion develops a deeper

---

4 *See* Final CWIS Rule, 79 Fed. Reg. at 48389 ("social costs" of the rule at 3% discount rate). If covered "new units" at existing facilities' costs were added, the estimate jumped to total $274.9 million at all in-scope facilities. Id.

5 *See* Final CWIS Rule, 79 Fed. Reg. at 48390. These cost estimates include the direct capital costs of the needed equipment, the cost of installation downtime, annual operating and maintenance costs, entrainment-related studies and reporting costs, and other administrative costs at the regulated facilities. *See* Final CWIS Rule, 79 Fed. Reg. at 48384.

6 *See* Final CWIS Rule, 79 Fed. Reg. at 48397.

7 *See* U.S. EPA, Economic Analysis for the Final Section 316(b) Existing Facilities Rule (EPA-821-R-14-001, May 2014) (hereafter "Final EA"); U.S. EPA, Technical Development Document for the Final Section 316(b) Existing Facilities Rule (EPA-821-R-14-002, May 2014) (hereafter "Final TDD"). The final rule preamble's discussion of "Cost Development and Economic Impact Analysis" runs to 17 *Federal Register* pages—not including a separate "Benefits" discussion—and alternatively describes costs of compliance, "social costs," "costs to households," and "economic impacts." *See* Final CWIS Rule, 79 Fed. Reg. at 48383–401.

8 *See* ConocoPhillips Co. v. U.S. EPA, 612 F.3d 822 (5th Cir. 2010); Riverkeeper, Inc. v. U.S. EPA, 475 F.3d 83 (2d Cir. 2007) ("Riverkeeper II"); Riverkeeper, Inc. v. U.S. EPA, 358 F.3d 174 (2d Cir. 2004) ("Riverkeeper I").

9 *See* Entergy Corp. v. Riverkeeper, Inc., 556 U.S. 208 (2009).

10 EPA has remained steadfast that CWA § 316(b) does not *mandate* cost-benefit balancing. *Cf.* Original CWIS Rule, 41 Fed. Reg. at 17388 (hereafter "Original CWIS Rule") ("The brief legislative history of section 316(b) states that the term 'best technology available' contemplates the best technology available commercially at an economically practicable cost. As with the statute, this language does not require a formal or informal 'cost/benefit' assessment.").

theory of these cost deliberations which EPA did not but perhaps should have offered.

The thermoelectric sector (fossil and nuclear combined) comprises the vast bulk of the cooling water withdrawals in the US and has done so for generations.[11] Cooling water is predominantly a function of electricity generation by means of "Rankine cycle," steam-powered turbines[12] and their reliance on this unpriced good. In arid regions, generating electricity without cooling water is cost feasible.[13] But this chapter traces a regulatory history almost as deep as that of auto emissions, demonstrating just how costs can skew standard-setting when cost-benefit balancing is not *required* yet still exerts powerful but loosely defined influences nonetheless. Water withdrawals were notorious environmental problems as the Clean Water Act (CWA) was being legislated.[14] But an already over-burdened agency (EPA) chose to permit each withdrawal individually until a judicial settlement in 1995 finally forced the issue of nationwide standards. This chapter traces the long arc toward national performance standards on cooling water at the intake and throughout the process, ultimately revealing how understanding the productive factors can determine cost analysis and, in turn, the standards themselves.

5.1 WHITHER A NATIONAL STANDARD, 1973–2001?

In 1973 EPA estimated that as much as 80 percent of the 70 trillion gallons of cooling water withdrawn annually in the US (a sum which it figured was about 15 percent of the annualized flow of all US rivers and streams combined[15]) was used by commercial steam-electric generating

---

[11] An exception is marine oil and gas development, which accounts for billions of gallons of withdrawals daily, as well.

[12] Rankine cycle, steam-powered turbines were, like the spark combustion engine, a pervasive force of American economic expansion throughout the twentieth century. *See* MAURY KLEIN, THE POWER MAKERS: STEAM, ELECTRICITY, AND THE MEN WHO INVENTED MODERN AMERICA (2008).

[13] *See* Kelly T. Sanders, *Critical Review: Uncharted Waters? The Future of the Electricity–Water Nexus*, 49 ENVTL. SCI. & TECH. 51, 55–56 (2015).

[14] *See* ROBERT D. LIFSET, POWER ON THE HUDSON: STORM KING MOUNTAIN AND THE EMERGENCE OF MODERN AMERICAN ENVIRONMENTALISM (2014).

[15] *See* U.S. EPA, Development Document for Proposed Best Technology Available for Minimizing Adverse Environmental Impact of Cooling Water Intake Structure (EPA-440-1-74-015, Dec. 1973) (hereafter "Development Document 1973") at iii.

facilities.[16] Some of the political impetus behind the 1972 CWA had stemmed from this massive environmental threat.[17] By 2005, the US Geological Survey (USGS) was more precise: the thermoelectric power sector withdrew an average of 201 billion gallons every day—about 49 percent of all the water withdrawn nationwide.[18] While water withdrawals had actually declined slightly since peaking in 1980,[19] that worked out to 23 gallons of water for every kilowatt hour of electricity marketed.[20] Ninety-two percent of it was in "once-through" cooling systems, predominantly clustered in the East and along the California coast.[21]

Clean Water Act § 316(a) governs thermal discharges,[22] whatever the "location, design, construction [or] capacity of [the] cooling water intake structures."[23] As discharger categories came under CWA §§ 301 and 306 effluent limitations,[24] thermal discharge parameters were gradually bundled into National Pollutant Discharge Elimination System (NPDES) permits.[25] The (modest) temperature constraints were easily combined

---

16 *See* id. at iii. That same figure was reiterated in the 1976 draft. *See* id. at iii.

17 *See* LIFSET, supra note 14 at 107–50; *see also* James R. May & Maya K. Van Rossum, *The Quick and the Dead: Fish Entrainment, Entrapment, and the Implementation and Application of Section 316(b) of the Clean Water Act*, 20 VT. L. REV. 373, 377–78 (1995); Karl R. Rábago, *What Comes Out Must Go In: Cooling Water Intakes and the Clean Water Act*, 16 HARV. ENVTL. L. REV. 429, 445–56 (1992).

18 *See* United States Geological Survey, Estimated Use of Water in the United States in 2005 at 38 (2009) (Circular 1344). Daily withdrawals of 410 billion gallons, id. at 1, yields an annualized total of 149.65 trillion gallons. USGS calculated that to be 5% less than the 1980 peak. Id.

19 *See* id. at 1.

20 *See* id. at 38.

21 *See* id. at 38.

22 33 U.S.C. § 1328(a). A thermal discharge is the excess heat cooling water absorbs in process which is conveyed to the environment at the outfall.

23 33 U.S.C. § 1328(b).

24 *See* Chapter 2, Section 2.3. Sections 316(a) and 316(b) cross-reference Sections 301 and 306 as jurisdictional prerequisites, tying cooling water intakes to the same new/existing dichotomy that effluent limitations guidelines practice struggled to tame. *See* Chapter 2, Section 2.3 above.

25 A comprehensive review of available data on the CWA permitting system in the 1990s found that attention to biological impairments had just barely begun and made no mention of thermal discharge limitations. *See* ROBERT W. ADLER ET AL., THE CLEAN WATER ACT: 20 YEARS LATER 137–70 (1993).

with sectoral effluent limits on discharges.[26] Variances played big roles in each:[27] The operating parameters of nuclear stations, for example, make even modest thermal limits into a mandate for on-site cooling of some kind.[28] Thus, thermal discharge criteria for new versus existing sources became the same challenges of distinguishing vintages of capital as were characteristic of NPDES permitting generally.[29]

The "location, design, construction *and capacity*"[30] of any withdrawal, as CWA § 316(b) makes clear, are distinct questions. It requires that these intakes "reflect the best technology available for minimizing adverse environmental impact."[31] But impingement and entrainment of biota and microbiota can vary greatly by location. Some intakes threaten particularly sensitive waters, others less so, with the location, pumping velocity, screening, and other engineering of the intake determining where along a continuum each withdrawal sits. The costs of alternatives to high-volume withdrawals are also quite variable, although there the numbers tend to be harder to obtain. Biologists can analyze various types of evidence suggesting population-level effects *in situ*,[32] but gathering that evidence on location, sorting it, and rating it is costly and usually requires the

---

[26] The 1977 Amendments realigned priorities as to certain sectors and pollutants—with thermal pollution from steam-electric power plant discharges becoming a principal concern. *See* Environmental Protection Agency, Proposed Rule—Effluent Limitations Guidelines, Pretreatment Standards and New Source Performance Standards under Clean Water Act; Steam Electric Power Generating Point Source Category, 45 Fed. Reg. 68328, 68329–30 (1980).

[27] The Supreme Court construed the CWA's treatment of variances no fewer than three times. *See* William Funk, *The Exception that Approves the Rule: FDF Variances Under the Clean Water Act*, 13 B.C. ENVT'L AFFS. L. REV. 1 (1985). Variances were a key issue in the setting of thermal discharge standards, as well. *See* Rábago, supra note 17 at 445–56 (1992).

[28] *See* Thomas J. Feeley III, *et al.*, *Water: A Critical Resource in the Thermoelectric Power Industry*, 33 ENERGY 1, 1–5 (2008). Nuclear is generally the most water-intensive thermoelectric factor. *See* id. at 4; Jordan Macknick *et al.*, *Operational Water Consumption and Withdrawal Factors for Electricity Generating Technologies: A Review of Existing Literature*, 7 ENVIRON. RES. LETTS. 045802 (2012) at 6 (Table 2).

[29] *See* Chapter 2, Section 2.3.

[30] 33 U.S.C. § 1328(b) (emphasis added).

[31] 33 U.S.C. § 1328(b). This is the so-called "BTA" standard. *See* Chapter 2, Section 2.3.

[32] One hypothesis that has dominated discussions of cooling water withdrawals is *density dependence*—where an oversupply of offspring is subsequently selected to small proportions thereof by prevailing conditions that limit the extent or density of the population. *See* Barry W. Brook & Corey J.A.

cooperation of the intake owner.[33] Finally, the economics of valuing whatever is lost on site were and have remained primitive.[34]

When EPA fashioned a pair of "development documents" for the design and operation of CWA § 316(b) intakes, first in 1973 and again in 1976,[35] it recorded the variety of potential means of reducing impingement losses.[36] But it also noted that "[r]eduction of cooling water intake volume (capacity) should in most cases, reduce the number of organisms that are subject to entrainment in direct proportion to the fractional flow reduction."[37] Indeed, EPA observed that, despite the "scarcity of detailed data on the constructed cost of intake structures" owed to the fact that "most intake structures [to that point had been] constructed as part of a larger general contract which include[d] other structures on the site, and in some cases, the complete plant,"[38]

Bradshaw, *Strength of Evidence for Density Dependence in Abundance Time Series of 1198 Species*, 87(6) ECOLOGY 1445 (2006).

[33] Species-specific density dependencies can be difficult to detect and prove and, in all events, require significant data gathering even with the use of sophisticated modeling and hypothesis testing. *See* id. at 1450.

[34] *Cf.* Charles Griffiths *et al., U.S. Environmental Protection Agency Valuation of Surface Water Quality Improvements*, 6(1) REV. ENVT'L ECON. & POL'Y 130, 135 (2012) (noting slow progress in valuation measures); Sheila M. Olmstead, *The Economics of Water Quality*, 4(1) REV. ENVT'L ECON. & POL'Y. 44, 50 (2010) ("About three-quarters of published estimates of the economic value of non-market goods and services in the United States that are provided by water quality are travel cost studies, suggesting that most measured benefits are recreational.").

[35] *See* Development Document 1973, supra note 15; U.S. EPA, Development Document for Proposed Best Technology Available for Minimizing Adverse Environmental Impact of Cooling Water Intake Structure (EPA-440-1-76-015A, April 1976) (hereafter "Development Document 1976").

[36] The first 150 or so pages of the 1976 version (Sections II–IV) reviewed alternatives for location, design, and construction. *See* Development Document 1976, supra note 35. Section V's turn to "capacity" noted the close relationship of an intake's volume and velocity to its "entrainment" mortality factor. Id. at 149–50.

[37] Development Document 1976, supra note 35 at 153. This echoed the conclusion in December 1973: "[T]he application of the best technology available on intake structures alone will do little to protect against the entrainment effects on small organisms passing through a cooling system. These effects are better controlled by either controlling the plant intake flow or the design of the cooling water systems." Development Document 1973, supra note 15 at 143.

[38] Development Document 1973, supra note 15 at 133.

> a prerequisite to the identification of [BTA] for any specific site should be a biological study and associated report to characterize the type, extent, distribution, and significant overall environmental relation of all aquatic organisms in the sphere of influence of the intake and evaluation of available technologies, to identify the site specific [BTA] for the location, design, construction, *and capacity* of cooling water intake structures for minimizing adverse environmental impact.[39]

The rulemaking that followed remains a monument to how *not* to create uniform national standards, though. In the rule's preamble, EPA repeatedly answered commenters with its observation that avoiding "adverse environmental impact" as § 316(b) commanded was a multidimensional mission, *i.e.*, that "[a]ll pertinent factors, rather than reliance on a single factor, should receive adequate consideration."[40] A commenter claimed that the substitutes for once-through cooling all entailed a prohibitive "energy penalty."[41] But in an "economic analysis" EPA said it prepared, it found that, in switching to recirculating or "closed-cycle" systems, "the increase in energy (fuel) consumption is less than one half of one percent of total fuel consumption by the power industry."[42] That triviality would become a theme. Still, EPA finalized that intakes rule by directing permitting personnel to the 1976 development document[43] without having published it in the *Federal Register* nor having obtained the requisite permission to "incorporate by reference" therein. And that doomed the rulemaking in a legal challenge brought by 50+ utilities.[44] Ironically enough, though, that development document did not even propose or suggest a uniform federal standard. It merely collected possible strategies

---

[39] Development Document 1976, supra note 35 at 176–77 (emphasis added).

[40] Original CWIS Rule, 41 Fed. Reg. at 17389.

[41] An "energy penalty" is the surplus energy consumption of one mode of production over another. For electricity production, the "energy return on investment" is a ratio of energy delivered to energy invested into capture/delivery for some project, fuel, *etc. See* Charles A.S. Hall *et al., EROI of Different Fuels and the Implications for Society*, 64 ENERGY POL'Y 141, 141–42 (2014).

[42] Original CWIS Rule, 41 Fed. Reg. at 17389.

[43] *See* Environmental Protection Agency, Final Rule—Part 402: Best Technology Available for the Location, Design, Construction, and Capacity of Cooling Water Intake Structure for Minimizing Adverse Environmental Impact, 41 Fed. Reg. 17387, 17390 (1976) (finalizing 40 C.F.R. § 402.12).

[44] In Appalachian Power Co. v. Train, 566 F.2d 451 (4th Cir. 1977), at the behest of 58 utilities challenging the rule, the Fourth Circuit invalidated and remanded EPA's intakes rulemaking as having failed to observe procedure required by law. *See* id. at 455–56.

and solutions given the overwhelming—seemingly immutable—demand for cooling water.[45]

The utilities' apparent opposition to *any* federal standard may have stemmed from the fact that reducing the *volume* of withdrawals was among the potential solutions commended in the development document.[46] That route would remain contentious even as it became evident that electricity production could do without massive cooling water withdrawals. But the 1976 document listed and analyzed at least a dozen distinct technologies for the design and operation of intakes, admonishing that the environmental effects of withdrawals are "highly site specific," and that, therefore, "adequate biological data would be needed in each case to determine the specific need and control strategy related to minimizing environmental impact."[47] It warned that location of intakes to minimize effects could only take place after detailed biological study,[48] while also stressing that many of the technologies reviewed could offer important complementarities under the right circumstances.[49]

One thing EPA could not do in 1976 was offer detailed estimates on the likely capital or operating costs of its many intake options.[50] It concluded that "[o]wing to the highly site specific characteristics of available technology for the location, design, construction and capacity of cooling water intake structure for minimizing adverse environmental impact, no technology can be presently generally identified as the best technology

---

[45] This was the first time EPA interpreted § 316(b) to require that EPA, in setting the performance standard, "not impose an impracticable and unbearable economic burden on the operation of any plant subject to section 316(b)." Original CWIS Rule, 41 Fed. Reg. at 17388.

[46] While both versions of the development document, 1973 and 1976, treated location and design options and operations and maintenance strategies, only the 1976 draft described "capacity" as a matter for consideration. *See* Development Document 1976, supra note 35 at 149–58. "Capacity" is one of CWA § 316(b)'s listed parameters.

[47] *See* Development Document 1976, supra note 35 at 175. Shortly after *Appalachian Power* EPA developed draft guidance for permit writers describing the type and means of biometric surveys and monitoring appropriate to individual, "best professional judgment" permitting for intakes. *See* U.S. Environmental Protection Agency, Draft Guidance for Evaluating the Adverse Impact of Cooling Water Intake Structures on the Aquatic Environment: Section 316(b) P.L. 92-500 (1977) (hereafter EPA, "*Draft BPJ Guidance*").

[48] *See* Development Document 1976, supra note 35 at 26.

[49] *See* id. at 177–94.

[50] *See* id. at 163–64.

available, even within broad categories of possible application."[51] A nationally uniform performance standard would wait at least 25 more years before an environmentalists' lawsuit would force the issue at EPA.[52]

Fish and other aquatic life can be managed away from intakes behaviorally or mechanically or they may be returned to the water by means of collect and return systems.[53] But if entrainment mortality of fish and shellfish is not simply to be converted to impingement mortality, the screening solutions used must ensure that these animals are not just pinned against the outer barriers of an intake.[54] Thus, importantly, microorganisms and fish and shellfish eggs and larvae remain at risk regardless of impingement countermeasures: Virtually *no* screening can exclude them.[55] So-called "traveling" screens used to keep intakes clog free had been employed for almost a century by the time EPA was at work.[56] Even in 1976 EPA was able, using vendor data, to rough out the difference between a "standard" intake designed merely to prevent fouling of the screen and one enhanced to minimize the mortality of the

---

[51] *See* id. at 176. According to EPA in that development document, "[t]he term 'best technology available' infers the use of the best technology available commercially at an economically practicable cost." Id. at 177. EPA paid no apparent attention to the judicial construction of CWA §§ 301, 304 and 306 then being entrenched, which inferred that the term "available," in place of the term "practicable," was Congress's CWA signal to EPA and the courts that cost be a minor factor for consideration. *See* American Frozen Food Inst. v. Train, 539 F.2d 107, 116–22 (D.C. Cir. 1976); Weyerhaeuser Co. v. Costle, 590 F.2d 1011, 1031–49 (D.C. Cir. 1978); Ass'n of Pac. Fisheries v. EPA, 615 F.2d 794, 804–09 (9th Cir. 1980).

[52] *See* Environmental Protection Agency, Final Rule—National Pollution Discharge Elimination System: Regulations Addressing Cooling Water Intake Structures for New Facilities, 66 Fed. Reg. 65256, 65261 (2001) (describing lawsuit and consent decree in Riverkeeper Inc., et al. v. Whitman, No. 93 Civ. 0314 (AGS) (1995)) (hereafter "Phase I Rule").

[53] *See* Final CWIS Rule 2014, 79 Fed. Reg. at 48330–31.

[54] *See* id. at 48330–31, 48334–35.

[55] The "entrainment" loss is, thus, linearly correlated to withdrawal volume throughout the history of § 316(b) standard-setting efforts. *See* Phase I Rule, 66 Fed. Reg. at 65284. An especially controversial aspect of egg/larvae mortality is the so-called density-dependence thesis, *i.e.*, that the vast majority of those lost to entrainment would have perished naturally in any event and, thus, do not constitute meaningful environmental harms.

[56] "Traveling" screens rotate periodically to reposition the screen relative to flow direction. *See* Development Document 1976, supra note 35 at 63–89; *see also* U.S. EPA, National Pollutant Discharge Elimination System—Regulations Addressing Cooling Water Intake Structures for New Facilities—Proposed Rule, 65 Fed. Reg. 49060, 49093 (2000) (hereafter "Phase I Proposal").

creatures that would ordinarily be that fouling.[57] Certain design measures intended to reduce intake velocity, for example, were expected to increase installation costs by up to 70 percent.[58] Newer, more impingement-conscious screens could add up to $1,000 per square foot based on the cross-sectional area of the screens.[59] And various "locational" steps—which were thought to be the most cost-effective measures in many contexts—varied greatly site to site, most especially as between new and existing facilities.[60] Many prototypes were tested. An experiment with sound barriers at one Virginia facility showed that although fish became acclimated to repetitive sound, rock and roll music's "varying frequencies and amplitudes" produced more sustained aversion.[61] Without meticulous control procedures and ample baseline data, however, the experiments could prove nothing about cost-effectiveness more generally.

The Tennessee Valley Authority, in conjunction with EPA, released a study in 1976 summarily concluding that

> [m]uch effort has been expended in recent years toward development and evaluation of fish protection systems at water diversions and power plant intakes. To date, however, there exists no one screening system that has been deemed "best technology available." ... Site specificity may require unique designs for each site to satisfy the "best technology" requirement. However, several proposed concepts, if sufficiently developed and evaluated, may be widely applicable to water intakes.[62]

In the face of the 1970s' energy shocks, TVA was alarmed at the projected costs of replacing its once-through cooling systems with dry- or closed-cycle cooling were EPA to deem either of them § 316(b) BTA.[63] Yet entrainment losses remained linearly correlated to withdrawal volumes. So TVA extolled the benefits of engineered "horizontal" traveling

---

[57] *See* Development Document 1976, supra note 35 at 169–74.

[58] *See* id. at 170.

[59] *See* id. at 169.

[60] *See* id. at 15–26, 169.

[61] *See* Tennessee Valley Authority & U.S. EPA, A State-of-the-Art Report on Intake Technologies: Interagency Energy-Environment Research and Development Program Report 13 (1976) (EPA-600/7-76-020) (hereafter TVA, "*Interagency Report*").

[62] *See* id. at 5.

[63] *See* Robert F. Durant, When Government Regulates Itself: EPA, TVA, and Pollution Control in the 1970s 45–64 (1985).

screens at intakes to minimize the impingement/entrainment of fish.[64] This enhanced traveling screen had been developed by US Fish and Wildlife Service engineers working to protect dwindling Pacific salmon populations and had demonstrated advantages over other intake designs.[65] But that research (and pronouncements like TVA's) reinforced the puzzle of water withdrawals under § 316(b): The better the solutions became for minimizing fish kills at the intake, the more water withdrawals—with their entrainment of microscopic biota—became just another cost of making electricity.

It is probably fair to say that the effort to set minimum federal standards bogged down in the variability and uncertainty of costs, a widespread belief that the engineering of intakes could minimize a withdrawal's harms, and a firm opposition from electric utilities deeply reliant on unpriced cooling water services.[66] "Amidst the changing political climate of the 1980s and the agency's enormous backlog of regulatory responsibilities under other federal environmental statutes, the EPA abandoned its Section 316(b) rulemaking efforts, leaving regulation of cooling water intake structures instead to the case-by-case decision making of [NPDES permit] issuers."[67] Further, that *should* have increased the "social costs" of permitting each facility on a fully individualized basis.[68] But an equally fair observation is that, by the time EPA proposed a national standard in 2000, water scarcity and the prevalence of unprecedented droughts loomed large in much of the US dependent on

---

[64] *See* TVA, *Interagency Report*, supra note 61 at 53–61. TVA also continued to maintain that cooling water withdrawals and thermal discharges were in fact harmful to surface waters. *See* DURANT, supra note 63 at 104–14.

[65] *See* TVA, *Interagency Report*, supra note 61 at 5; Development Document 1973, supra note 15 at 68–74; Development Document 1976, supra note 35 at 81–97.

[66] *See* DOUGLAS A. KYSAR, REGULATING FROM NOWHERE: ENVIRONMENTAL LAW AND THE SEARCH FOR OBJECTIVITY 203–05 (2010); May & Van Rossum, supra note 17 at 378–84. EPA might well have believed in 1976 that permit writers would individually guide intakes owners toward recirculating systems—which would drastically reduce water withdrawals. *Cf.* Rábago, supra note 17 at 458–60 (concluding that the substance of the 1976 Development Document and the 1977 permitting guidance suggest that EPA believed permit writers would generally require closed-cycle cooling systems).

[67] KYSAR, supra note 66 at 205.

[68] EPA several times noted the governance costs its intakes rules would impose, adding them into each rule's "social cost" without once pausing to note that the fully individualized permitting envisioned by the 1977 guidance would likely have been costlier than permitting guided by a uniform performance standard. *See, e.g.*, Phase II Rule, 69 Fed. Reg. at 41650.

cooling water withdrawals for its electricity production,[69] to say nothing of the technological advances that had amassed in electricity generation in the intervening quarter century.[70] Once-through systems withdraw on average 35,000 gallons per megawatt hour (MWh) to closed-cycle systems' 660 gallons per MWh.[71] But repowering away from thermoelectric altogether can eliminate the need for cooling water. And that is the kind of productivity gain research has long suggested may be spurred by environmental, health and safety risk regulation.

5.2 A STATIC PICTURE OF THERMOELECTRIC COOLING WATER: PHASED AND CONFUSED

In 2001, EPA finalized a BTA standard for *new* withdrawals designed for ≥ 10 MGD based on a projection that some 121 such facilities would open from 2001 to 2020.[72] It found that closed-cycle cooling technology withdrawing only the water needed to replenish a recirculating system

---

[69] *See* National Energy Tech. Lab., *Impact on U.S. Steam Electric Power Plant Cooling Water Intakes and Related Water Resource Management Issues* 1–3 (2009) (DOE/NETL-2009/1364); Benjamin K. Sovacool & Kelly E. Sovacool, *Preventing National Electricity-Water Crisis Areas in the United States*, 34 COLUM. J. ENVTL. L. 333, 358–68 (2009). Any Rankine cycle electricity generating unit, whether powered by nuclear fission or fossil fuel combustion, will have some need for cooling. The steam power's conversion in a dynamo generator necessitates a condenser or heat exchanger which cycles the steam back into liquid water. Because Rankine cycle generation has long accounted for roughly four-fifths of the electricity produced in the US, this technology's need for cooling has long been tied to America's electricity services market.

[70] By 2000, the technological advances in and experience with combined cycle natural gas generation were significantly more advanced than had been the case in the 1970s. *See* Ulrika Claeson Colpier & Deborah Cornland, *The Economics of the Combined Cycle Gas Turbine—An Experience Curve Analysis*, 30 ENERGY POL'Y 309 (2002). *See* Section 5.2.2.

[71] *See* James S. Meldrum *et al.*, *Life-Cycle Water Use for Electricity Generation: A Review and Harmonization of Literature Estimates*, 8 ENV'TL. RES. LETTS. 015031 (2013), at 8.

[72] *See* Phase I Rule, 66 Fed. Reg. at 65337–45. EPA projected that 656 *total* new facilities in the target sectors would open in that interval but only 121 would be large enough to meet its volume threshold. *Cf.* U.S. EPA, Economic Analysis of the Final Regulations Addressing Cooling Water Intake Structures for New Facilities 5–35 (EPA-821-R-01-035, 2001).

was "available and economically practicable" nationally while dry, water-free cooling was not.[73] Yet this "Phase I" rule reignited an old, at times acrimonious legal debate over the role of cost-benefit analysis in the setting of environmental performance standards.[74] For EPA's findings were based on a static analysis and a questionable statutory interpretation.[75] Its rule rejected uniform performance standards in favor of separate compliance "tracks"[76] with one track even leaving impingement and entrainment mortality minimization to a facility's "demonstration" of its own mixture of solutions.[77] When this led to a Phase II rule for

---

[73] *See* Phase I Rule, 66 Fed. Reg. at 65270–71. From proposal to finalization, EPA remained convinced that taking a "barrier to entry" approach to settling "how-much-cost-is-too-much" was the best interpretation of CWA § 316(b). *See* Phase I Proposal, 65 Fed. Reg. at 49094–95; Phase I Rule, 66 Fed. Reg. at 65282–83. "EPA has determined that higher capital and operating costs associated with dry cooling may pose barrier [*sic*] to entry for some new sources in certain circumstances. (In general, barrier to entry means that it is too costly for a new facility to enter into the marketplace.)." Id. at 65282.

[74] *See* Winston Harrington, *The Cooling Water Intake Structures Rule, in* REFORMING REGULATORY IMPACT ANALYSIS 160 (Winston Harrington *et al.*, eds., 2009); *see also* ELIZABETH ANDERSON, VALUE IN ETHICS AND ECONOMICS (1995).

[75] *See, e.g.*, Douglas A. Kysar, *Fish Tales, in* REFORMING REGULATORY IMPACT ANALYSIS 190 (Winston Harrington *et al.*, eds., 2009).

[76] On "Track I," new facilities designed to withdraw ≥ 10 MGD were required to limit their flow to that of a comparable closed-cycle/recirculating wet cooling system—a reduction EPA maintained could approach 98%. *See* Phase I Rule, 66 Fed. Reg. at 65273. New facilities designed to withdraw ≥ 2 MGD were required to restrict intake velocities to 0.5 feet per second and intake volume to a proportion of the water's mean annual flow or to within that water's thermal stratification norms, depending on water-type. Id.

[77] Most controversially, this included the use of "restoration" measures like artificial propagation and habitat enhancement. *See* Phase I Rule, 66 Fed. Reg. at 65280–81. The reviewing court vacated and remanded this part of Phase I Track II as inconsistent with CWA § 316(b). *See* Riverkeeper, Inc. v. U.S. EPA, 358 F.3d 174, 189–91 (2d Cir. 2004) ("*Riverkeeper I*"). That opinion was published four months before EPA finalized its "Phase II" rule for existing withdrawals. *See* U.S. EPA, Final Rule—National Pollution Discharge Elimination System: Regulations to Establish Requirements for Cooling Water Intake Structures at Phase II Existing Facilities, 69 Fed. Reg. 41576, 41682–693 (2004) (hereafter "Phase II Rule"). Finally, new marine oil and gas extraction facilities were omitted from the Phase I rule and became the subject of a "Phase III" rule in June 2006. *See* U.S. EPA, Final Rule—National Pollutant Discharge Elimination System—Final Regulations to Establish Requirements for Cooling Water Intake Structures at Phase III Facilities, 71 Fed. Reg. 35006 (2001) (hereafter EPA,

existing facilities offering *five* alternative tracks to performance improvement rejecting not only dry cooling on cost grounds, but also the recirculating closed-cycle systems by similar reasoning,[78] an environmentalist opposition went kinetic.

The 2001 Phase I and 2004 Phase II rules were meticulously groomed over the course of almost five years of rulemaking.[79] Standards governing a core segment of the economy like thermoelectric power, EPA seemed to say, should be *efficient*—or at least cost effective.[80] Large flow thresholds would, for example, exclude facilities least able to absorb regulatory costs while still governing the bulk of the cooling water withdrawn.[81] Impingement-reducing technologies were much cheaper than cooling towers, cooling ponds, repowering, *etc.*, so the nationally uniform requirements were all impingement related.[82] Projected changes in the power sector complicated EPA's task, though.[83] So the rules evolved into

---

"Phase III Rule"). The challenges to that rule were rejected in ConocoPhillips Co. v. U.S. EPA, 612 F.3d 822 (5th Cir. 2010).

[78] *See* Phase II Rule, 69 Fed. Reg. at 41584–93, 41650–55.

[79] The August 2000 proposal of Phase I, *see* U.S. EPA, Proposed Rule—National Pollutant Discharge Elimination System—Regulations Addressing Cooling Water Intake Structures for New Facilities, 65 Fed. Reg. 49060 (2000) (hereafter EPA, "Phase I Proposal"), was followed up almost a year later (and after the change of administrations) with a notice of new information, *see* U.S. EPA, Proposed Rule—Notice of Data Availability; National Pollutant Discharge Elimination System—Regulations Addressing Cooling Water Intake Structures for New Facilities, 66 Fed. Reg. 28853 (2001) (hereafter "Phase I NODA"). Likewise, the Phase II proposal, *see* U.S. EPA, Proposed Rule—National Pollutant Discharge Elimination System—Proposed Regulations to Establish Requirements for Cooling Water Intake Structures at Phase II Existing Facilities, 67 Fed. Reg. 17122 (2002) (hereafter EPA, "Phase II Proposal"), was followed up almost a year after that with a similar notice. *See* U.S. EPA, National Pollutant Discharge Elimination System—Notice of Data Availability; Proposed Regulations to Establish Requirements for Cooling Water Intake Structures at Phase II Existing Facilities, 68 Fed. Reg. 13522 (2003) (hereafter "Phase II NODA").

[80] *Cf.* Phase I Proposal, 65 Fed. Reg. at 49101–03 (presenting intakes rules' first "cost/benefit analysis" counting facility-level and national balances).

[81] At proposal, EPA considered setting a flow threshold of up to ≥ 30 MGD for its Phase I rule, *see* Phase I Proposal, 65 Fed. Reg. at 49068, and eventually set a ≥ 50 MGD "design intake flow" (DIF) threshold for the Phase II rule. *See* Phase II Rule, 69 Fed. Reg. at 41611.

[82] *See* Phase I Rule, 66 Fed. Reg. at 65270–85; Phase II Rule, 69 Fed. Reg. at 41598–610.

[83] *See* Phase I Rule 66 Fed. Reg. at 65267 (projecting 35 total new and 14 new in-scope coal-fired electric generating facilities 2001–20); Phase II Rule, 69

a labyrinth of compliance possibilities dividing new (Phase I) from existing (Phase II) withdrawals.[84] All of EPA's rules began with the acknowledgement of grave environmental consequences which had been associated with poorly designed intakes.[85] But each of them finished by deferring, one way or another, to business as usual.

EPA justified rejecting strict capacity reductions by claiming that its "wholly disproportionate" cost test in CWA technology standards[86] was "very imprecise" when applied to new facilities[87] and then by insisting

---

Fed. Reg. at 41608–09 (rejecting dry cooling as a national BTA standard for existing facilities based on the costs of retrofitting some facilities to dry cooling but observing that it may still be the best overall solution for some existing facilities' retrofits). The Phase I rule's "economic analysis" projected 83 new in-scope electric generation facilities incurring a total of $34.7 million in compliance costs from 2001 to 2020 and 38 new in-scope manufacturing facilities incurring a total of $13 million in compliance costs from 2001 to 2020. 66 Fed. Reg. at 65323–24. The Phase II rule's analogous effort projected some $385 million in total costs of compliance across 1065 facilities, although these estimates grew much more contingent and uncertain in the projection of facility-level and firm-level costs. *See* Phase II Rule, 69 Fed. Reg. at 41650.

[84] *See* Phase I Rule, 66 Fed. Reg. at 65270–85; Phase II Rule, 69 Fed. Reg. at 41598–610. In the Phase I rulemaking, EPA was especially keen to note the projected energy penalties of dry cooling systems, as well as the consequent air pollution increases, revenue losses, and space demands associated therewith, *see* 66 Fed. Reg. at 65283, concluding that § 316(b)'s "adverse environmental impact" phrase meant to sweep in such factors in EPA's balance. *See* Phase I Rule, 66 Fed. Reg. at 65291–92. In the Phase II rulemaking, EPA set the flow threshold for coverage at ≥ 50 MGD and rejected its estimated $490 million annualized costs of dry cooling retrofits (to a projected 121 facilities) in favor of its "economically practicable" menu of five compliance tracks differentiated by waterbody, volume of withdrawal, and a facility's capacity utilization rate. *See* Phase II Rule, 69 Fed. Reg. at 41604–06.

[85] *See* Phase I Rule, 66 Fed. Reg. at 65262–65; Phase II Rule, 69 Fed. Reg. at 41587–90. Several major intakes built in the 1960s had become notorious for their fish kills. *See, e.g.*, LIFSET, supra note 14 at 69–71.

[86] In several CWA §§ 301 and 306 contexts, EPA has maintained that "best" available or achievable technology includes all those options available at costs not "wholly disproportionate" to their effectiveness and that setting the performance standard according to such technologies is a means for preventing a race to the-bottom among individual permitting locations. *See* Chapter 2, Section 2.3.

[87] *See* Phase I Proposal, 65 Fed. Reg. at 49094; Phase I Rule, 66 Fed. Reg. at 65282. Interestingly, EPA seemed to return to the "wholly disproportionate" standard in the Phase III rulemaking. *See* Phase III Rule, 71 Fed. Reg. at 35010 ("When the costs of establishing a national categorical rule substantially outweigh the benefits of such a rule, a national categorical section 316(b) rule may

that existing facilities would have to compete with new ones.[88] In rejecting dry cooling's equivalent as the uniform standard for new plants,[89] EPA had argued that it would put new thermoelectric capacity at a competitive disadvantage to existing capacity.[90] The base compliance "track" required updated impingement precautions and imposed the entrainment expectations of a comparably scaled closed-cycle system withdrawing only enough water to replace consumptive losses.[91] But a second track allowed covered facilities to present their own comparably effective solutions on entrainment losses—including by the use of "restorative" tools like fish hatcheries and other offsetting techniques[92]—if they could prove the equivalence to their permitting authority.[93] The supposed "energy penalties" and a cost-effectiveness gap separating dry cooling from various other solutions figured prominently in EPA's justification.[94] That same reasoning then arranged the compliance options in the Phase II rule, as well.[95]

---

not be economically practicable, and therefore not the "best technology available for minimizing adverse environmental impact.").

[88] *See* Phase II Proposal, 67 Fed. Reg. at 17168 (rejecting dry cooling options as likely to create "unfair" competitive disadvantage for existing facilities, especially existing facilities in warmer areas such as the South).

[89] In the Phase I rule, EPA created two tracks, only the first of which would necessarily be equivalent to closed-cycle cooling's performance on entrainment/impingement mortality. *See* Phase I Rule, 66 Fed. Reg. at 65273–82. The track II alternative offered several sources of flexibility for individual facilities seeking to meet different location, intake velocity, or volume parameters—including "restoration" measures like artificial propagation of burdened species. *See* id.

[90] *See* Phase I Rule, 66 Fed. Reg. at 65283 ("New facilities are competing against the many … facilities already in the marketplace or slated for substantial expansion that use wet, closed-cycle cooling systems or even once-through cooling systems. The potential economic impact should EPA not similarly require dry cooling for some or all existing facilities might cause some firms to, at the least, delay their entry into the marketplace …").

[91] *See* Phase I Rule, 66 Fed. Reg. at 65278.

[92] *See* id. at 65279–81.

[93] *See* id. at 65271–78.

[94] *See* id. at 65270–71, 65281–84.

[95] The Phase II rule differentiated the impingement/entrainment mortality reduction obligations by (1) facility location, (2) rate of production (capacity utilization rate), and (3) proportion of the waterbody withdrawn and included design, construction, and restorative options. *See* Phase II Rule, 69 Fed. Reg. at 41590–93. It thus created five separate compliance tracks, four of which were set by rule and a fifth by a facility's own demonstration of unique controls meeting EPA's impingement and entrainment improvement ranges. *See* Phase II Rule, 69 Fed. Reg. at 41599–601. EPA stated in its "basis" for this approach that it had

To estimate how compliance costs might be minimized in Phase II, EPA developed what it called "technology modules," replacing its traditional least-cost assumption for each installation required to retrofit.[96] The technology modules were a kind of decision tree wherein a hypothetical existing facility (composed of familiar variations within the regulated universe) could proceed to the "best" mix of techniques for minimizing its own impingement and entrainment losses—all at uniquely minimized costs of compliance.[97]

But the straight-line calculations—the assumption that electricity demand would steadily increase from 1998 to 2020 being emblematic[98]—led EPA to some dubious conclusions. For example, in each of the rules EPA's assumption that a block of the covered facilities would be compliant regardless of the rule helped keep the costs of compliance at ≤ 1 percent of affected facility revenues.[99] EPA also projected a 0.0028 percent increase in annual CO_2 emissions, a 0.0026 percent increase in

judged closed-cycle recirculating systems to be not "economically practicable" for all in-scope facilities in the Phase II rule, id. at 41602, a unique legal standard the agency traced to CWA § 361(b)'s legislative history. *See* Phase I Proposal, 65 Fed. Reg. at 49094 & n.52 ("[T]he legislative history of section 316(b) indicates that the term 'best technology available' should be interpreted as 'best technology available commercially at an economically practicable cost.'").

[96] *See* Phase II NODA, 68 Fed. Reg. at 13526–27; Phase II Rule, 69 Fed. Reg. at 41648–50.

[97] *See* Phase II Rule, 69 Fed. Reg. at 41648–50 (describing the pairing of "model" facilities with permutations of over a dozen technological options to minimize impingement and entrainment losses); id. at 41603 (noting EPA's surveying of existing facilities).

[98] EPA had plenty of indication as of 2001 that, in fact, growth in electricity consumption would not "steadily" increase from 2001 to 2020 (which, in fact, it did not) and that electricity generation by fossil fuel-fired Rankine cycle units would not continue to grow either. *See* Richard F. Hirsh & Jonathan G. Koomey, *Electricity Consumption and Economic Growth: A New Relationship with Significant Consequences?*, 28(9) 74–76 ELECTRICITY J. (2015). It also had plenty of data indicating that growth in the thermoelectric sector would come in the form of combined-cycle plants—which increased efficiencies over coal-fired facilities considerably. *See* Phase I Rule, 66 Fed. Reg. at 65265 (noting that of 361 in-scope facilities then being built, 320 were combined-cycle). By 2014, when EPA finalized an amended rule for intakes, its perspective on growth in the fossil fuel-fired thermoelectric sector had matured considerably. *See* Section 5.2.2.

[99] *See* Phase II Rule, 69 Fed. Reg. at 41654–55 (estimating that 314 out of 554 will incur annualized costs of > 0.5% of revenues); Phase I Rule, 66 Fed. Reg. at 65323–34 (EPA assumes that only 47 of the projected 121 in-scope new facilities would incur *any* cost of compliance created by the rule).

annual mercury emissions, a 0.0024 percent increase in annual NO_x emissions, and a 0.0011 percent increase in annual SO_2 emissions were it to set dry cooling as BTA.[100] Of course, to conclude as much, EPA had to ignore the Clean Air Act[101] and the fact that, somehow, despite the supposedly "serious energy impacts"[102] of dry cooling, "dry cooling technology in the United States ha[d] been growing rapidly since the early 1980s and represent[ed] approximately 27 percent of new [generating] capacity since 1985."[103] For Phase II, EPA rejected a uniform standard equivalent to closed-cycle (recirculating) systems for withdrawals $\geq$ 50 MGD on the grounds that, for some number of high-volume facilities, the costs would be substantially higher than the costs imposed at even the costliest new facilities affected by the Phase I Rule.[104] Though it was admittedly aware of the opportunities presented when a facility elects to repower,[105] EPA refused to concede that retrofitting to recirculating systems would, in some number of cases—especially in drought-prone areas—be the least-cost option.[106] In short, new facilities were not forced to strive given competition from existing facilities and existing facilities' (statically) estimated retrofitting costs were capped at what little had been required of new facilities!

---

100 *See* Phase I Rule, 66 Fed. Reg. at 65269 (Exhibit 3).

101 For its calculations, EPA had to assume that "the energy lost by the facility cannot be replaced through additional fuel consumption at that facility, but rather, the energy will be replaced by the entire grid as a whole." Phase I Rule, 66 Fed. Reg. at 65269.

102 Phase II Rule, 69 Fed. Reg. at 41608.

103 Phase I Rule, 66 Fed. Reg. at 65304.

104 *See* Phase II Rule, 69 Fed. Reg. at 41605. EPA used this reasoning despite including a variance mechanism in the rules. In its 2014 rule, EPA would later deny that it was rejecting closed-cycle cooling at existing facilities *solely* on the basis of cost—instead emphasizing the space demands of cooling towers and their associated air emissions. *See* Final CWIS Rule, 79 Fed. Reg. at 48340.

105 *See, e.g.*, Phase II Rule, 69 Fed. Reg. at 41609 (agreeing that when facilities repower, new efficiencies can be found in using dry cooling, especially where access to cooling water is constrained).

106 Tidwell and colleagues developed a simple search and costing algorithm to step through each of 1,178 power plants in the US using freshwater in a steam cycle and determine the costs of retrofitting to dry cooling and/or the use of non-potable water. *See* Vincent C. Tidwell *et al.*, *Transitioning to Zero Freshwater Withdrawal in the U.S. for Thermoelectric Generation*, 131 APPLIED ENERGY 508, 509–10 (2014). Their results show that many retrofits were low difficulty/cost and that a median value in the change of "levelized cost of electricity" (ΔLCOE) produced at each plant was $3.53 MWh. Id. at 515.

EPA's supposedly "complete" cost analyses[107] showing big Pareto imbalances in both Phase II ($306 million in costs/$83 million in benefits)[108] and Phase I ($13 million in costs to undetermined benefits[109]) were, it is worth mentioning, exactly the sort of analysis the Office of Management and Budget had prescribed.[110] But this was no Pareto optimization. In the Phase II rule EPA also prepared what it termed a "market level analysis" of projected price effects electricity ratepayers could expect from EPA's cooling water rules.[111] This was closer to a general equilibrium account: Electricity producers meet a demand—presumably an elastic demand.[112] But even there EPA ignored the fact that firms exist to minimize exchange and production costs. It opted to straight-line the costs to end-users without any attention to the possibility

---

107 *See* Phase II Rule, 69 Fed. Reg. at 41666.

108 *See* Phase II Rule, 69 Fed. Reg. at 41666.

109 *See* Phase I Rule, 66 Fed. Reg. at 65324–26. EPA refused to estimate the benefits of its Phase I rule but did note analyses done at five facilities with once-through cooling systems and its estimate that nine of a projected 83 "new power plants would be built [in the next 20 years] without recirculating systems in the absence of this rule." Id. at 65326.

110 The intakes rules were among the "major" rulemakings falling within Executive Orders 12866 and 13563's ambit and included substantial OMB involvement. *See* Cass R. Sunstein, *The Office of Information and Regulatory Affairs: Myths and Realities*, 126 HARV. L. REV. 1838, 1851–53 (2013). The rules' regulatory impact analyses each featured virtually all of what OMB has said good practice requires: the use of 3% and 7% discount rates, a statement of need, evaluation of alternatives, *etc. See* Art Fraas & Randall Lutter, *The Challenges of Improving the Economic Analysis of Pending Regulations: The Experience of OMB Circular A-4*, 2011(3) ANN. REV. RESOURCE ECON. 71. OMB also urges that cost-benefit estimates present formal uncertainty analyses, *see* id. at 74, which the intakes rules did not do. Chapter 6 delves into a particular OMB-guided "regulatory impact analysis" and its political odyssey.

111 *See* Phase II Rule, 69 Fed. Reg. at 41651 (describing the "Integrated Planning Model" used to "identify potential economic and operational impacts of various regulatory options considered for the Phase II regulation"). The estimated price impacts to ratepayers from the Phase II rule were infinitesimal, ranging from 0.007 cents to 0.019 cents per kilowatt hour regionally. Id. at 41654.

112 *See* Chapter 3, Section 3.1.1. Ignoring demand elasticities may have simplified EPA's analysis, but it was not particularly realistic to do so—especially with a product (electricity) traded in large markets and having well-known price effects. *See* Daron Acemoglu *et al.*, *The Environment and Directed Technical Change*, 102(1) AMER. ECON. REV. 131 (2012) (presenting a model highlighting the market size and price effects for policymaking seeking to encourage innovation).

of optimization through trade.[113] It became evident from the work EPA revealed that the lion's share of the costs, energy penalties, and other reasons not to set stringent cooling standards which it was conjuring came from a baseline comprised of (1) a single-cycle coal or nuclear facility;[114] (2) otherwise unconstrained in the volume, capacity, or location of its intake;[115] (3) unconstrained in its air emissions;[116] and (4) unable to improve on industry-average thermoelectric performance efficiencies.[117] That baseline was not at all realistic. Its phased "barrier to

---

[113] *Cf.* Phase II Rule, 69 Fed. Reg. at 41651–54 (projecting "economic closures" of ≤ 0.1–0.2% of generating capacity as a result of the rule).

[114] *Compare* Phase I Rule, 66 Fed. Reg. at 65267 (projecting 14 of 35 new in-scope facilities to be built 2001–20 would be coal-fired), *with* id. at 65282 (noting, as one reason dry cooling should be rejected as BTA, that for 12 of the in-scope facilities projected, dry cooling's costs would be ≥ 10% of revenues); *compare* Phase II Rule, 69 Fed. Reg. at 41605 (noting, as one reason closed-cycle cooling should be rejected as BTA, that the total capital costs for "individual high-flow plants ... to convert ... generally ranged from $130 to $200 million with annual operating costs in the range of $4 to $20 million."), *with* Phase II Proposal, 67 Fed. Reg. at 17133 (reporting results of EPA surveys of 961 steam-electric generating plants and review of available datasets finding that out of 65 in-scope facilities planning a repowering, 36 were planning to repower with natural gas combined-cycle (NGCC) units and 34 of those would reduce cooling water use).

[115] In water-stressed regions, water costs have been prohibitive for years—leading to a regionalized gradient of cooling water approaches and electricity generation (and resultant ΔLCOE). *See* Vincent C. Tidwell *et al.*, *Transitioning to Zero Freshwater Withdrawal in the U.S. for Thermoelectric Generation*, 131 APPLIED ENERGY 508, 509–10 (2014). Indeed, as the GAO found by analyzing the same summary statistics available to EPA, thermoelectric generation in the most water-stressed regions of the US is significantly less prevalent. *See* Gov't Accountability Office, *Technology Assessment—Water in the Energy Sector: Reducing Freshwater Use in Hydraulic Fracturing and Thermoelectric Power Plant Cooling* 40–41 (2015) (GAO-15-545).

[116] In both the Phase I and Phase II rules, EPA made prominent mention of the possibility that cooling technology choices could in turn augment a facility's air emissions without making *any* mention of the Clean Air Act constraints that would materialize either in the event an existing thermoelectric stationary source was "modified" or in the greenfield construction of a new source. Suffice to say that those constraints, depending on the facility's location and other circumstances, could be cost-prohibitive. *See* Shi-Ling Hsu, *The Real Problem with New Source Review*, 36 ENVTL. L. RPTR. 10095 (2006).

[117] This assumption was evident despite the fact the turn toward combined cycle generation was quite evidently under way even in 2001. *See* Phase I Rule, 66 Fed. Reg. at 65265. EPA tipped off its awareness of coal's innate efficiency disadvantages to NGCC generation in its "economic analysis" in the Phase I rule.

entry" theory of cost acceptability allowed EPA essentially to ignore both innovation and influences from outside the sector.

The bulk of the costs EPA used to disqualify stringent intake limits were at hypothetical facilities that would never be built in competitive markets, in places governed by actual environmental laws, or where investment decisions reflected the panoply of threats, opportunities, and technological changes in progress.[118] Yet, quite unlike the mobile source emissions dynamic of Chapter 4, by the time EPA got around to setting § 316(b) standards it was no longer strategically obliged to seek the regulated community's cooperation. The justification of its BTA decisions reached neither for Kaldor/Hicks nor the pursuit of mutual advantage.[119] Had EPA studied the competitive advantages that natural gas combined-cycle (NGCC) turbines had gained in the marketplace,[120] even a presumption of linear growth in the fossil thermoelectric sector could not have sustained its decisions.[121] Coal's protracted supply-cost advantage over natural gas was its only competitive edge and that was clearly

---

See id. at 65323–25. There, EPA noted that, of the 83 new generating facilities projected 2001–20, 69 of them would be NGCC with costs of compliance dramatically in favor of NGCC. *See* id. And, indeed, NGCC capacity growth outpaced even this projection—leaping from 7% of all electricity produced in 2001 to 23% in 2013. *See* Govn't Account. Office, *Electricity: Generation Mix Has Shifted, and Growth in Consumption Has Slowed, Affecting System Operations and Prices* 13–14 (GAO-15-524) (May 2015) (hereafter GAO, "*Generation Mix*"). Though EPA remained mostly silent on thermoelectric nuclear's comparative disadvantages throughout the intakes rulemakings, it is even less efficient than coal and has been in a prolonged contraction within the industry. Id. at 22.

[118] The amended rule's attention to space constraints and remaining useful lives of the existing plants was purportedly decisive, *see* Final CWIS Rule, 79 Fed. Reg. at 48340–42, but there is good reason to believe that concern was mistaken. *See* Section 5.2.1.

[119] *See* Chapter 1, Section 1.2 and Chapter 2, Section 2.1. EPA's surveys for its § 316(b) rulemakings were completely voluntary (and yields reflected that fact). It otherwise used publicly available data, either from EIA form-data sets, vendor data, or published reports of particular intakes and, of course, its efforts came after three decades of inaction at the centralized level.

[120] *See* Sanders, supra note 13 at 53–54.

[121] The increasing penetration of combined-cycle efficiencies (inherently better than single-cycle technology) added to the tremendous expansion in natural gas production should have alerted EPA to a changing market in thermoelectric power. *See* Section 5.2.2.

dwindling by the turn of this century.[122] As the superior efficiencies of NGCC capacity combined with its reduced cooling demands and grid adaptability, closures of coal and nuclear thermoelectric capacity grew increasingly common.[123] The rapid diffusion of renewables throughout the grid has punctuated this shift.[124]

A legal challenge to the Phase I rule's rejection of dry cooling and heavily qualified use of closed-cycle cooling was swift. It targeted EPA's weighing of costs. But in response to the environmentalists' challenge that EPA had essentially weighted costs too heavily, Judge Katzmann, for the Second Circuit panel hearing the case, shrewdly observed that a

> [c]ourt is not well equipped … to meaningfully weigh a 95 percent reduction in entrainment against .027 percent of new generating capacity, 300 pounds of mercury, and $443 million dollars. It is certainly true that dry cooling is an available technology, at least in some regions and industries, and it is better than closed-cycle cooling at reducing impingement and entrainment … but the [CWA] allows EPA to make a choice among alternatives based on more than impingement and entrainment.[125]

The panel upheld most of EPA's choices as *reasonable*, invalidating only its offer of restorative, *ex situ* compliance options as contrary to the text of § 316(b).[126] The panel hearing the Phase II challenges went much further, though, remanding not just the restoration measures, but also

---

[122] *See* Scott L. Montgomery, The Powers That Be: Global Energy for the Twenty-First Century and Beyond 81–110 (2010); Colpier & Cornland, supra note 70.

[123] *See* Richard L. Revesz & Jack Lienke, Struggling for Air: Power Plants and the "War on Coal" 141 (2016) ("[A]s of August 2014, utilities planned to shutter a full 80 percent of the pre-1970 units by 2025. In 2012 alone, about 10.2 [gigawatts] of coal capacity retired—just over 3 percent of the U.S. total. The retiring units had an average age of 51 years.") (citations omitted). A study of Texas' transition away from coal and toward NGCC, for example, showed a saving of 60% of the water needed for levelized electricity demand. *See* Emily A. Grubert *et al.*, *Can Switching Fuels Save Water? A Life Cycle Quantification of Freshwater Consumption for Texas Coal- and Natural Gas-Fired Electricity*, 7(4) Envtl. Res. Letts. (2012). As water-stressed regions facing prolonged droughts and rising surface temperatures confront the efficiencies to be gained in the thermoelectric sector, retrofitting to closed-cycle and/or dry cooling is sure to become a more heavily studied alternative.

[124] EPA elsewhere acknowledged that annual growth in electricity demand has been on a steady downward trajectory for years. *See* Michael Wara *et al.*, *Peak Electricity and the Clean Power Plan*, 28(4) Elec. J. 18, 19–20 (2015).

[125] *Riverkeeper I*, 358 F.3d at 196.

[126] *See* id. at 189–91.

EPA's BTA determination rejecting closed-cycle cooling.[127] This second panel maintained that *any* use of cost-benefit balancing in determining BTA was, if not forbidden by the statute's text and history, at least presumptively suspect.[128] The Supreme Court intervened there.[129]

As discussed in Chapter 2, Section 2.3, the Supreme Court's opinion in *Entergy* headlines a list of bouts over ambiguous delegations to regulate risk and the weighing of costs. It includes *Michigan v. EPA*,[130] *EPA v. EME Homer City Generation*,[131] *Utility Air Regulatory Group v. EPA*,[132] *Alaska Dept. of Envtl. Conserv. v. EPA*, and *Whitman v. American Trucking Ass'ns*.[133] Justice Scalia's *Entergy* opinion viewed EPA's work as a reasonable approach to performance standards' defining ambiguity: When are the costs of compliance too great?[134] The Court held that absent statutory text to the contrary, the specific weighting of costs in regulatory settings like § 316(b)'s BTA is the agency's choice to make.[135] As a Fifth Circuit panel hearing challenges to the Phase III rule later remarked, *Entergy* "lucidly establishe[d] that the EPA *may* employ cost-benefit analysis," that EPA "is not *required* to do so," and that, overall, EPA "is afforded discretion to consider to what degree, if any, costs and benefits should be weighed in determining the 'best technology available to minimizing adverse environmental impact.'"[136] When an incoming Obama Administration reconsidered the intakes rules, however, that discretion was again cloaked in cost calculations which ignored ongoing changes in the thermoelectric sector.

---

[127] *See* Riverkeeper, Inc. v. U.S. EPA, 475 F.3d 83, 98–105 (2d Cir. 2007) ("*Riverkeeper II*").

[128] *See Riverkeeper II*, 475 F.3d at 99.

[129] Entergy Corp. v. Riverkeeper, Inc., 556 U.S. 208 (2009).

[130] 135 S. Ct. 2699 (2015).

[131] 134 S. Ct. 1584 (2014).

[132] 134 S. Ct. 2427 (2014).

[133] 531 U.S. 457 (2001).

[134] *See Entergy*, 556 U.S. at 222–25.

[135] *See* id. at 224–26. "While the EPA's prior 'wholly disproportionate' standard may be somewhat different from its current 'significantly greater than' standard [of benefits-to-costs], there is nothing in the statute that would indicate that the former is a permissible interpretation while the latter is not." Id. at 225.

[136] ConocoPhillips Corp. v. U.S. EPA 612 F.3d 822, 828 (5th Cir. 2010) (emphases in original).

5.2.1 The Relevance of Trivial Effects?

EPA's justifications in its intakes rules rested squarely in the economics of thermoelectric power and its substitutes.[137] Curiously enough, despite spending 15+ years trying to optimize its intakes rules, they still purported to generate more costs than benefits! That disparity attracted much of the attention (most of it critical[138]). Of course any comparison of costs to benefits highlights the *relative* merits of two different evaluations.[139] But the intakes rules' soft benefits estimates[140] should have prompted some harder questions about why the cost-of-compliance figures mattered at all. For EPA's years of work on intakes surely accentuated how an "economic" analysis can, by persistently ignoring technological innovation like factor switching, introduce a form of blindness to the very policymaking it is supposedly informing.

EPA worked through its economic analyses in all three phases of the intakes rules to show that the final rules would mostly exert ≤ 1 percent cost-to-revenue effects at the national, firm, and facility levels. It also

---

[137] The thermoelectric sector is but a segment of the larger electricity generation industry—competing with other factors of production therein on a single LCOE. Within that segment, EIA and others have long projected that, by LCOE (let alone water demand), NGCC production would outcompete coal in the US for the foreseeable future. Sanders, supra note 13 at 53–54, 60–61. Beyond it, "sources" of electricity services like wind, solar, conservation, and other renewables with low water intensities may well offer least-cost alternatives as well, although these projections are much more uncertain.

[138] *See, e.g.*, Kysar, supra note 75, at 196–99; KYSAR, supra note 66 at 211–28.

[139] *See* Chapter 1, Section 1.1.

[140] Without detailed biological data on actual intakes, confidently estimating the benefits of dry- or closed-cycle cooling requirements in place is impossible. *See* Brook & Bradshaw, supra note 32. Despite its 1977 guidance urging permitting authorities to undertake or to require such investigations before issuing permits, the record documenting actual intakes' effects in the environment remained anecdotal even after 15+ years of rulemaking. *See* Phase I Rule, 66 Fed. Reg. at 65262–65; Final CWIS Rule, 79 Fed. Reg. at 48351–52 (noting site-based variabilities lost in aggregate assessments). Indeed, it is especially telling that after three decades of operational experience with the Indian Point once-through intakes and New York State's eventual order requiring a closed-cycle cooling system be retrofitted there in 2014, the decision was still at least perceived to be (and may have been) a deeply "political" decision. *See* Scott Waldman, *Seeing Cuomo's Hand, or Not, in a State Move on Indian Point*, POLITICO, July 31, 2014, *available at* https://www.politico.com/states/new-york/albany/story/2014/07/seeing-cuomos-hand-or-not-in-a-state-move-on-indian-point-014723.

predicted that the Phase I and II rules' expected effects on electricity supply would be infinitesimal. It followed this same approach in the remand after *Entergy*.[141] At that point, EPA reopened its BTA judgments for existing intakes,[142] redoubling efforts to track what costs an intakes rule would make essentially unavoidable.[143] It again adopted alternatives with trivial expected impacts on regulated parties, leading to the conclusion that the indirect impacts in the wider economy would be trivial as well.[144] Indeed, even after cutting the coverage threshold from ≥ 50 MGD to ≥ 2 MGD and treating new units at existing facilities like new facilities, EPA *still* concluded that its rules would mostly cost ≤ 1 percent of revenues.[145] And the cursory evaluation EPA did showed miniscule effects on variable production costs at either a regional or national level.[146] By 2014 the agency had been rebuked by members of Congress on the issue,[147] so it also paused to note that EPA had no information suggesting significant employment effects from its rule, either.[148]

Did these "trivial effect" evaluations signal some underlying, if also tacit norm? They arguably reflect the normative priorities some commentators have ascribed to feasibility-based regulation more generally: Society ought to take the practicable steps in its power to reduce the risks

---

141 *See* Final CWIS Rule, 79 Fed. Reg. at 48390–91.

142 EPA remained committed to assessing costs using a combination of facility-specific and model facility approaches. *See* Final CWIS Proposal, 76 Fed. Reg. at 22213; *see also* Final CWIS Rule, 79 Fed. Reg. at 48308–10. EPA also removed the restorative alternatives in the Phase I rule, which the Second Circuit had ruled were incompatible with the statute's text. Id. at 22183–84.

143 By 2011, EPA had concluded that roughly 43% of in-scope existing facilities were already employing closed-cycle cooling, whether because their states had required it or because they lacked access to needed water supplies. *See* Final CWIS Proposal, 76 Fed. Reg. at 22216.

144 *See* Final CWIS Proposal, 76 Fed. Reg. at 22235.

145 *See* Final CWIS Rule, 79 Fed. Reg. at 48399 ("Under the final rule, between 90 and 95 percent of all entities are estimated to incur compliance costs of less than 1 percent of revenue."); id. at 48390 ("EPA estimates that over all … 86 percent of regulated facilities will incur compliance costs of less than 1 percent of revenue."). EPA also reiterated its belief that the costs-of-compliance and administrative costs associated with the rule would comprise the rule's "social costs," straight-lining them 51 years into the future. *See* id. at 48387–88.

146 *See* Final CWIS Rule, 79 Fed. Reg. at 48396.

147 *See* Jonathan S. Masur & Eric A. Posner, *Regulation, Unemployment, and Cost-Benefit Analysis*, 98 VA. L. REV. 579, 580 (2012).

148 *See* Final CWIS Rule, 79 Fed. Reg. at 48399–400.

imposed on others.[149] On this view, society can and should demand that of a regulated party which no one could, in similar circumstances, *reasonably* reject.[150] Of course, 1 percent can be the difference between some actual firm's profitability and insolvency.[151] Triviality here is the objective sort but that arguably makes it a better proxy for *fairness* than for utility. As Scanlon put it, "an act is wrong if its performance under the circumstances would be disallowed by any set of principles for the general regulation of behavior that no one could reasonably reject as a basis for informed, unforced, general agreement."[152] But supposing this was the intended effect, was EPA's approach even arguably still about *optimizing*? If the standards were grounded in fairness to the utilities involved, they should have been justified explicitly in those terms.

EPA's assurances in 2014 that impingement and entrainment losses remain significant kept the onus on intakes.[153] A 2012 analysis of public data sets suggested that the impacts of once-through cooling systems on freshwater temperatures in the US from 1996 to 2005 were extreme. Maximum reported temperature discharges averaged 37°C—which meant they were 9.5°C to 10°C higher than maximum reported intake temperatures during the summer.[154] At those extremes, many if not most applicable CWA water quality standards would be violated, especially if current trends in surface water temperatures continue.[155] Capacity

---

[149] *See* Dov Waisman, *Equity and Feasibility Regulation*, 50 U. RICH. L. REV. 1263, 1275–97 (2016).

[150] The ethical program as such is explored in T.M. SCANLON, WHAT WE OWE TO EACH OTHER (1998).

[151] In its final rule following the remand in *Entergy*, EPA estimated that 91–94% of all parent entities would incur annualized costs of ≤ 1% of revenues under the final rule. *See* Final CWIS Rule, 79 Fed. Reg. at 48390.

[152] SCANLON, supra note 150 at 153.

[153] *See* Final CWIS Rule, 79 Fed. Reg. at 48318–21, 48401–14. "EPA has determined that the majority of surveyed facilities including 71 percent of electric generators and 79 percent of sampled manufacturing facilities are within two miles of an impaired … waterbody." Id. at 48319.

[154] *See* N. Madden *et al.*, *Thermal Effluent from the Power Sector: An Analysis of Once-Through Cooling System Impacts on Surface Water Temperature*, 8 ENVIRON. RES. LETT. 035006 (2013).

[155] *See* Sovacool & Sovacool, supra note 69 at 337–43; 352–53; *cf.* Madden *et al.*, supra note 154 at 4–5 (finding that all five thermoelectric plants studied in one watershed had exceeded the temperature change limits in applicable state water quality standards and all five had been granted variances to do so). Lui and colleagues' modeling results suggest thermal limits in state water quality standards could become a significant barrier for thermoelectric generation as surface temperatures increase throughout this century. *See* Lu Liu *et al.*,

limitation at intake would necessarily correlate to outflow but not necessarily to the temperature of that outflow. So what if the trivial effect model of costs-as-veto over more stringent standards obscured a still more discriminating approach to these questions—one that conceived of costs more as a *motivational force* than as a proxy for harm?

5.2.2 Entrenchment's Cost: Beyond Partial Equilibrium Welfarism

Thermoelectric power is but one factor for producing widely traded energy services, *i.e.*, grid-delivered electricity at 60Hz. Substitutes are abundant (if also imperfect) and the grid-reliability of thermoelectric factors is increasingly questionable.[156] A team of US Energy Department engineers recently showed from newly public Energy Information Administration (EIA) datasets that about a third of all the cooling water withdrawn by thermoelectric generators occurs while the plants are not even generating electricity.[157] Where they sit on their regional dispatch curve strongly affects this idling cost.[158] But thermoelectric technology is pervasive and has advanced enough that its head-start in the market may also be locking out competing factors to a significant degree.[159] Whether

---

Vulnerability of US Thermoelectric Power Generation to Climate Change When Incorporating State-Level Environmental Regulations, 2 NATURE ENERGY 17109 (2017) (DOI: 10.1038/nenergy.2017.109).

156 *See, e.g.*, Ariel Miara *et al.*, *Climate and Water Resource Change Impacts and Adaptation Potential for US Power Supply*, 7 NATURE CLIMATE CH. 793, 793 (2017). Nuclear is often touted as "emissions free," but its inefficiencies—starting with its use of 1940s vintage single steam-cycle technology to harness the fission's heat energy—have kept it among the highest-cost sources of electricity for five decades. *See* Lucas W. Davis, *Prospects for Nuclear Power*, 26(1) J. ECON. PERSP. 49, 63 (2012).

157 *See* Zachary Clement *et al.*, Effects of Cooling System Operations on Withdrawal for Thermoelectric Power (POWER-ICOPE2017-3763), *available at* http://proceedings.asmedigitalcollection.asme.org/proceeding.aspx?articleid=2653553. Clement and colleagues were able to estimate that coal-fired plants withdrew the largest total volume of water and the most water while at idle among all thermoelectric. Id. at 2.

158 *See* Clement *et al.*, supra note 157 at 4 (reporting that coal- and gas-fired single-cycle plants "are the major contributors to water withdrawal while not generating electricity" due to the fact that "these are used as peaking plants because they are older and less efficient plants that are lower on the dispatch curve").

159 *See* Thomas Covert *et al., Will We Ever Stop Using Fossil Fuels?*, 30 J. ECON. PERSP. 117, 126–34 (2016). Some have modeled this lockout effect (and

or not this lock-in effect is afoot, the "trivial costs" approach EPA took assured controlling influence to the cost leaders in its standard-setting studies.

Throughout its intakes rulemakings, EPA essentially ignored the broader competitive landscape on which its calculations were grounded, thereby ignoring basic relationships that may have been much more informative than its straight-line arithmetic. For example, it ignored the fact that covered manufacturers were only covered because they were generating their own thermoelectric power, *i.e.*, had elected to make not buy power produced by that very factor.[160] EPA ignored the fact that from 2001 to 2014, industrial electricity consumption *decreased* by 4 percent, reducing its share of total consumption from 29 percent to 26 percent.[161] EIA data suggest that multiple influences were at work in this trend,[162] some of which implicate "competitiveness" concerns, *i.e.*, production's leakage out of the US.[163] But EIA maintains that "energy intensity" in US manufacturing *also* declined,[164] suggesting industry was doing more with less over EPA's interval. EPA's tunnel vision focused it on the "trivial effect" projections it could show for its covered manufacturers.[165] What if EPA had instead investigated whether manufacturers

---

its neutralization), although their results are sensitive to the size of the technology gaps and the expected profitability of innovations in "cleaner" substitutes. *See* Daron Acemoglu *et al.*, *Transition to Clean Technology*, 124(1) J. POL. ECON. 52 (2016).

160 In theory, owning a factor rather than contracting for it is cost minimization at work. *See, e.g.*, Sanford J. Grossman & Oliver D. Hart, *The Costs and Benefits of Ownership: A Theory of Vertical and Lateral Integration*, 94(4) J. POL. ECON. 691, 693–95 (1986).

161 *See* GAO, *Generation Mix*, supra note 117 at 24.

162 *See* id. at 25 (EIA views changes in the economy, efficiency gains, demand response, and other factors as causes).

163 *See, e.g.*, Daniel J. Henderson & Daniel L. Millimet, *Pollution Abatement Costs and Foreign Direct Investment Inflows to U.S. States: A Nonparametric Reassessment*, 89 REV. ECON. & STAT. 178 (2007); Tim Jeppesen *et al.*, *Environmental Regulations and New Plant Location Decisions: Evidence from a Meta-Analysis*, 42 J. REGIONAL SCI. 19 (2002); Smita B. Brunnermeier & Arik Levinson, *Examining the Evidence on Environmental Regulations and Industry Location*, 13 J. ENV'T & DEV. 6 (2004).

164 *See* U.S. Energy Information Admin., *Manufacturing Energy Consumption Survey* (2014), *available at* https://www.eia.gov/consumption/manufacturing/reports/2014/enduse_intensity/.

165 *Cf.* Final CWIS Rule, 79 Fed. Reg. at 48397 (announcing EPA finding that of 500 covered facilities, 496 would incur costs < 1% of revenue and four would incur costs of 1–3%).

seeking new efficiencies—in NGCC or beyond thermoelectric—were distinguishable from their competitors?[166] What if EPA had investigated who could *not* phase out a reliance on thermoelectric altogether because, for example, of its complementarities with other factors, and who was already doing so? What might the cost projections of stringent cooling water rules have looked like then? Might they have supported choices in the intakes rules that minimized still *more* costs?

For example, where should averted operating losses of temperature-constrained electricity generation in the future figure into a rule which prompts factor and/or process substitutions today away from cooling water-dependent technology? How might EPA have projected the social costs of a continued grid dependency on generating capacity likely to face so many drought-induced frictions in the future?[167] That sort of grid vulnerability could entail truly socialized costs.[168] In its 2011 proposal of the amended rule, EPA acknowledged that "[u]se of a comprehensive, market analysis system is important in assessing the potential impact of the options because of the interdependence of electricity generating units in supplying power to the electric transmission grid."[169] What it was apparently unwilling to do is acknowledge any possible role for innovation in reducing cooling water demand by factor substitution.

---

[166] Such an investigation would at least have been in pursuit of more instrumentally valuable insights into the changing markets of electricity generation. Indeed, in that much it may also have been better calculated to identify those utilities that would have struggled most with an ambitious performance standard and growth-enhancing ways of helping them. *Cf.* RICHARD G. LIPSEY ET AL., ECONOMIC TRANSFORMATIONS: GENERAL PURPOSE TECHNOLOGIES AND LONG-TERM ECONOMIC GROWTH 520 (2005) (describing a governmental role in "[o]vercoming the disincentive of sunk costs" wherein government disseminates technical knowledge and thereby subsidizes factor switching that firms may otherwise be incapable of undertaking).

[167] *See, e.g.*, David M. Ward, *The Effect of Weather on Grid Systems and the Reliability of Electricity Supply*, 2(1) CLIMATIC CHANGE 103 (2013).

[168] *See* U.S. DEPT. OF ENERGY, QUADRENNIAL ENERGY REVIEW: ENERGY TRANSMISSION, STORAGE, AND DISTRIBUTION INFRASTRUCTURE 3-3 (April 2015), *available at* https://www.energy.gov/epsa/downloads/quadrennial-energy-review-first-installment; *see also* C.B. Harto & Y.E. Yan *et al.*, Analysis of Drought Impacts on Electricity Production in the Western and Texas Interconnections of the United States, Argonne Nat'l Lab. (ANL/EVS/R-11/14) (2011), *available at* http://www.ipd.anl.gov/anlpubs/2012/02/72096.pdf.

[169] U.S. EPA, National Pollutant Discharge Elimination System—Cooling Water Intake Structures at Existing Facilities and Phase I Facilities, 76 Fed. Reg. 22174, 22229 (2011) (hereafter "Final CWIS Proposal").

Of course, nothing in such a normative project alleviates the need to count—and count carefully—the unavoidable costs a rule would impose on the regulated. But the integrity of the efforts surely rests on why factor substitution—away from a relative high cost factor and in favor of untold other possibilities—was left unexplored. Utilities conceive of such rule-makings as of a piece with the problem they have faced since delegations like § 316(b) emerged: a totality of regulatory constraints that cumulatively frustrate rational investment decisions under uncertainty.[170] These constraints (frictions) intersect market-facing decisions to invest in generation, transmission, and storage infrastructure against the backdrop of, if not falling demand, then demand that is no longer doubling every decade and may well have leveled off permanently.[171] And if that is the firm-level decision-making framework, then EPA most definitely should have explored how its intakes rules were going to change the "entire friction load" then confronting utilities—if at all. Social "costs" attributed to regulation demands no less from rulemaking efforts that persisted for 14+ years which came after 20+ years of refusing to make any national standard at all.

---

[170] *See* DURANT, supra note 63 at 142–45; Clifford P. Case III & David Schoenbrod, *Electricity or the Environment: A Study of Public Regulation without Public Control*, 61 CAL. L. REV. 961, 965–73 (1973); LIFSET, supra note 14. It is telling that in negotiating with environmental and community opponents to its Storm King Mountain pumped storage project in the early 1970s, Consolidated Edison ultimately elected to trade away its Storm King project for its opponents' concession to a once-through cooling system for ConEd's nuclear station at Indian Point. *See* id. at 163–65, 183.

[171] *Compare* Case & Schoenbrod, supra note 170, *with* QUADRENNIAL ENERGY REVIEW, supra note 168 at 1–8.

6. Freight rail's productivity puzzle: offsetting regulatory costs

To its customers, rail transport is a cost of doing business pure and simple. It is not a key to creating social welfare.[1] To the railroad, it is quite the opposite: Linking producers to consumers is the essence of creating value.[2] Identifying *social* costs from regulations diminishing the productivity of rail transport surely takes one perspective on that difference or another.[3] When the matter for transport is hazardous, the testing and characterization, packing and shipping, transport, and delivery thereof is governed by an amalgamated regulatory apparatus in the US: component bureaus of the Department of Transportation (DOT).[4] Its "hazardous materials regulations" (HMR[5]) include elements from the Federal Railroad Administration (FRA), the Pipeline and Hazardous

---

[1] *Cf.* Harold Demsetz, *The Problem of Social Cost: What Problem? A Critique of the Reasoning of A.C. Pigou and R.H. Coase*, 7 REV. L. & ECON. 1, 10 (2012) (arguing that if transport costs are too high, the transaction is rationally left undone—but that nothing can be changed in the parties' respective rights or duties to change that).

[2] *See* ALFRED D. CHANDLER, JR., THE VISIBLE HAND: THE MANAGERIAL REVOLUTION IN AMERICAN BUSINESS (1977) (linking the rise of large, integrated firms and mass production to the creation of the first modern railroads and their managerial and technological innovations); *cf.* OLIVER E. WILLIAMSON, THE ECONOMIC INSTITUTIONS OF CAPITALISM 107 (1985) ("Without the low cost, reliable, all-weather transportation afforded by the railroad ... the incentive to integrate [vertically] would have been much less.").

[3] One might, for example, identify it as a basic "competitiveness" question—with regulatory costs driving production/consumption elsewhere as the same kind of retardants as first-generation economic criticism cast environmental, health, and safety regulations. *See* Adam B. Jaffe *et al.*, *Environmental Regulation and the Competitiveness of U.S. Manufacturing: What Does the Evidence Tell Us?*, 33 J. ECON. LIT. 132 (1995).

[4] U.S. Dept. of Transp., Pipeline and Hazardous Materials Safety Admin., Final Rule—Enhanced Tank Car Standards and Operational Controls for High-Hazard Flammable Trains, 80 Fed. Reg. 26644, 26644–45 (2015) (hereafter "HHFT Final Rule").

[5] *See* 49 C.F.R. parts 101, 106–107, 171–180 (2017).

Materials Safety Administration (PHMSA), and others.[6] With pipelines promising to replace freight rail transport of the subject matter wholesale, the economics of regulatory cost here can seem especially dim.

This chapter examines one recent HMR amendment and how costs figured into the deliberations. The advent of new technologies for "tight" oil and gas production from tar sands and shale coincided for a time with historically high oil prices.[7] That created a hydrocarbon production tsunami from about 2005 to 2014.[8] Besides the tsunami's grave environmental concerns,[9] it also faced an infrastructure bottleneck, most noticeable in the case of pipelines.[10] Tightening things further, the crude transport demand surge coincided with an ethanol boom (of the Clean Air Act's making[11])—which all had the effect of focusing the public's attention on long, combustible trains moving rapidly.[12] It was a powerful but not unprecedented political prompt: the public's "discrete and salient

---

[6] *See* id. §§ 171.1(a)–(g) (2018) (distributing HMR applicability to covered "persons" and "functions" transporting designated "hazardous materials").

[7] *See* U.S. Energy Information Admin., *Spot Prices for Crude Oil and Petroleum Products, available at* https://www.eia.gov/dnav/pet/hist/LeafHandler.ashx?n=PET&s=RWTC&f=D (hereafter "EIA Spot Prices").

[8] *See* Daniel Raimi, The Fracking Debate: The Risks, Benefits, and Uncertainties of the Shale Revolution (2018); Russell Gold, The Boom: How Fracking Ignited the American Energy Revolution and Changed the World (2014).

[9] *See* Mark Squillace, *Managing Unconventional Oil and Gas Development as if Communities Mattered*, 40 Vt. L. Rev. 525 (2016).

[10] *See* Raimi, supra note 8 at 25–29.

[11] The combined effects of excise tax credits to gasoline blenders using ethanol and the CAA's renewable fuel standards (RFS) increased ethanol production and transport from 2007 to 2012—due in good part to an EPA cost-benefit analysis showing ethanol's substantial social cost advantages over gasoline. *See* Robert Hahn & Caroline Cecot, *The Benefits and Costs of Ethanol: An Evaluation of the Government's Analysis*, 35 J. Reg. Econ. 275, 277–80 (2009). Subsequent analyses drew that conclusion into doubt. *See* Gabriel E. Lade *et al., Ex Post Costs and Renewable Identification Number (RIN) Prices under the Renewable Fuel Standard* (Resources for the Future 2015) (RFF DP 15-22), *available at* http://www.rff.org/files/sharepoint/WorkImages/Download/RFF-DP-15-22.pdf.

[12] *See* U.S. Dept. of Transp., Pipeline and Hazardous Materials Safety Admin., Notice of Proposed Rulemaking—Hazardous Materials: Enhanced Tank Car Standards and Operational Controls for High-Hazard Flammable Trains, 79 Fed. Reg. 45016, 45019 (2014) (hereafter "HHFT NPRM") ("In 2008 there were around 292,000 rail carloads of ethanol. In 2011, that number increased over 40 percent, to 409,000.").

threat" raised in Chapter 2.[13] From 2011 to 2012, the volume of crude carried by rail increased > 400 percent and by 2013 more than 400,000 rail carloads of crude were shipped.[14] An accident in July of that year where one of these trains crashed and torched a Quebec town, killing 47 people—along with several less deadly accidents—sent FRA and PHMSA in search of a response.[15]

By 2014, crude-by-rail had clearly peaked. Oil prices were collapsing[16] and the demand that only months before had seemed assured was vanishing even as pipeline proposals continued to emerge. But freight rail's capital maintenance costs are, at best, imperfectly demand-elastic.[17] To make matters worse, rail loses much of its cost advantage over trucking when diesel fuel prices are low[18] and freight rail casualties remained on trend in a decline that had begun more than a half-century ago.[19] Such has long been the freight rail sector's predicament: With multiple asset indivisibilities, density-dependent profits often turning on network effects and other returns to scale, and price competition from modally distinct competitors (trucking, aviation, shipping, *etc.*), the freight rail business has long struggled to keep firm and cost structures fit for unpredictable business cycles.[20]

---

[13] *See* MARK ALDRICH, BACK ON TRACK: AMERICAN RAILROAD ACCIDENTS AND SAFETY, 1965–2015, 111–12 (2018).

[14] *See* HHFT Final Rule, 80 Fed. Reg. at 25544.

[15] *See* HHFT NPRM, 79 Fed. Reg. at 45019–22 (describing the disaster at Lac Mégantic and other similar train explosions).

[16] *See* Robert J. Samuelson, *Key Facts About the Great Oil Crash of 2014*, WASH. POST, Dec. 3, 2014, at A3.

[17] Freight rail's track maintenance cost structure is very nearly a "fixed" cost in the conventional sense of the term. *See* Section 6.1.2.

[18] *See* TRANSP. ECONOMICS & MNGT. SYSTEMS, INC., TECHNICAL REPORT—IMPACT OF HIGH OIL PRICES ON FREIGHT TRANSPORTATION: MODAL SHIFT POTENTIAL IN FIVE CORRIDORS 31–35 (2008), *available at* https://www.marad.dot.gov/wp-content/uploads/pdf/Modal_Shift_Study_-_Technical_Report.pdf.

[19] Rail safety historian Professor Mark Aldrich concluded that the steep decline in rail-related fatalities in the latter part of the twentieth century was largely a function of federal subsidies for track, grade crossing, and other capital improvements. *See generally* ALDRICH, BACK ON TRACK, supra note 13. The largest railroads persuaded Congress to subsidize track maintenance and research beginning in the late 1970s, id. at 89–96, which, in turn, improved the engineering and R&D expenditures, bringing what Aldrich calls a "technological revolution" in materials, powering, and train control. *See* id. at 96–105.

[20] *See* Theodore E. Keeler, *Railroad Costs, Returns to Scale, and Excess Capacity*, 56(2) REV. ECON. & STATS. 201 (1974). The largest ("Class I") railroads immediately began abandoning tracks to shrink their cost bases. *See*

As the search for safety improvements ebbed forward in 2014–15, some familiar dilemmas came into focus. Train accidents are, from a railroad's perspective, about energy transfer. Thus, if *kinetic energy* = ½(*mass*) *x* (*velocity*)^2, the potential solutions address mass, velocity, or their combined product taking the form of a massive, hazardous payload.[21] In contrast, the HMR-251 rulemaking's "High Hazard Flammable Trains" (HHFT)[22] evoked the public dread of "bomb trains" that followed from the Lac Mégantic disaster.

A different perspective emphasizes train accidents' *imposed* risks on whomever or whatever in the vicinity might be jeopardized by an accident.[23] Safety concerns in the 1970s led to the first FRA tank car

---

Tenpao Lee *et al.*, *Market Structure, Conduct, and Performance of the Class I Railroad Industry, 1971–1984*, 26(4) TRANSP. J. 54, 57 (1987) ("The size of the Class I railroad system declined by ... 22.4 [percent] during the 1971–1984 period."). Because over long enough intervals, all costs are "variable," the causal relations between rail service in the past, present, and future confounded the setting of minimum service, rate, and other standards while the Interstate Commerce Commission was at work. This often entailed endless debate over what constituted marginal costs in the presence of competition. *See* ALFRED KAHN, THE POLITICS OF REGULATION: PRINCIPLES AND INSTITUTIONS 159–80 (1988) (showing how attempts to approximate marginal costs in railroading can leave firms with excess capacity and wide discrepancies between allowable rates and average total costs). And that left many railroads in desperate competitive shape. *See* Keeler, supra, at 207–08.

21 Thus, a typical freight rail tank car as a risk vector might be (1) designed or built differently; (2) propelled or controlled differently; (3) loaded differently; or (4) operated at greater or lesser distances from any potential dangers.

22 "High Hazard Flammable Trains" (HHFT) would include any train transporting ≥ 20 loaded tank cars containing Class 3 flammable liquids in a continuous block and any train transporting ≥ 35 such cars throughout the train. A "High Hazard Flammable Unit Train" (HHFUT) includes any train transporting ≥ 70 such cars. *See* 49 C.F.R. § 171.8 (2017). Class 3 flammable liquids include (with some exceptions) liquids having a flash point of not more than 60°C (140°F) and any material in a liquid phase with a flash point at or above 37.8°C (100°F) that is intentionally heated and offered for transportation or transported at or above its flash point in a bulk packaging. Id. at § 173.120(a). Crude oil and ethanol are at least Class 3 flammable liquids. Crude may be classified more restrictively depending on its origins and treatment.

23 *Cf.* JOHN OBERDIEK, IMPOSING RISK: A NORMATIVE FRAMEWORK 10 (2017) ("In modern life, dependent upon risk as it is, everyone's lives are in the hands of others to some extent. But the investiture of this authority in others is only partial; there is a limit to the extent that our lives can permissibly be in another's hands and still be our lives in the relevant respect.").

safety specifications like head and thermal protection systems and, in turn, revealed a tank car fleet that had mostly been offloaded to shippers (or their vendors).[24] So with railroads dependent on shippers to provide sound equipment that could be a matter of long- or short-term contracting,[25] characterizing shipments, routing cars across different railroads, pairing the correct equipment, and handling protocols had often devolved into (strategized) efforts to capture surplus value.[26] Thus, enhancing (1) train control, (2) crash-worthiness, or (3) emergency preparedness could thus each become their own welfare- and cost-optimization struggles. The owners (or crew) of locomotives, tracks, and/or train cars would surely bear the costs (and risks) quite differently from proximate communities, residents, bystanders, or passenger train-goers involved in crashes.

As FRA and PHMSA conducted the HMR-251 rulemaking, 3,200 "public" comments were amassed while detailed and sustained conversations with shippers and railroads progressed.[27] The projections of

---

[24] *See* TRANSPORTATION RESEARCH BOARD, ENSURING RAILROAD TANK CAR SAFETY 107–11 (1994) (hereafter "ENSURING TANK CAR SAFETY"). "Many large shippers operate their own tank car maintenance and repair shops and employ tank car engineers to help design new tank cars and periodically inspect the fabrication and repair shops used to supply and service the fleet." Id. at 53.

[25] *See* id. at 54.

[26] *See* Thomas M. Palay, *Comparative Institutional Economics: The Governance of Rail Freight Contracting*, 13 J. LEGAL STUD. 265, 270–86 (1984) (reviewing the informal sanctions and other means available to carriers and shippers engaged in repeat-play dealings); *cf.* Transport. Safety Bd. of Canada, *Railway Investigation Report R13D0054: Runaway and Main-Track Derailment: Montreal, Maine & Atlantic Railway* 112–13 (2013) (concluding that crude at Lac Mégantic was improperly handled by railroad because its classification documents were not properly reconciled after lading), *available at* http://www.tsb.gc.ca/eng/rapports-reports/rail/2013/r13d0054/r13d0054.pdf. Even co-operative parties may struggle under such circumstances to share the surpluses created. *See* Steven N.S. Cheung, *The Contractual Nature of the Firm*, 36 J. L. & ECON. 1, 3–10 (1983). But given their frequent encounters with insolvency, railroads' structuring their assets to avoid tank car ownership may have had more to do with access to credit than anything else. *See* George Triantis, *The Personification and Property of Legal Entities, in* RESEARCH HANDBOOK ON THE ECONOMICS OF PROPERTY LAW 190 (Kenneth Ayotte & Henry E. Smith eds., 2011).

[27] *See* HHFT Final Rule, 80 Fed. Reg. at 26723; *see also* Hannah J. Wiseman, *Negotiated Rulemaking and New Risks: A Rail Safety Case Study*, 7

future shipments, derailments, and potential damages all sharpened the divides among those participating. When the final rule emerged, it mixed speed limits, enhanced shipment characterization requirements, a tank car redesign and retrofit schedule, routing, and crew integrity constraints.[28] Nothing aroused as much rancor, however, as the requirement that trains carrying flammable liquids in bulk have installed so-called "electronically controlled pneumatic" (ECP) braking systems.[29] ECP brakes came to be at the center of a regulatory mêlée, prompting Congress to legislate a resolution—or something like it.[30]

In the 1870s, after more than 40 years of stopping trains with hand brakes, American railroads began equipping their passenger trains with the Westinghouse airbrake.[31] But it took an Act of Congress to force the adoption of airbrakes by many of those same firms on their freight trains by the turn of the twentieth century.[32] Railroads resisted the expense, confident that they could do without the brake.[33] Gradually, as experience on some western railroads mounted, it became evident that the airbrake was a superior technology which could lead to significant business gains in rail[34]—after a massive capital turnover. That chapter of rail history

---

WAKE FOREST J. LAW & POL'Y 207, 221–26 (2017) (describing the range of industry groups participating in the rulemaking and the close relationships with FRA).

28 *See* HHFT Final Rule, 80 Fed. Reg. at 26649–53.

29 *See* HHFT Final Rule, 80 Fed. Reg. at 26692–703; U.S. Government Accountability Office, *Train Braking: DOT's Rulemaking on Electronically Controlled Pneumatic Brakes Could Benefit from Additional Data and Transparency* (Oct. 2016) (GAO-17-122) (hereafter GAO, "*ECP Report*"), *available at* https://www.gao.gov/products/GAO-17-122.

30 *See* Section 6.2.

31 *See* Steven W. Usselman, *Air Brakes for Freight Trains: Technological Innovation in the American Railroad Industry, 1869–1900*, 58(1) BUS. HIST. REV. 30, 30–31 (1984). The Westinghouse airbrake was revolutionary in its time for the use of compressed air lines governed from a locomotive that exerted as much braking power as handbrakes applied by brakemen from individual cars. Id. at 32–33.

32 *See* id. at 47–48. The railroads fought Westinghouse in a variety of ways, including through very public "trials" of his brakes where they supposedly failed to operate to the railroads' satisfaction, and only relented to Congress's "Safety Appliance Act" in 1893 because of the overwhelming public support behind the bill. Id. That law provided ample lead time and was twice amended to provide more. By 1900, the airbrake was finally standard equipment for all trains. Id.

33 *See* id. at 34.

34 This was the era of track gauge standardization as well. *See* id. at 35 ("The standard gauge enabled railroads to ship goods long distances over tracks

frames the question posed in crude-by-rail's ECP brake problem: Was enhanced braking technology a step to a better rail system or merely an unjustified burden on a perennially struggling sector?

6.1 DESIGN STANDARDS, COST AVOIDANCE, AND CAPTURE: REGULATING THE REGULATORS?

The US rail sector had barely escaped the struggles of rate, wage, and service regulation[35] when it took on contemporary risk regulation.[36] It was the first industrial sector to convince the American public and its representatives that corporate decision making will ignore the common good wherever corporate costs can be externalized.[37] Since the end of rate/service regulation, railroads struggled to achieve consistent profitability[38] while economists have struggled to measure rail's productivity.[39] As technology has evolved, so has the industry's capital—both human

---

owned by many companies without transferring the merchandize to cars of different gauges. This practice simplified the movement of goods but complicated the movement of cars. ... A fifty-car train might include cars owned by twenty or more railroads."). Western roads faced steep grades and fewer interchangeability issues, which is where Westinghouse had his first success selling the airbrake to freight railroads. Id. at 34–39.

35 *See* K. AUSTIN KERR, AMERICAN RAILROAD POLITICS, 1914–1920: RATES, WAGES AND EFFICIENCY (1968); THE RAILROADS: THE NATION'S FIRST BIG BUSINESS (Alfred D. Chandler, Jr., ed. 1965); GABRIEL KOLKO, RAILROADS AND REGULATION, 1877–1916 (1965) (1970).

36 *See generally* MARK ALDRICH, DEATH RODE THE RAILS: AMERICAN RAILROAD ACCIDENTS AND SAFETY, 1828–1965 (1985); ALDRICH, BACK ON TRACK, supra note 13.

37 *See* THOMAS K. MCCRAW, PROPHETS OF REGULATION 25–31, 40–44 (1984).

38 *See* Lee *et al.*, supra note 20 at 54–56. Many predicted that deregulation would lead railroads back to profitability. *See* John D. Bitzan & Theodore E. Keeler, *Economies of Density and Regulatory Change in the U.S. Railroad Freight Industry*, 50 J. LAW & ECON. 157, & n.1 (2007).

39 *See* Tae Hoon Oum *et al.*, *A Survey of Productivity and Efficiency Measurement in Rail Transport*, 33(1) J. TRANSP. ECON. & POL'Y 9, 9–10 (1999); Douglas W. Caves *et al.*, *Productivity in U.S. Railroads, 1951–1974*, 11(1) BELL J. ECON. 166, 166 (1980). "Since 1945, railways in most countries have experienced a declining market share, rising input prices, and increasing competition from other modes of transport." Oum *et al.*, supra, at 9. This has arguably increased the importance of input factor costs in judging rail's productivity gains. *See* Caves *et al.*, supra, at 180.

and physical.[40] Once deregulation freed railroads to pursue only the business they expected to be profitable, they shed passenger operations and aimed for traffic-dense commodity hauls[41]—making tank car contracts vital. By some measures, productivity soared: From 1980 to 2002, revenue ton-miles per employee hour increased about 320 percent while gallons of fuel per revenue ton-mile dropped more than 40 percent.[42] But the search for tank car engineering and control standards—whether public or private—remained assiduously cost conscious.[43]

Neither FRA nor PHMSA lacks the statutory authority to use less prescriptive standards nor even to use tools like taxes or fees.[44] Of course, calibrating and using such tools entails informational burdens of perhaps insuperable magnitude under their circumstances.[45] The Hazardous

---

[40] *Cf.* John D. Bitzan & Theodore E. Keeler, *Productivity Growth and Some of its Determinants in the Deregulated U.S. Railroad Industry*, 70(2) SOUTH. ECON. J. 232, 233–34 (2003) (noting that the substitution of steam with diesel locomotives should have entailed immediate crew-size shrinkage but that labor unions and labor laws probably prevented such cost-cutting actions from being taken); Lee *et al.*, supra note 20 at 58 (finding that Class I railroads shrank locomotive and car fleets by 10% and 16%, respectively, and employees by 37% from 1971 to 1984).

[41] *See* Bitzan & Keeler, *Economies of Density*, supra note 38 at 166–71.

[42] *See* Jose Manuel Vassallo & Mark Fagan, *Nature or Nurture: Why Do Railroads Carry Greater Freight Share in the United States than in Europe?*, 34 TRANSPORTATION 177, 180 (2007).

[43] *See* ENSURING TANK CAR SAFETY, supra note 24; ALDRICH, BACK ON TRACK, supra note 13 at 81–113.

[44] FRA was created by the Department of Transportation Act of 1966, Pub. L. No 89-670, 80 Stat. 931 (1966), and has long been tasked with the safety and security of US rail transit. Since 1970, FRA has had the authority to "prescribe, as necessary, appropriate rules, regulations, orders, and standards for all areas of railroad safety … ." Pub. L. No. 91-458, 84 Stat. 971, 971 (1970) (§ 202), *codified at* 49 U.S.C. § 5103(b).

[45] Usefully categorizing risk regulatory actions distributes them according to (1) who pays; (2) who decides; and (3) which of these roles government either assumes or structures. *See* Kenneth R. Richards, *Framing Environmental Policy Instrument Choice*, 10 DUKE ENVTL. L. & POL'Y F. 221, 232–54 (2000). Finally, tool choice, *e.g.*, Pigovian taxes over performance standards, must necessarily include consideration of the institution making that choice and the information available to it. *See, e.g.*, DANIEL H. COLE, POLLUTION AND PROPERTY: COMPARING OWNERSHIP INSTITUTIONS FOR ENVIRONMENTAL PROTECTION 46–84 (2002); NEIL K. KOMESAR, LAW'S LIMITS: THE RULE OF LAW AND THE SUPPLY AND DEMAND OF RIGHTS 35–52 (2001).

Materials Transportation Act of 1975[46] empowered the Secretary of Transportation (Secretary) to "prescribe regulations for the safe transportation, including security, of hazardous material in intrastrate, interstate, and foreign commerce,"[47] authority the Secretary has delegated to PHMSA.[48] Unlike PHMSA's pipeline safety and security standards (which face stringent cost-benefit testing required by statute[49]), its delegated authority to regulate hazardous materials transport includes *no* mandate that it weigh costs. Yet Executive Orders 12866 and 13563 ostensibly imposed duties on PHMSA in HMR-251 that it take only those measures it could show "maximize net benefits,"[50] that "impose the least burden on society, including individuals, businesses of different sizes and other entities" and that, "consistent with obtaining the regulatory objectives, taking into account, among other things, and to the extent practicable, the costs of cumulative regulations,"[51] PHMSA determines (subject to OMB review), using "the best available techniques to quantify anticipated present and future benefits and costs as accurately as possible,"[52] are cost justified.[53]

---

46 Pub. L. No. 93-933, 88 Stat. 2156 (1975), *codified at* 49 U.S.C. §§ 5101–28.

47 49 U.S.C. § 5103(b).

48 *See* 49 C.F.R. § 1.97(b) (2017).

49 *See* 49 U.S.C. § 60102. In terms, PHMSA's pipeline standards must be "practicable" and must balance "relevant available" pipeline safety information, hazard information, the "reasonableness" of the standard, the "reasonably identifiable or estimated" benefits and costs of the standard, and input from the principal constituencies thereon. Id. at § 60102(b)(2).

50 Executive Order 12866—Regulatory Planning and Review, 58 Fed. Reg. 51735, 51735 (1993) (§ 1(a)). Notably, PHMSA prefaced its new tank car, the DOT 117, by explaining that it had sought "to ensure that the car selected will have the greatest net social benefits, with benefits primarily generated from mitigation of accident severity." HHFT Final Rule, 80 Fed. Reg. at 26666.

51 Executive Order 12866—Regulatory Planning and Review, 58 Fed. Reg. 51735, 51736 (1993) (§ 1(b)(11)); Executive Order 13563—Improving Regulation and Regulatory Review, 76 Fed. Reg. 3821, 3821 (2011) (§ 1(b)(2)).

52 Executive Order 13563—Improving Regulation and Regulatory Review, 76 Fed. Reg. 3821, 3821 (2011) (§ 1(c)).

53 Executive Order 12866—Regulatory Planning and Review, 58 Fed. Reg. 51735, 51735 (1993) (§ 1(b)(6)); Executive Order 13563—Improving Regulation and Regulatory Review, 76 Fed. Reg. 3821, 3821 (2011) (§ 1(b)(1)). Executive Order 12866 variously orders that regulations, upon completion, be the result of a "reasoned determination that the benefits of the intended regulation justify its costs," id. at § 1(b)(6), and that it "design its regulations" in the most "cost-effective manner to achieve the regulatory objective." Id. at § 1(b)(5). Though

Notably, no judicial challenge was brought against the weighing of all that in the shadow of two statutory delegations that were silent on regulatory costs.[54]

For 30+ years, successive presidential administrations have issued orders like this.[55] The Trump Administration's order purports to create a "[r]egulatory [c]ap" wherein any new regulatory costs must supposedly be "offset by the elimination of existing costs associated with at least two prior regulations,"[56] although it also cautioned that the order is to be "implemented consistent with applicable law" and does not create "any right or benefit, substantive or procedural enforceable in law or in equity."[57] The Obama Administration's orders governing PHMSA's HMR-251 "regulatory impact analyses" (RIAs)[58] ostensibly *required* the detailed, quantitative analysis of braking, speed limit, crew integrity, rail routing, hazard notification, spill response, packing protocol, and car integrity alternatives which PHMSA prepared.[59]

Executive Order 13563 reiterates many of 12866's enumerated "principles," it made no mention of this "cost-effectiveness" criterion.

[54] Of course, Clean Air Act § 109(b)'s silence on the factoring of costs into the setting of its "national ambient air quality standards" was held to preclude US EPA's weighing of costs therein. *See* Chapter 1, Section 1.3.

[55] *See* Exec. Order 12291, § 3, 3 C.F.R. 127, 128–30 (1982), *revoked by* Exec. Order No. 12866 § 11, 3 C.F.R. 638, 649 (1994); Exec. Order 13563, 3 C.F.R. 215, *reprinted in* 5 U.S.C. § 601 app. at 101–02. *See also* Christopher C. DeMuth & Douglas H. Ginsburg, *White House Review of Agency Rulemaking*, 99 Harv. L. Rev. 1075 (1986).

[56] Executive Order 13771—Reducing Regulation and Controlling Regulatory Costs, 82 Fed. Reg. 9339, 9339 (2017) (§§ 1–2); *see also* Executive Order 13777—Enforcing the Regulatory Reform Agenda, 82 Fed. Reg. 12285 (2017). This pair of orders may not be the last effort to overhaul regulatory review. The George W. Bush Administration's order was not issued until late in the second term. *See* Executive Order 13422—Further Amendment to Executive Order 12866 On Regulatory Planning and Review, 72 Fed. Reg. 2763 (2007), *abrogated by* Executive Order 13497—Revocation of Certain Executive Orders Concerning Regulatory Planning and Review, 74 Fed. Reg. 6113 (2009).

[57] Executive Order 13771—Reducing Regulation and Controlling Regulatory Costs, 82 Fed. Reg. 9339, 9339 (2017) (§ 2(c)).

[58] The Obama White House retained Executive Order 12866 but aimed to build significantly thereon. *See* Nina A. Mendelson & Jonathan B. Wiener, *Responding to Agency Avoidance of OIRA*, 37 Harv. J. L. & Pub. Pol'y 447, 457–63 (2014).

[59] *See* HHFT Final Rule, 80 Fed. Reg. at 26649–54, 26718–24; *see also* U.S. Pipeline and Hazardous Materials Safety Admin., Final Regulatory Impact Analysis—Hazardous Materials: Enhanced Tank Car Standards and Operational Controls for High-Hazard Flammable Trains (May 2015), *available at* https://

On one hand, this approach, begun in President Reagan's Executive Order 12291,[60] is a curious path to improving regulation.[61] It arguably elevates generic approximations of rationality above practiced professional judgments by subject matter experts in context.[62] Several of the economists of that era, miffed at Porter and others suggesting that their cost assessments needed to improve, stammered that "[i]t is impossible to escape the conclusion that the U.S. devotes significant resources, *net of cost savings*, to environmental protection each year."[63] Except that it was *not* impossible to escape that conclusion, at least if by "cost" we mean costs not balanced out by someone else's benefits.

Both FRA and PHMSA have long been accused of being "captured" by the industries they ostensibly regulate.[64] But centralizing their authority in the hands of a White House office may do no better.[65] Still, an RIA

---

www.regulations.gov/document?D=PHMSA-2012-0082-3442 (hereafter "HHFT Final RIA").

60 *See* Executive Order 12291—Federal Regulation, 46 Fed. Reg. 13193, 13193 (1981) (§ 2(b)) (requiring that regulatory action, "to the extent permitted by law," "shall not be undertaken unless the potential benefits to society for the regulation outweigh the potential costs to society").

61 *Cf.* Alan B. Morrison, *OMB Interference with Agency Rulemaking: The Wrong Way to Write a Regulation*, 99 HARV. L. REV. 1059, 1060–63 (1986) (observing that "[t]o understand how a President [Reagan], who campaigned in part on his abhorrence of centralized power, came to place the entire federal regulatory process under the control of a single office [OMB]," the origins of broad delegations to regulate risk by rulemakings and the inevitability of occasional agency mistakes is needed background).

62 *See* THOMAS O. MCGARITY, REINVENTING RATIONALITY: THE ROLE OF REGULATORY ANALYSIS IN THE FEDERAL BUREAUCRACY 6–16 (1991). This is often brought to the defense of OMB-imposed cost-benefit analysis's "neutrality" among ultimate goods/ends. *See, e.g.*, RICHARD L. REVESZ & MICHAEL A. LIVERMORE, RETAKING RATIONALITY 165–68 (2008).

63 Karen Palmer *et al.*, *Tightening Environmental Standards: The Benefit-Cost or the No-Cost Paradigm*, 9(4) J. ECON. PERSP. 119, 128 (1995) (emphasis in original). Then-Vice President Al Gore had famously touted one of Porter's exemplars, 3M, in his book. *See* AL GORE, EARTH IN THE BALANCE: ECOLOGY AND THE HUMAN SPIRIT 342 (1992). This had the noticeable effect of politicizing Porter's work, a fact evident in the strident tone of Palmer and colleagues' attempted rebuttal.

64 *See, e.g.*, Nicholas Bagley, *Agency Hygiene*, 89(1) TEX. L. REV. *See also* 1, 3–10 (2010) (*discussing* PHMSA); ALDRICH, BACK ON TRACK, supra note 13 at 106 (*discussing* FRA).

65 *Cf.* Michael A. Livermore, *Cost-Benefit Analysis and Agency Independence*, 81 U. CHI. L. REV. 609 (2014) (finding that cost-benefit analysis's effects on agency autonomy and independence from the President are ambiguous).

prepared by one agency (PHMSA) estimating proposed solutions' costs in another agency's industry (FRA's) for "generalist" reviewers lacking ties to or exchanged personnel in that industry[66] would at least raise the political responsibility for balancing decisions that might otherwise remain rather obscure.[67]

PHMSA estimated the expected costs of the final rule's five different "requirement areas," *i.e.*, routing, tank car design, speed limits, braking, and crude classification, versus the expected benefits thereof.[68] After trimmings meant to eliminate double counting, its RIA identified the final rule's mix of requirements as yielding the highest expected net benefits of the alternatives examined.[69] The rule combined phased implementation of new braking equipment and new tank cars (with lead times out to 2021), speed limits, and train sizing thresholds for the foregoing in an impressive optimization effort.[70] *Assuming continued growth* in domestic crude and ethanol production, the agencies concluded that a growing number of train accidents involving these shipments would raise the probability of a "catastrophic" train accident and that, therefore, the benefit-cost balance over the ensuing 20 years would be (at a 7 percent discount rate) approximately $2.48 billion in costs of compliance and between $912 million and $2.9 billion in averted-risk benefits.[71] Those costs were the result of a static, partial equilibrium analysis,[72] perhaps justified given the

---

[66] *Cf.* McGarity, supra note 62 at 281–88 (noting that interagency disclosures can be an important source of transparency and accountability which RIAs create).

[67] *See* Revesz & Livermore supra note 62 at 1359–60.

[68] *See* HHFT Final RIA, supra note 59 at 288–95.

[69] Id. at 295 ("The Final Rule appears to be the best compromise between enhanced safety and cost.").

[70] *Cf.* HHFT Final Rule, 80 Fed. Reg. at 26698 ("By focusing the ECP brake system requirements on trains over [a] 70-car threshold that travel in excess of 30 mph, we ensure that trains with the greatest associated risk (based on volume of product) will be equipped with the advanced brake signal propagation system that has the highest known effectiveness in reducing the kinetic energy of a train during a derailment.").

[71] *See* HHFT Final Rule, 80 Fed. Reg. at 26723–24 (Table 4). This key assumption would later occasion a significant revision of the RIA in 2017 after Congress had become involved. *See* Section 6.2.

[72] The vast majority of the costs comprising the aggregate estimates were from the purchase prices of new tank cars, new braking equipment, and the retrofitting of existing DOT-111 legacy tank cars. *See* HHFT Final RIA, supra note 59 at 12 (Table ES3). That total aligned against damage estimates for continued allowance of the status quo. Id. That the agencies' focus began and remained on high-profile accidents like Lac Mégantic was evident from the

tool choice, *i.e.*, design standards.[73] But it left the analysis wide open to powerful objections if/when the straight-line assumptions from which it proceeded, *e.g.*, assuming continued growth in crude and ethanol by rail, failed.[74] And despite the industry's structure—with shippers owning/leasing the vast majority of tank cars—no uncertainty seemed to qualify the cost estimates reported in the final rulemaking notice. (This was especially curious given the contentious accounting the agencies offered of the business benefits from rail's adoption of ECP brakes.[75])

A range of estimated benefits expresses uncertainty—about future rail traffic, accident rates, how penetration of the required technologies would affect these values, *etc.*[76] FRA and PHMSA were both well initiated in the use of design standards,[77] often stemming from specific tragedies and the technology that was thought to have been available but missing at ill-fated events.[78] To them, speed limits, whether applied to "high-consequence" urban areas or throughout the rail system for all so-called

---

structure of their amendments to the HMR. *Cf.* id. at 27 ("Our intent is to address the risks posed by large blocks or unit train shipments of flammable liquids.").

[73] The tank car specification adopted (new "DOT 117"), *see* HHFT Final Rule, 80 Fed. Reg. at 26666–75, was complemented by a "performance standard compliance alternative," id. at 26679–80, where the car proponent could receive DOT approval based on stringent criteria amounting, in practical effect, to the spec car.

[74] *See* Section 6.2.

[75] *See* Section 6.1.2.

[76] *See* HHFT Final RIA, supra note 59 at 73–85.

[77] *See* Cary Coglianese *et al.*, *Performance-Based Regulation: Prospects and Limitations in Health, Safety, and Environmental Protection*, 55 ADMIN. L. REV. 706, 709 (2003) ("In contrast to a design standard or a technology-based standard that specifies exactly how to achieve compliance, a performance standard sets a goal and lets each regulated entity decide how to meet it.").

[78] *See* ALDRICH, BACK ON TRACK, supra note 13 at 223–24 (Appendix I). FRA's railroad safety mandates stem from a patchwork of authorizing statutes, beginning from the Federal Railroad Safety Act of 1970, Pub. L. No. 91-458, 84 Stat. 971 (1970), the Railroad Safety Enforcement and Review Act, Pub. L. No. 102-365, 106 Stat. 972 (1992), the Rail Safety Improvement Act of 2008, Pub. L. No. 110-432, 122 Stat. 4848 (2008), and the Fixing America's Surface Transportation Act, Pub. L. No. 114-94, 129 Stat. 1312 (2015), *codified at* 49 U.S.C. §§ 20101 *et seq.* The statutes pre-empting state and local laws pertaining to railroad safety are numerous and dissonant. *See* Auburn v. United States, 154 F.3d 1025 (9th Cir. 1998); Norfolk So. Rwy. Co. v. City of Alexandria, 608 F.3d 150, 157–58 (4th Cir. 2010). PHMSA's various authorities stem from the Natural Gas Pipeline Safety Act, Pub. L. No. 90-481, 82 Stat. 720 (1968), the Hazardous Liquid Pipeline Act, Pub. L. No. 96-129, 93 Stat. 989 (1979), and, more recently, the Hazardous Materials Transportation Uniform Safety Act, Pub. L. No.

HHFTs, entailed imprecision: Slow trains can slow anyone behind them, anyone waiting for them to pass, or anyone waiting on their rolling stock.[79] Improving the technology of trains is something else: It always presents the prospect of productivity enhancements. So the struggle that ensued over the *distribution* of on-train regulatory costs as between railroads—large and small—and shippers grew both contentious and public.[80] Indeed, the magnitude and distribution of the equipment costs to befall railroads and tank car fleet owners were difficult even for the agencies to pin down, ultimately having to back them out of the component changes' expected costs to the average unit.[81]

From its very beginnings before common law courts confronting similar choices, however, the accuracy of estimates like this has determined the coherence of utilitarian arguments.[82] Minimizing the costs of society's supra-compensatory responses to risk has sustained a long,

---

101-615, 102 Stat. 3244 (1990), and the Pipeline Safety Improvement Act, Pub. L. No. 107-355, 116 Stat. 2985 (2002), *codified a*t 49 U.S.C. § 5101–5128.

[79] *See* HHFT Final Rule, 80 Fed. Reg. at 26686 (relaying comments of American Association of Private Rail Car Owners, Amtrak, and others that slowing of the entire rail system would result from HHFT speed limits).

[80] *Cf.* Robert Wright, *Union Pacific Takes Aim at Oil Train Rules*, FINAN. TIMES, June 1, 2015, at 16 (noting railroads' attacks on new braking requirements and complaints that tank car standards were not stringent enough). In its denial of appeals—a prerequisite to any judicial challenge of the rulemaking—the agencies heard competing attacks on the tank car redesign and retrofit requirements (from shippers) and the advanced braking options (from railroads). *See* Dept. of Transp., Pipeline and Hazardous Materials Safety Administration, Hazardous Materials: Enhanced Tank Car Standards and Operational Controls for High-Hazard Flammable Trains, 80 Fed. Reg. 71952, 71959–73 (2015) (hereafter PHMSA, "Appeals Denial").

[81] *Compare* HHFT ANPRM, 78 Fed. Reg. at 54855 (reporting that PHMSA had "received an estimate of the increased costs associated with" upgrading tank cars to the CPC-1232 standard of "approximately $18,000 more than a car built to the standard [then] required by the HMR"), *with* Dept. of Transp., Pipeline and Hazardous Materials Safety Admin., Hazardous Materials: FAST Act Requirements for Flammable Liquids and Rail Tank Cars, 81 Fed. Reg. 53935, 53944 (2016) (noting that "tank car purchase prices are difficult to obtain" and estimating car cost differentials from build material and spec differences).

[82] *See* GERALD J. POSTEMA, BENTHAM AND THE COMMON LAW TRADITION 440–64 (1986).

contentious search for mechanisms that optimize in the face of both cost- and benefit-uncertainty.[83] If cost-uncertainty is high enough, though, even conducting a rational search for the right tools becomes a challenge.[84] So it may have been fully rational, once the ECP brake and tank car upgrades were identified, simply to stop searching for other potential solutions.

We have seen throughout that mandatory capital turnovers can lead in different directions, some of which may offset the lost opportunities or other costs incurred as the capital expense.[85] Among the major determinants in such dynamics are the efficiencies and/or bottlenecks arising from enforced diffusion—two questions that arose repeatedly in the HMR-251 rulemaking.[86] Experience suggests that it will usually come down to granular technical details, the strategies and opportunity sets of the regulated, and the savvy with which regulators can scheme out the requirements they ultimately set. In the HMR-251 notice of proposed rulemaking, PHMSA identified 27 different factors to be balanced in distributing the costs of enhanced freight rail safety.[87] At finalization, this had become a 20-year costs-to-benefits comparison of particular stand-alone regulatory amendments, with benefits all expressed in (massive) ranges and costs simply discounted to present values at 7 percent.[88] Lurking within the numbers, however, were the many uncertainties of potential cost offsets.

---

[83] *See generally* Louis Kaplow & Steven Shavell, *Property Rules versus Liability Rules: An Economic Analysis*, 109 HARV. L. REV. 713 (1996); Steven Shavell, *Liability for Harm versus Regulations of Safety*, 13 J. LEGAL STUD. 357 (1984).

[84] *Cf.* Stewart E. Sterk, *Property Rules, Liability Rules, and Uncertainty About Property Rights*, 106 MICH. L. REV. 1285, 1299–304 (2008) (demonstrating ways in which parties searching for information clarifying their respective rights and duties can incur search costs far in excess of any benefits to be gained from added increment of right- or duty-certainty).

[85] *See* Stefan Ambec *et al.*, *The Porter Hypothesis at 20: Can Environmental Regulation Enhance Innovation and Competitiveness?*, 7(1) REV. ENVTL. ECON. & POL'Y 22, 3–9 (2013) (reviewing "variations" and the candidate causal explanations behind the "Porter Hypothesis" that business benefits often accrue to those motivated to change by regulatory action).

[86] *See, e.g.*, HHFT Final Rule, 80 Fed. Reg. at 26676–77 (*discussing* industry "shop capacity" to produce replacement cars); id. at 26695–98 (*discussing* purported flaws and weaknesses like the possibility of "crosstalk" between electronic brake systems from train to train).

[87] *See* HHFT NPRM, 79 Fed. Reg. at 45029 (Table 10).

[88] *See* HHFT Final Rule, 80 Fed. Reg. at 26649 (Table 4).

6.1.1 Train Control Economics: Of Brakes, Business Benefits, and Human Error

Every specification/design standard trades off innovation in the thing specified for the potential benefits of enforced diffusion.[89] Making a widget to someone else's design specifications, all things equal, will be costlier than having the freedom to design it but a guaranteed demand for that widget will surely defray the excess costs' impacts. That standardization is so often the key to profits in transporting energy merely raised the stakes in tank car/flammable liquid standards.[90] Enforced diffusion, we might say, could spur increasing returns in the sector[91] but it could also backfire if supply fails and/or the design itself was flawed.[92] The industry's own efforts to enhance tank car specifications in 2011 illustrate.[93] Rail was at least united against its modal competition and a

---

[89] *See* Coglianese *et al.*, supra note 77 at 713. Regulators can avoid *prohibiting* innovation with the right attention to leaving open the possibility of a performance-based alternative. *See* id. at 713 ("One approach is to require specific technologies or designs, but to add to the regulation so-called equivalency clauses or provisions for alternative compliance mechanisms."); *cf.* Nicholas A. Ashford *et al.*, *Using Regulation to Change the Market for Innovation*, 9 HARV. ENVTL. L. REV. 419, 425–29 (1985) (observing that this innovation/diffusion curve may be wholly within the regulated sector or may involve vendors and/or related industries); Herman R.J. Vollebergh & Edwin van der Werf, *The Role of Standards in Eco-innovations: Lessons for Policymakers*, 8(2) REV. ENVTL. ECON. & POL'Y 230, 232–41 (2014) (arguing that the larger the market touched by any kind of standardization, the larger the incentives to invent around or in concert with the standard(s)).

[90] *See* John W. Bagby, *How Standardization Will Balance Sustainability Goals in the Transport Component of Energy Supply Chains: Efficiency versus Environmental Safety*, 54(1) TRANSP. J. 136 (2015). From the outset of the HMR-251 rulemaking it was known that ethanol and crude were the only flammable liquids known to be transported by freight rail in ≥ 20 carloads at a time. *See* HHFT NPRM, 79 Fed. Reg. at 45040.

[91] *See* Ashford *et al.*, supra note 89 at 463; Vollebergh & van der Werf, supra note 89 at 236–37.

[92] *See* Richard B. Stewart, *Regulation, Innovation, and Administrative Law: A Conceptual Framework*, 69 CAL. L. REV. 1256 (1981).

[93] In 2011, the American Association of Railroads (AAR) issued Casualty Prevention Circular (CPC) 1232, setting forth key upgrades to the DOT Specification 111 (DOT-111) tank car construction. *See* HHFT NPRM, 79 Fed. Reg. at 45026. CPC 1232 was issued after the National Transportation Safety Board (NTSB) had concluded from a notorious derailment at Cherry Valley, Illinois, that DOT-111 tank cars should be expected to breach in virtually all derailments involving car-to-car impacts. Id. at 45025–26. In a September 2013 notice,

private standard tank car upgrade offered the prospect of forestalling costlier public action.[94] By the time PHMSA's proposed rule emerged, however, the industry's own upgraded tank car had become but a feasibility demonstration;[95] a means of challenging rail to do better still.[96]

New tank car specifications and old car retrofitting schedules (which included lengthy lead-in intervals) were eventually set.[97] Coordinating with Rail Canada would ensure that the North American DOT-111 tank

---

PHMSA announced a petition from AAR for rulemaking establishing new DOT specifications for a tank car based on the CPC 1232-enhanced DOT-111. *See* U.S. Dept. of Transp., Pipeline and Hazardous Materials Safety Admin., Advance Notice of Proposed Rulemaking—Hazardous Materials: Rail Petitions and Recommendations to Improve the Safety of Railroad Tank Car Transportation (RRR), 78 Fed. Reg. 54849, 54854–55 (2013). The CPC 1232 enhancements were projected to add $18,000 in construction costs and 23,000 pounds in weight per car—increasing the fees railroads could charge per car but also increasing per-car shipments by 13–16,000 pounds. *See* id. at 54855–56.

[94] *See* Michael P. Vandenbergh, *Private Environmental Governance*, 99 CORNELL L. REV. 129, 186–87 (2013).

[95] Hardening tank cars and their puncture resistance makes them more robust in the event of a derailment but also increases the car's gross tare weight. *See* HHFT NPRM, 79 Fed. Reg. at 26675. Shippers eventually argued that this made the DOT 117 specification means-ends irrational because more cars/trains would be needed to transfer the same volume. *See* HHFT Final Rule, 80 Fed. Reg. at 26675. When tank car fabricators noted that the assumptions underlying that argument were faulty, PHMSA concluded that no such means-ends issues were presented, *see* id., perhaps because "PHMSA firmly believe[d] that reliance on HHFTs to transport millions of gallons of flammable liquids is a risk that must be addressed." Id. at 26676.

[96] *See* HHFT NPRM, 79 Fed. Reg. at 45030 ("DOT ... challenged the industry to consider additional improvements in puncture resistance, thermal protection, top fitting protection, bottom outlet protection, and braking, as well as railroad operations."); id. at 45031–33. The retrofit requirements for CPC-1232 cars were minor by comparison. *See* HHFT Final RIA, supra note 59 at 143. Ultimately, the CPC-1232 cars, if not upgraded to the standards of the new DOT-117R (by 2023 or 2025, depending on the version of CPC-1232), would only become ineligible for service in HHFT trains—not all of "Packing Group III." *See* HHFT Final Rule, 80 Fed. Reg. at 26675–76.

[97] The adopted specifications all aimed to increase the tank car's survivability, thereby mitigating damages in the event of derailment. *See* HHFT Final Rule, 80 Fed. Reg. at 26666 (describing tank shell thickness and material, bottom outlet protection, head shields, jacketing, and thermal blanket and top fittings protection).

car fleet of approximately 272,000 cars[98]—86,000 of which were estimated to be transporting crude and ethanol—faced a single transition.[99] Yet the industry's car set the baseline from which a new DOT-117's costs of compliance would be calculated.[100] The regulators chose their baseline from which to count deliberately. In effect, the enforced diffusion of hardened tank car enhancements, with a recent industry upgrade that had easily been shown to embody compromise and half measures,[101] slipped some of the cost (and deliberative) frictions which enhancing cars would have otherwise met by coming safely in the wake of Lac Mégantic and other derailments.[102] Hardened tank cars may be minimal insurance against *any* form of human error, but their incremental costs—at least when not held in comparison to other possible measures like speed limits[103]—probably would have been harder to justify were human error not as prominent an overall concern in the freight rail industry.

---

[98] This total represented substantial growth in the fleet from the Transportation Research Board's 1994 estimate of approximately 162,000 DOT-111 and similar AAR non-pressure tank cars then in service. *See* ENSURING TANK CAR SAFETY, supra note 24 at 43 (Table 2-2).

[99] *See* HHFT Final RIA, supra note 59 at 141. The DOT-111 and CPC-1232 cars were assumed to have life spans of 40 years and 50 years, respectively, id. at 149, and the fleet of cars in crude- and ethanol service was mostly built since 2000—about 28% of which were figured to be retired rather than retrofit. Id. at 151.

[100] *See* HHFT Final RIA, supra note 59 at 149 ("The CPC-1232 has been the industry standard for orders placed after October 2011, and PHMSA assumed that 100 percent of the newly constructed tank cars will be CPC-1232 … .").

[101] *Cf.* HHFT Final Rule, 80 Fed. Reg. 26669–70 (noting tank car fabricator's objection to CPC-1232 specifications as flawed and fabricator's argument that if a flawed standard were adopted by DOT it might require reconsideration soon thereafter).

[102] One principal ground of dispute over the CPC-1232 car and a more robust design was the weight penalty of using 9/16ths inch-thick steel for the tank shell over the CPC-1232's (and DOT-111's) 7/16ths. *See* Final HHFT Rule, 80 Fed. Reg. at 26675. The grade of steel was the same industry standard used for decades, as was the steel to comprise the tank "jacket." Id. at 26667 (Table 13). Although a tank car builder ultimately undermined the industry's arguments that the weight differences would make the standards means/ends irrational, PHMSA did not prepare a marginal analysis of weight-to-strength differences between the cars (at least not that it shared).

[103] *See* HHFT NPRM, 79 Fed. Reg. at 45040–45 (announcing the range of measures that would be considered with rough estimates of cost).

When attention turned to train control and revealed an industry mired in the transition to "positive train control" (PTC) automation (a legislative mandate which had come in response to the tragic Chatsworth commuter rail accident of 2008[104]), however, things tensed up. What the Rail Safety Improvement Act of 2008 (RSIA) said about PTC had left wide discretion to FRA.[105] FRA at least claimed it was aiming to balance the costs of retrofitting existing systems with the benefits of automated crash avoidance.[106] In superintending that transition for rail systems with intercity passenger operations and/or those carrying poison- or toxic-by-inhalation freight, FRA found that a range of technologies could potentially fulfill the precautionary functions Congress expected.[107] The projected costs of the performance standard FRA adopted in 2010 were almost 20 times the projected benefits,[108] though, fomenting a long struggle over the specifics thereafter.[109] Yet after a preliminary skirmish,

---

104 *See* HHFT Final Rule, 80 Fed. Reg. at 26697–703; *see also* ALDRICH, BACK ON TRACK, supra note 13 at 163–64 (describing collision of a freight train and a Metrolink passenger train because Metrolink driver missed a signal, killing 25 and seriously injuring 130 others). Chatsworth punctuated a series of such accidents involving failed "block" signaling and avoidable human errors. Id. at 159–67.

105 PTC as named in the RSIA was less a performance or technology mandate than an express preference for automation over human control in speed and track-switching meant to avoid train-to-train crashes and incursions into work zones. *See* RSIA, Pub. L. No. 110-43, 122 Stat. 4848, 4858 at § 104(i)(3), *codified at* 49 U.S.C. § 20157(i)(3) (defining "positive train control").

106 *See* U.S. Dept. of Transp., Federal Railroad Administration, Final Rule—Positive Train Control Systems, 75 Fed. Reg. 2598 (2010) (finalizing rules implementing RSIA and positive train control systems required thereby); *see* Pub. L. No. 110-432, 122 Stat. 4848, 4856 at § 104 (2008), *codified at* 49 U.S.C. § 20157 (requiring each covered railroad establish a "positive train control system"). Although PTC systems had been under voluntary development since 2006, "the widespread deployment of … various [PTC systems] remained very much constrained by prohibitive capital costs." 75 Fed. Reg. at 2601.

107 *See* Final Rule—Positive Train Control Systems, 75 Fed. Reg. at 2604–05. This led the agency to require that each covered railroad create its own PTC-implementation plan from among a menu of approved or suggested technologies. Id. at 2637–57.

108 *See* id. at 2684–85 (projecting expected costs of PTC mandate around $13.21 billion (present discounted value at 3%) and expected benefits around $674 million (same)).

109 Several subsequent adjustments to the rules were aimed at reducing costs of compliance where only marginal safety gains were available. *See* Dept. of Transp., Federal Railroad Admin., Final Rule—Positive Train Control Systems (RRR), 79 Fed. Reg. 49693, 49694 (2014) (reporting as "benefits to society" the

an industry challenge to the final PTC rule had gone nowhere because of how FRA had schemed its rule.[110]

Tellingly, the opposition to the "advanced braking signal propagation" mandate emerged early as HMR-251 settled on an ECP brake design standard.[111] ECP brakes, to the agencies, offered multiple avenues for cost-reducing efficiencies, *i.e.*, business benefits, in operation. ECP-equipped trains need fewer stops for brake inspections and tests, operate better in cold weather, improve handling of longer trains (potentially allowing train sizes to increase), improve braking ratios (allowing more time at optimal speed), reduce wear and tear on wheels, and improve fuel efficiency.[112] *Railway Age*, the premiere trade magazine, called ECP brakes the "most significant development in freight train braking since George Westinghouse."[113] Norfolk-Southern reportedly saved 800–900 gallons of fuel on one trip with a beta-test train operating ECP brakes.[114] But with so much projected as business benefits, *i.e.*, cost offsets, the ECP question quickly shifted: Why were railroads not adopting the brakes themselves?[115]

Predicting business benefits (cost avoidance), as noted throughout, is fraught with uncertainty. Matters worsen when the strategic dynamics between repeat-play business partners with divergent interests (for example shippers and railroads), the existence of modal competition like pipelines, and the hard ceiling of an "energy return on investment"

---

avoided costs of compliance being cut in the rulemaking's expansion of an exemption from PTC for various railroads and track systems).

[110] *See* Chlorine Institute, Inc. v. Federal Railroad Admin., 718 F.3d 922, 927–29 (D.C. Cir. 2013) (dismissing challenge to PTC rulemaking as not "ripe" for testing by federal courts in light of rule's requirement that each railroad fashion its own PTC implementation plan individually).

[111] *See* U.S. Government Accountability Office, Train Braking: DOT's Rule-making on Electronically Controlled Pneumatic Brakes Could Benefit from Additional Data and Transparency (Oct. 2016) (GAO-17-122) (hereafter "GAO, ECP Brake Audit"). In its proposal, PHMSA suggested an exception that would reduce ECP brakes' burden for "small carriers that may not have the capital available to install new braking systems—a speed limit for such carriers (30 mph). *See* HHFT NPRM, 79 Fed. Reg. at 45051.

[112] *See* HHFT Final RIA, supra note 59 at 234–37; HHFT Final Rule, 80 Fed. Reg. at 26693.

[113] ALDRICH, BACK ON TRACK, supra note 13 at 100.

[114] *See* id.

[115] *Cf.* HHFT Final RIA, supra note 59 at 34 ("One may question why, if ECP brakes have been widely accepted in Australia, railroads in the United States have not adopted ECP brakes at the same rate.").

profitability cap must factor into the calculus.[116] The ECP brake mandate would be costly to both roads and shippers and its projected business benefits would be contingent on learning, intra-industry cooperation, crew training, and the cost of capital.[117] Their united challenge to ECP brakes took aim at the *marginal* superiority of braking performance in the event of a (threatened) derailment as compared to standard air brakes.[118] From an epistemic standpoint, it was a shrewd gauntlet to throw down.

There is no standard or representative derailment from past occurrences, so the only tools available to PHMSA to answer the challenge were computer models.[119] PHMSA's modeling confirmed the intuitive: A braking system that deploys evenly, immediately, train-wide and that can modulate braking forces rather than locking up steel wheels on steel rails performs better, both overall and in the event of derailment, than a fully mechanical system.[120] NTSB's modeling agreed.[121] In-depth GAO interviews after the fact, however, showed that the American Association of Railroads (AAR) and its members came to view the agencies as deliberately understating the issues that would arise from an ECP braking mandate.[122] AAR and major shipper organizations had emphasized that, for ECP brakes to yield their benefits and achieve practical interoperability with other equipment, most of the freight rail rolling stock would have to be retrofitted and/or built for purpose.[123] So both shippers and

116 The "energy return on investment" (EROI) measures the quality of a fuel by calculating the ratio between the energy delivered thereby to its consumers and the energy needed for its capture and delivery. EROI can focus either on the net or surplus for a given project, industry, nation, *etc.*, and, for fuels like domestically produced corn-based ethanol, can raise unique challenges in having to account for public subsidies and/or mandates.

117 *See* HHFT Final RIA, supra note 59 at 218–28.

118 *See* id. at 213–16.

119 *See* HHFT Final Rule, 80 Fed. Reg. at 26699–700.

120 *See* HHFT Final RIA, supra note 59 at 207–12.

121 *See* National Transp. Safety Bd., *Train Braking Simulation Study: Train Derailment, Opposing Train Struck Derailed Car and Derailed, Fire and Evacuation* (July 20, 2015), copy on file with author.

122 *See* GAO, ECP Brake Audit, supra note 11 at 14–20 (noting that, contrary to agencies' statements that industry would need to equip about 2,500 locomotives and 60,000 tank cars with ECP brakes under HMR-251, AAR maintains the mandate would actually entail about 20,000 locomotives and 133,000 tank cars).

123 *Cf.* Dept. of Transp., Pipeline and Hazardous Materials Safety Admin., Hazardous Materials: Enhanced Tank Car Standards and Operational Controls for High-Hazard Flammable Trains—Response to Appeals, 80 Fed. Reg. 71952, 71962–64 (2015) (reviewing experiences with ECP brakes in Canada and

railroads opposed it, with the two roads that had originally petitioned FRA to allow ECP brake usage becoming vocal opponents after PHMSA had cited them in arguing potential business benefits.[124] They emphasized some (clearly fixable) glitches that had been observed in certain trials.[125] Mostly, though, they complained that ECP brakes were costly and would reduce risks only marginally.[126]

Of course organizing asset classes to minimize own production/transaction costs can put business partners at cross purposes when regulators have a choice of means at their disposal for constraining risk.[127] And railroad/shipper antagonisms surely run deep.[128] But what cost avoidance should we expect from among firms known to have structured and restructured their assets and organizations over time? The wave of mergers following deregulation allowed the largest railroads to

---

Australia and finding that, contrary to industry argument, interoperability with standard air brakes has not been problematic).

124 *See* HHFT Final Rule, 80 Fed. Reg. at 26697–98; *see also* GAO, ECP Brake Audit, supra note 11 at 48 (railroads generally refused to share information on ECP braking experiences).

125 *See* HHFT Final RIA, supra note 59 at 225 ("AAR has raised crosstalk and interoperability as the two primary technological issues that [affect] the ability of trains to operate in ECP brake mode. ... After further investigation into this problem, the ECP brake manufacturers were able to resolve this by updating the ECP brake software program.").

126 *See* GAO, ECP Brake Audit, supra note 11 at 10–48.

127 Optimizing asset assignment by contract and/or firm boundaries is the proverbial bread and butter of industrial organization and transaction cost economics. *See, e.g.*, Oliver Hart & John Moore, *Property Rights and the Nature of the Firm*, 98(6) J. POL. ECON. 1119 (1990). Whether firms generally tend to engage in rent-seeking, adaptation, incentive optimization, or some combination of the foregoing remains unsettled. *See* Robert Gibbons, *Four Formal(izable) Theories of the Firm?*, 58 J. ECON. BEHAV. & ORG. 200 (2005). A freight railroad ("carrier") that is self-insured, owns its tracks and locomotives, employs its own crews, and presumably develops expertise on those factors to reap returns to scale will be the *residual claimant* and risk bearer at least as to those factors of production. But such a carrier may or may not be able to charge higher rates for more dangerous freights, making the design of its dealings with shippers at best difficult to optimize (whatever the organizational arrangement). *See* Steven N.S. Cheung, *The Contractual Nature of the Firm*, 26(1) J. L. & ECON. 1, 3–10 (1983).

128 *See, e.g.*, KERR, supra note 35 at 14–38 (describing the struggles in rate regulation by the Interstate Commerce Commission between variously organized shippers and railroads); KOLKO, supra note 35 at 7–29 (describing collusion between shippers and between railroads, one attempting to gain leverage over the other, 1877–1883).

achieve scale returns smaller competitors could not, for example, but it also increased cost bases leading to clear inefficiencies.[129] By coincidence of many factors US railroads (and shippers) have come to a unique mix of assets, capital, and geographic/market shares which is still evolving.[130] One of the principal ECP brake business benefits is fuel savings (from more accurate, optimized braking ratios), which would seemingly be a cost saving for all except fuel suppliers.[131] Should PHMSA have supposed that competitive forces in freight rail (or beyond) would *not* eventually return some of this advantage to shippers? In a market where modal competition from pipelines looms so large, it would seem to deny the importance of production and productivity to suppose that technological improvement can never trim costs *tout court*. But would the market participants recognize their opportunities? The "market failure" of trainsets' losses being insufficient motive for railroads to insure fully against disasters like Lac Mégantic or the others suggests they might not.[132] Yet braking, a technology uniquely capable of empowering operators with a last clear chance to avert losses, is arguably more precise than any other target in its reconciliation of rail's risks to others with rail's capital costs.[133]

---

129 *See* Alison Chapin & Stephen Schmidt, *Do Mergers Improve Efficiency? Evidence from Deregulated Rail Freight*, 33(2) J. TRANSP. ECON. & POL'Y 147 (1999).

130 *See* Vassallo & Fagan, supra note 42 at 179–80, 182–86. With coal having reached as much as a quarter of rail ton-miles in the US—but as little as 1% of ton-miles being accounted for by value-added, manufactured goods—freight rail is facing other demand shifts, as well. Id. at 185.

131 *See* HHFT Final RIA, supra note 59 at 234–35; HHFT Final Rule, 80 Fed. Reg. at 26693.

132 *Compare* HHFT Final RIA, supra note 59 at 22–23 (reporting that in October 2014 a major insurer expanded the excess casualty liability limits for the seven Class I railroads to $1 billion per accident and that most of those railroads self-insure to, at most, $50 million), *with* Gregory C. Keating, *Pressing Precaution Beyond the Point of Cost-Justification*, 56 VAND. L. REV. 653, 677 (2003) ("The circumstances in which we voluntarily expose ourselves to risks in the pursuit of our own ends is very different from the circumstance in which others involuntarily expose us to risks in the pursuit of their ends."). Note that AAR and all Class I railroads had voluntarily committed to a 50 mile per hour speed limit with all HHFTs in February 2014. *See* HHFT Final RIA, supra note 59 at 199. Of course, reducing that speed limit from 50 to 40 MPH would reduce the trains' kinetic energy by 36% and any accident's expected severity by that much as well. Id. at 201.

133 Such a justification could succeed from beginnings in fairness if not in welfarism. *Cf.* Keating, supra note 132 at 678 ("It is reasonable to expose other

All the same, the trade association, AAR, went to lengths to argue that, from its modeling, ECP braking benefits relative to conventional air brakes under the forces prevailing in derailments were vastly outweighed by their cost.[134] No one disputed that immediate brake signal propagation was better than the delayed, erratic, easily interrupted braking signals of standard equipment.[135] No party disagreed with that advantage's potential safety benefits in either probabilities or severities of derailments.[136] The dispute was purely a matter of the relevant quantities—event probabilities, train forces, exact timing and locations of derailment, *etc*. And the industry never seemed to notice (or to care) that the rulemaking itself became, in its engulfing dispute over these numbers, a public subsidy to the understanding of the production factors at issue.

6.1.2 What Capital to Change? Of Firm Incentives and Opportunity Sets

The one fact about research and development (R&D) on which critical and mainstream economics seem to converge is the strategic role of uncertainty in R&D expenditures.[137] When those expenditures are

people to risks of serious injury and even death when it is fair to do so; and it is fair to do so when they also stand to gain, ex ante and over time, from the imposition of those risks. ... When the gains to each person's freedom outweigh the losses to each person's liberty, the imposition of risk benefits each member of the community.").

[134] *See* HHFT Final RIA, supra note 59 at 213–45; *see also* GAO, ECP Brake Audit, supra note 11 at 36–37. GAO noted of the lack of "physical" evidence on PHMSA's part, *see* id. at 37, that "seven of the 13 experts" interviewed thought that both AAR and PHMSA "could have bolstered their modeling efforts by performing physical tests," id., and that OMB's "Circular A-4" on the preparation of RIAs requires agencies to obtain all "reasonably obtainable scientific, technical, and economic information reasonably available." Id. at 30.

[135] *See* GAO, ECP Brake Audit, supra note 11 at 41–42.

[136] *See* id.

[137] *See* David Popp, *Uncertain R&D and the Porter Hypothesis*, 4(1) CONTRIBS. ECON. ANALYSIS & POL'Y 1, 1–2 (2005). The orthodox treatment of induced innovation at a microeconomic level has long focused on factor prices and their effects on R&D choices. *See, e.g.*, Hans P. Binswanger, *A Microeconomic Approach to Induced Innovation*, 84 ECON. J. 940 (1974). An unorthodox account, rooted in the premise that R&D expenditures are not typically profit maximizing, has long separated market from nonmarket "selection environments." *See* Richard R. Nelson & Sidney G. Winter, *In Search of Useful Theory of Innovation*, 6 RESEARCH POL'Y 36, 64–70 (1977).

"nonmarket" and/or required, the separation of interests between firms and customers is at least not as sharp as in market environments.[138] Capturing the benefits to be found in ECP braking may or may not be done by first movers—which is obviously important to the firms making the expenditures. But if innovation by firms is ordinarily aimed at either stimulating demand or minimizing costs, it would stand to reason that shippers and railroads both stand to benefit from enhanced braking. A better service means surplus; its division is altogether separate. Furthermore, with so public an exploration of a factor's design and prospects for improvement as that which overtook the ECP braking mandates (especially in the regulation's proffered performance-based option[139]), the HMR-251 rulemaking came to be the equivalent of subsidized R&D. It could not but shift the "natural trajectory" of available research and engineering talent studying the efficiencies to be found in train control.[140] Any resulting efficiencies would presumably be subject to capture by attentive competitors.[141] In that much, unified industry opposition was simply anticompetitive.

Train propulsion and control technologies have continued to evolve over recent decades, even as much of North America's freight rail infrastructure has stagnated technologically.[142] Train formation planning

---

[138] Nelson & Winter, supra note 137 at 67.

[139] *See* HHFT Final Rule, 80 Fed. Reg. at 26748 (*finalizing* 49 C.F.R. § 174.310(a)(3)(v) ("Alternate brake systems may be submitted for approval through the processes and procedures outlined in 49 C.F.R. part 232, subpart F.").

[140] *Cf.* Nelson & Winter, supra note 137 at 56–58 (arguing that path-dependent, self-reinforcing search strategies tend to address R&D expenditures to ordered problem sets along a "natural trajectory"); Wesley M. Cohen, *Fifty Years of Empirical Studies of Innovative Activity and Performance, in* 1 HANDBOOK OF THE ECONOMICS OF INNOVATION 129, 176 (Bronwyn H. Hall & Nathan Rosenberg eds., 2010) ("The notion is that in certain instances technological development proceeds along a relatively clear path, as if moving toward some physical limit. Engineers do not move myopically from one bottleneck to the next; they repeatedly focus on a particular class of engineering problems, drawing upon and strengthening a familiar method of solution.").

[141] Assuming the railroad is free to pursue those efficiencies, it is equally plausible to assume some will do so and that all will do so evenly. In examining cost-cutting measures adopted by Class I roads following deregulation, Bitzan and Keeler found that one railroad—the very firm that had pioneered elimination of caboose-cabining crews—failed to realize gains from the step because a state with much of its track prohibited the measure. *See* Bitzan & Keeler, *Productivity Growth*, supra note 40 at 247.

[142] Besides the century-old air brake technology still standard in American freight operations, track and wheel materials and propulsion and powering

capacities for optimizing the use of locomotives, cars, and crews have likewise improved.[143] Thus, optimizing ECP retrofits for interoperability and compliance by 2021–23 was a solvable R&D problem. It was just not one the freight rail firms wanted. If returns to R&D increase with the level of output over which the fixed costs of innovation can be spread,[144] the cyclical boom–bust nature of freight railroading may have mattered less to roads' vulnerabilities than the individual railroad's own capacities to adapt and successfully capture business from a competitor.[145] The imperfectly competitive structure of the sector—geographically lumpy as the distribution of Class I railroads is—complicates that deduction, but it does not refute it.

The major point of contention throughout the struggle remained the extent of the necessary conversion to ECP-braked rolling stock. From the time of proposal to finalization the agencies' estimates ranged from as few as 900 locomotives to 2,500+ in the final rule.[146] By contrast, AAR put that number at over 20,000.[147] Experience in Australia where ECP brakes were widely adopted in the freight train mining sector on the

---

systems have advanced well beyond the technologies most commonly employed by North American freight rail operations. The "network effects" or increasing returns to scale of the industry may explain this technological plateau. *See* W. Brian Arthur, *Competing Technologies, Increasing Returns, and Lock-In by Historical Events*, 99 ECON. J. 116, 125–26 (1989). The legacy effects of rate, wage, and service regulation may also still account for it. *See* Aaron J. Gelman, *Barriers to Innovation in the Railroad Industry*, 25(4) TRANSP. J. 4, 6–9 (1986).

[143] *See* William C. Vantuono, *Boosting Asset Utilization: The Hunt for Percentage Points*, RAILWAY AGE (May 30, 2013), *available at* https://www.railwayage.com/freight/class-i/boosting-asset-utilization-the-hunt-for-percentage-points/.

[144] *See* Cohen, supra note 140 at 138–39.

[145] *Cf.* id. at 140–53 (collecting empirical evidence on the correlation(s) between firm size and capabilities and the incentives to innovate); David J. Teece *et al.*, *Dynamic Capabilities and Strategic Management*, 18(7) STRAT. MNGNT. J. 509, 511–12 (1997) (describing a pivot in business strategy theory toward the tools of game theory and strategic manipulation of sunk costs and rivals' vulnerabilities when cost containment efforts can be misguided but cautioning that game theoretic explanations likely cannot explain competitive advantages grounded in path-dependent factors).

[146] *See* HHFT Final RIA, supra note 59 at 219–20; HHFT Final Rule, 80 Fed. Reg. at 26701. FRA and PHMSA estimated that about 60,000+ tank cars would need to be ECP equipped. Id. at 26702.

[147] *See* GAO, ECP Brake Audit, supra note 11 at 16 (reporting that AAR estimates that railroads and shippers would need to equip 20,000 locomotives and 133,000 tanks with ECP brakes).

expectation of business benefits went a long way to convincing PHMSA and FRA of their cost estimates and of the cost achievability of a transition to ECPs.[148] Delayed transition would presumably lower transition costs—which was why PHMSA elected to phase in the mandate in 2021 and 2023.[149] The industry was known to purchase ≥ 1,000 locomotives per year on ordinary retirements and expected growth.[150] So to maintain that *no* opportunities could be found in that turnover, whether in the "demand-pull" on ECP unit costs or in optimizing locomotive-to-train operations, seems incredible in the light of all the work on R&D and the real sources of innovation and productivity.[151]

AAR answered that Australia's experience was limited to "unit" trains—captive, dedicated train sets traveling point to point—and that "manifest" training (where train assembly from multiple demands and points of origin predominates[152]) would force a greater, more immediate transition here.[153] If there is a generalized railroad cost function it would seem to confirm a vulnerability of this kind[154] (although it could just as readily confirm railroads' incentives to maximize unit- over manifest training[155]). But there is also reason to question a formalized cost function when so little is understood about the microeconomics of rail firms.

---

[148] *See* HHFT Final RIA, supra note 59 at 33–35.

[149] *Cf.* HHFT Final Rule, 80 Fed. Reg. at 26645 (limiting ECP brake mandate to "high-hazard flammable unit trains" (HHFUTs) of ≥ 70 cars of crude traveling at 30+ miles per hour by 2021 and HHFUTs of ethanol traveling at 30+ miles per hour by 2023).

[150] *See* HHFT Final Rule, 80 Fed. Reg. at 26701.

[151] *See* Cohen, supra note 140 at 172–82.

[152] *See* Bitzan & Keeler, *Economies of Density*, supra note 38 at 160–62.

[153] *See* GAO, ECP Brake Audit, supra note 11 at 15–20. GAO found that "[s]ix out of the eight experts [interviewed] who commented on equipping fleets with ECP brakes, said that railroads could operate a dedicated fleet of [unit trains transporting crude and ethanol] with four of those six experts adding that doing so would create manageable logistical challenges." Id. at 16.

[154] Thus, if the cost function is specified as follows: $C = C(\boldsymbol{w}, \boldsymbol{y}, \boldsymbol{a}, T)$, where $\boldsymbol{w}$ is a vector of factor prices, $\boldsymbol{y}$ is a scalar representing outputs, $\boldsymbol{a}$ is a vector of technological attributes, and T is a time-trend variable accounting for technological change, a regulatory constraint forcing $\boldsymbol{w}$ or T forward will invariably increase costs. *See* Bitzan & Keeler, supra note 38 at 167–69.

[155] *See* Carl D. Martland, *Productivity Improvements in the U.S. Rail Freight Industry, 1980–2010*, 51(3) J. Transp. Res. F. 83, 94–102 (2012) (finding that productivity rose fastest for unit trains in the era of deregulation and the shift to competition in freight railroading); *cf.* Vassallo & Fagan, supra note 42 at 190

In general, economists expect robust R&D expenditures (if perhaps also less R&D efficiency) from larger, mature firms like our Class I railroads.[156] Hardening tank cars could prevent some punctures in derailments. Speed limits could prevent certain human errors. And crew training might do the same. But the improved control of kinetic energy that comes from better braking has been the hallmark of technical advance in every mode of transport from buggies to bicycles for centuries.[157] If productivity gain in railroading is a quantity best measured over a long run,[158] it seems myopic at best to focus on the marginal superiority of ECP brakes over conventional air brakes in the event of a derailment.

Rapidly declining oil prices—so rapid that the entire crude-by-rail sector seemed in jeopardy as HRM-251 was being finalized—changed the calculus on ECP braking before any of this could be resolved, though. Shortly after its finalization, railroads and shippers took their complaints to Congress.

6.2 REGULATORY IMPACT ANALYSES IN POLITICS: (CERTAIN) UNCERTAINTIES TO THE FORE

With the HMR-251 rule finalized and united opposition to ECP brakes dug in from the fight but unbuoyed by the prospects in court, the focus shifted to Congress. Unlike many other risk areas, Congress has remained active in rail safety, passing omnibus reforms repeatedly over the last two decades.[159] It quickly took up the ECP brake's achievability and cost questions, dispensed with objections to the hardened tank car standards, and fashioned a compromise into a short subtitle of the

(observing that competition in US freight rail sector benefited the sector as a whole when compared to freight rail in the EU).

[156] *See* Cohen, supra note 140 at 132–40. The seven Class I railroads were the principal opponents of the ECP brake mandate probably because they were HMR-251's target. *See* GAO, ECP Brake Audit, supra note 11 at 2–6 (noting applicability of ECP brake mandate to HHFUTs and the Class I railroads' concentrated opposition).

[157] *Cf.* Usselman, supra note 31 at 48–50 (concluding that Westinghouse was largely to credit for getting passenger trains on air brakes because the transition costs and challenges were minor by comparison to those in freight rail where industry structure made interoperability challenges much more acute and costly).

[158] *See* Oum *et al.*, supra note 39 at 35–36.

[159] *See* ALDRICH, BACK ON TRACK, supra note 13 at 104–13.

massive Fixing America's Surface Transportation (FAST) Act of 2015.[160] Sorting out the relevance of regulatory costs within that compromise is instructive.

The FAST Act legislated the tank car standards of HMR-251 (shifting the phase-ins slightly),[161] and required that any flammable liquid must be transported in some version of the DOT-117 by dates specified.[162] It also required that, before an ECP mandate could take effect, the GAO first prepare "an independent evaluation of ECP brake systems, pilot program data, and the [FRA's] research and analysis on the costs, benefits, and effects of ECP brake systems."[163] (GAO's audit ten months later ended with a caution to the agencies that the uncertainty in future crude-by-rail markets must inform any cost-to-benefit evaluation.[164]) Critically, however, in further specifying that the Secretary of Transportation must also engage the National Academy of Sciences (NAS) to fully evaluate ECP braking[165] as part of a so-called "[e]vidence-[b]ased [a]pproach,"[166] the FAST Act required an NAS study that seemed to entail actual train derailment experiments and a completion date of 18 months![167] As soon as that study was estimated to cost $100+ million to complete, NAS declined to participate.[168] That left the Department to a mere revision of

---

160 *See* Pub. L. No. 114-94, 129 Stat. 1312, 1594–1604 (2015).

161 *See* Pub. L. No. 114-94, §§ 7304–06, *codified at* 49 U.S.C. §§ 20155–57 (2017).

162 49 U.S.C. § 20155(a).

163 Pub. L. No. 114-94, § 7311(a)(1), *codified at* 49 U.S.C. § 20141 (note).

164 *See* GAO, ECP Brake Audit, supra note 11 at 48–49.

165 *See* Pub. L. No. 114-94, § 7311(b)(1), 129 Stat. 1312, 1602. The "complete testing of ECP brake systems during emergency braking application" that Congress quite specifically ordered was to "objectively, accurately, and reliably [measure] the performance of ECP brake systems relative to other braking technologies or systems." Id. at §§ 7311(b)(2), (3).

166 Pub. L. No. 114-94, § 7311(c), 129 Stat. 1312, 1603.

167 Pub. L. No. 114-94, § 7311(c), 129 Stat. 1312, 1603.

168 *See* U.S. Dept. of Transp., Pipeline and Hazardous Materials Safety Admin., Hazardous Materials: Announcement of the Dept. of Transp.'s Decision on Electronically Controlled Pneumatic Braking, 82 Fed. Reg. 58582, 58583 & n.5 (2017) (hereafter "ECP Final Determination") ("In a March 17, 2016, letter, NAS declined to perform the testing, citing preliminary cost estimates to perform the testing in excess of $100 million and expressing concern about meeting the statutory deadline."). The FAST Act states that the "Secretary [of Transportation] *shall* enter into an agreement with" NAS for the preparation of the study, *see* Pub. L. No. 94-114, § 7311(b)(1), 129 Stat. 1312, 1602, and also states that the "Secretary *shall* provide funding. ..." Id. at § 7311(b)(4) (emphasis added). Apparently the Secretary's judgment was that neither this provision of the FAST

the 2015 RIA with GAO's cautionary pronouncements in mind, this time with an enlarged record of crude- and ethanol-by-rail shipments and little else.[169] This time the RIA concluded that a range of expected compliance costs was appropriate: at the high end, 20-year total costs might reach $491.7 million (net present value, discounted at 7 percent) or be as low as $375.6 million.[170] Much would depend on how quickly the crude-by-rail market sank and whether it ever came back.[171]

"Starting in 2013 and continuing through 2015 carloads spiked dramatically to over 500,000 carloads in 2014 and 2015," the Department noted, "followed by a decline to less than 300,000 in 2016."[172] So the reworked ECP RIA shifted to the US Energy Information Administration's (EIA) crude oil production forecasts,[173] took fuller account of expected pipeline capacities servicing the Bakken oil-producing region,[174] and added what amounted to a rudimentary sensitivity analysis of the demand parameter.[175] Unsurprisingly, the 20-year benefit-cost projections shifted noticeably in just that small change of inputs: Having

---

Act nor Circular A-4's mandate to base RIAs on "the best reasonably obtainable scientific, technical and economic information available" required that the NAS study be completed. *But cf.* Office of Management and Budget, Circular A-4: Regulatory Analysis 17 (Sept. 17, 2003) ("Because of its influential nature and its special role in the rulemaking process, it is appropriate to set minimum quality standards for regulatory analysis."), *available at* https://www.transportation.gov/regulations/omb-circular-no-4-0.

[169] *See* U.S. Dept. of Transp., Electronically Controlled Pneumatic Braking: Regulatory Impact Analysis (Dec. 2017) (hereafter "ECP FAST RIA"), *available at* https://www.regulations.gov/docket?D=PHMSA-2017-0102. In the December 2017 RIA revision the agencies also adjusted their car estimates upward with a "high range" figure of 43,000+ tank cars and 1900+ locomotive retrofits. Id. at 43–44.

[170] *See* ECP FAST RIA, id. at 49. The more striking change was in predicted safety benefits—for the same 20-year period discounted at 7%: between $131 and $198 million. Id. at 6 (Table E1).

[171] *Cf.* id. at 89 (noting that HMR-251 RIA of 2015 was prepared on the assumption that, at its peak, over 1 million carloads of crude would be transported and that for the 2017 updated RIA, that assumption had been changed to 679,000+ carloads). DOT concluded that ethanol traffic had been and will remain relatively stable with about half of it traveling by unit train. Id. at 33.

[172] Id. at 20.

[173] *See* id. at 21.

[174] *Cf.* id. at 85 (assuming that pipeline capacity would expand to keep crude-by-rail carloads at about 120,000 per year and never increasing). A great majority of Bakken crude was transported to refineries by rail until the Dakota Access and Energy Transfer Crude Oil pipelines came into service in June 2017.

[175] *See* id. at 85–89.

to retrofit capital with costly equipment where the capital would be productive less frequently (causing fewer accidents) and the retrofit costs remained constant increased the ratio of expected costs to expected benefits.[176] The tight focus was telling, though. It ignored the larger dynamics and uncertainties inherent in what the Department was attempting to predict: an evolutionary path to enhanced train control and a superior service.[177] OMB/OIRA's critics will argue this is "epistemic capture," a kind of influence multiplier for those able to shade cost assessments.[178] But it may be more mundane: the fragility of *any* cost estimates consisting of straight-line arithmetic from contested origins.

To be sure, the agencies' prediction of business benefits from ECP brakes tackled uncertainty with precious few of the tools necessary to quantify or explain any underlying sources of that uncertainty. Even the ensuing effort to reduce the targeted uncertainties was questionable. Congress's hollow command of the (ill-fated) NAS study staging actual derailments lent an air of even-handedness to the FAST Act even as that air dissipated faster than it blew in. Although subsequent review of FRA and PHMSA's cost-benefit figuring—taken up by "external" reviewers at OMB, GAO, and in Congress—also suggested a kind of clinical impartiality, the information available to those reviewers was no better than it had been before the agencies. The record of ECP brakes in the sector and that sector's capacity to adapt remained unchanged and no more insight was shared with the reviewers than had been shared with the agencies.[179]

---

176 *Cf.* id. at 13 ("Within the 20-year period of this analysis, costs are assessed in terms of changes in the current regulatory burden being addressed by these rule changes. In economics, this type of analysis is referred to as a *marginal analysis*.") (emphasis added). The Department also added certain component costs to the ECP brake units and their upkeep on tank cars, id. at 43–44, increasing that cost number slightly.

177 *Cf.* Sidney G. Winter, *Pursuing the Evolutionary Agenda in Economics and Management Research*, 41 CAMB. J. ECON. 721, 730–31 (2017) (explaining the "evolutionary theory of economic change" as a "Neo-Schumpeterian" framework in which profit-seeking—if not profit-*maximizing*—firms must constantly probe their surroundings for beneficial technological changes which, when found, can enhance their opportunities and fitness).

178 *See* Cass R. Sunstein, *The Office of Information and Regulatory Affairs: Myths and Realities*, 126 HARV. L. REV. 1838, 1861 (2013).

179 None of the subsequent reviews, for example, made any attempt to predict innovation within the freight rail sector to capture the business benefits hypothesized in ECP braking nor made attempts to quantify the effects that enforced diffusion of ECP brakes might have had within the sector.

For a presidential administration that made bold—perhaps rash—campaign promises to undo the regulatory state, the ECP brake episode may be especially illuminating. Selectively targeting uncertainties in risk regulation and rescinding a rule if a highly specific uncertainty cannot be resolved is surely one way to cultivate a hawkish appearance on regulatory costs. In that light, the ECP brake mandate was a rule that the Trump Administration successfully did in—at least for now. In another light, scrapping a mandate after years of regulatory and Congressional study (much of that focused on the productive factors in freight rail and their potential for improvement) based on nothing more than a tendentious use of uncertainty simply ignores the well-known relationship between product quality and demand stimulation. Our "*Overton Park* consensus" may eventually insulate this rescission from searching judicial scrutiny,[180] but it cannot erase the social costs evident from the record. For if freight rail has another heyday like the tight oil boom of 2005–14 in the near future, whatever productivity gains economists think they can back out of that "growth" should be discounted by a special fraction that captures the embedded, coordinated industry opposition to improving their product which has kept it the transport service most easily replaced for all but a diminishing portfolio of goods. Specific design standards may not be the best mechanism for spurring innovation or microeconomic cost avoidance, but they can be a strategic means of imposing collectively agreed upon minimum standards at manageable cost. And better braking in freight rail may yet have a day in court.

---

[180] *See* Chapter 1, Section 1.1. The Department's notice of December 2017 purported to be but a "final determination" and not a rescission of the ECP brake mandate of August 2015. *See* ECP Final Determination, 82 Fed. Reg. at 58583 ("PHMSA and FRA will initiate a rulemaking to rescind the necessary regulatory provisions."). Thus, it would arguably not be "ripe" for judicial challenge in its own right. Nevertheless, the RIA supporting it and the statutory prompt in the FAST Act occasioning that "final determination" will almost certainly feature prominently in any subsequent judicial challenge to the rescission.

Conclusion

> It is tempting to occupy the aesthetic high ground and to say that tragic choices cannot be evaluated. But decisions have to be made, and thinking in terms of numerical indices makes decision-makers face trade-offs explicitly.[1]

Cost has always been a reason to temper, to delay, or to reject a risk-regulating action by government. But costs have evolved into a multifaceted arena in contemporary risk regulation, playing a subtly distributed array of roles in legislative, judicial, and regulatory choice. Cost factors quite variably into those deliberations: It has become a factor with utilitarian, fairness, and deliberative significance. It is tempting to see in the consideration of costs a mere differentiation of means and ends.[2] But cost is often the mechanism by which we recognize our true ends regarding risk, the means by which *we* as a society come to agree on the priorities that will guide collective action. As the temporal, factoral, and geographic scales at which we measure and evaluate regulatory costs expand or contract, their nature as genuinely *social* costs—or not—can be brought into sharper focus. Like any representation, cropping cost assessments or expanding them to unusually broad scales changes their meaning. Like our parable at the outset about money and its practical value, the selection of time scales, of feasible substitutes and purposes for use, and of spatial frames of reference can make all the difference.

Costs that can be avoided through innovation, competition, industry consolidation or other microeconomic changes are no (economic) costs at all. Some costs are unavoidable given the state of technology or its productive uses and how regulators choose to regulate. But it usually takes deliberate and directed study to distinguish the avoidable from the unavoidable, often with a healthy skepticism toward information gathered from the regulated parties. This conclusion briefly summarizes the

1 PARTHA DASGUPTA, HUMAN WELL-BEING AND THE NATURAL ENVIRONMENT 23 (2003).

2 *See, e.g.*, David M. Driesen, *The Ends and Means of Pollution Control: Toward a Positive Theory of Environmental Law*, 2017 UTAH L. REV. 58, 77–81.

contours traced throughout the case studies and the scaffolding which the first three chapters built up to them.

Chapter 4 was fundamentally a study of performance standards driving production to evolve. It involved the original performance standards and industry's coordinated opposition thereto. But that evolution was eventually channeled toward a vast societal transition—electric powertrains—which is still unfolding. It ranged over several notoriously confounding influences in the estimation of costs of compliance. Variables such as increasing returns to scale in production and how costs-of-compliance accountants assess a sector's evolving competitive landscape over time proved vital. We traced a transition from static, partial equilibrium accounting to fully dynamic, general equilibrium methods—and also glimpsed the limits of those methods. Congress's episodic interventions in the Clean Air Act and later Corporate Average Fuel Economy standards evidenced a continuing concern for costs of compliance without nearly as much concern for how those costs were counted or weighed. The importance of innovation, learning-by-doing, and the regulated firms' capacities to avoid costs of compliance given long enough lead times became undeniable as experience with EPA's performance standards mounted. Finally, with automobile emissions in particular, public support for continued research and development (R&D), first in the area of catalysis and the control of conventional pollutants and later in the area of fuel efficiency and repowering, became a significant subsidy in overall social cost minimization.

Congress, it will be recalled, originally gave regulators (US EPA) the power to relent in its "technology-forcing" emissions limits—withholding the authority to redesign the constraints wholesale.[3] That authority fully to design the performance standards being set was later delegated. By then, though, the strategic dimensions of information sharing were evident to all involved. Later, the strength and weakness of the automobile sector, its sources of productivity gains and its losses thereof, came to weigh heavily in EPA's design of its emissions standards. After years of studying and working with the production and technology involved, the regulators found themselves embedded in any decision to relent; their agency had become bound up with the strategic dimensions of cost and cost avoidance in the auto sector.[4] This is one of the lessons of cost factoring as a welfare- and fairness-facing considerations. If part of the reason we care about regulatory costs is out of

---

[3] *See* Chapter 4, Section 4.1.
[4] *See* Chapter 4, Section 4.1.1.

concerns for fairness to the regulated and if our regulators, in seeking to trim regulatory costs, will so easily find themselves enmeshed in long-term relationships with the regulated, we must take care to investigate and express cost estimates conscious of this hybridized and potentially conflicted role. Especially as the macroeconomic drivers of auto sector fortunes came to dominate cost-of-compliance estimation and evaluation, and the transition to greenhouse gas emissions as pollutants of concern shifted the focus to fuel efficiency, the ability of auto manufacturers to *spread* costs of compliance took on central importance. By that point, however, the theory of emissions' social costs had expanded so extravagantly that some welfarists had a change of heart, turning on the very methods they had once so fully embraced.[5] The "social cost of carbon" analyses from general equilibrium growth modeling proved too manipulable (or arcane) even for them.

Agency reasonableness in court has long been about justification, not motive. But outside of court it has just as long turned on a recognition that some degree of regulator/regulated mutuality is necessary, perhaps never more so than in setting performance standards. The more our regulators have studied the cost achievability of proposed performance standards, the more directly they studied the innovation frontiers and microeconomic trends at work in their subject production sectors (or risk vectors). If the firm's boundaries and structure are any reflection of its know-how, "innovation" of any significance will disrupt them. Hence, innovation in risk-regulatory standard-setting entails some tolerance of factoral and perhaps even sectoral change. For automobile emissions at EPA, reasonableness in the assessment of compliance costs did not preclude the agency from peering into the future and projecting the possibility of major, structural changes in the products being marketed or the firms marketing them.[6] But it did first entail developing methods to split the costs of necessary R&D among the products devised and enhanced in response to their performance standards. It entailed refining tools for estimating innovation's costs on a marginal basis. A long lead time and a finely tailored menu of fleet-wide standards maximized each manufacturer's opportunities to develop products and compliance strategies in order to minimize its own costs of compliance.[7]

Chapter 5 offers a contrast: the same regulator (US EPA) choosing not to set nationwide performance standards, multiplying its own

---

[5] *See* Chapter 4, Section 4.5.
[6] *See* Chapter 4, Section 4.4.
[7] *See* Chapter 4, Section 4.5.1.

administrative costs over the ensuing decades and doing virtually nothing to protect the natural capital at risk. For all that could be told from the rulemaking record when the agency finally did act to set national standards, the decades-long interval spent permitting facilities individually yielded precious little useful information. And once buckled into the task, EPA set a standard that required little-to-no performance at all, seemingly persuaded by the disparity between its cost figures and the anemic benefits estimates which could be monetized.[8] Cooling water intakes are a prime example of reliance on unpriced natural capital which a large but increasingly diversified sector—such as electricity generation—grew dependent upon. And yet this thermoelectric power has begun, in the changing North American climate, to present grid-reliability risks and local environmental costs which its host communities and regions find increasingly problematic. EPA's repeated encounters with setting nationally uniform performance standards for thermoelectric cooling water intakes from 2001 to 2014 remained remarkably aloof of the larger technological transition then ongoing within the sector. EPA could not get itself unstuck from the geographic variability of cooling water intakes as local environmental problems or thermoelectric power as a grid contributor. Yet with its rulemaking becoming so public (a trip to the Supreme Court and a turnover of party in power will do that), the longer EPA avoided setting a performance standard on the "capacity" of intakes (their total throughput) the more that transition to lower water-demanding generation factors like natural gas combined-cycle turbines undermined EPA's performance standard *as* a performance standard. The longer EPA's obsession with costs of compliance idled it, the less its performance standards seemed to cost, but the less they resembled actual *performance* standards.

Now the Clinton Administration that agreed finally to impose national standards was not the Bush Administration that had to create them nor the Obama Administration that later found itself (having come to office a month before the case was argued in the Supreme Court[9]) reviewing and revising them.[10] But EPA's analytical focus remained steady throughout: how to scheme out national standards for both the intake mechanism and the scale of overall withdrawals with justifiable (monetized) costs and benefits. EPA's solution, specifying the system of constraints so as to

---

[8] *See* Chapter 5, Section 5.2.

[9] *See* Chapter 2, Section 2.3 and Chapter 5, Section 5.2.

[10] *See* ConocoPhillips Co. v. EPA, 612 F.3d 822, 825–30 (5th Cir. 2010); Entergy Corp. v. Riverkeeper, Inc., 556 U.S. 208, 213–14 (2009); Riverkeeper, Inc. v. EPA, 475 F.3d 83, 89–95 (2d Cir. 2007).

reduce its unavoidable costs to fractional shares of the regulated parties' annual profits, arguably shifted the relevance of compliance costs into a question of fairness or of reasonableness. Yet EPA did little to justify its performance standards in terms of their fairness to the utility sector or anyone else.[11] It was only ever implicitly motivating the rulemaking. The net result was a standard reliant upon a cost evaluation consisting in weak partial equilibrium methods that ignored possibilities for innovation, impending sectoral changes, and increasingly proven harms to the environment.

Finally, that saga contrasts sharply with the crude- and ethanol-by-rail derailment rulemaking undertaken by Department of Transportation regulators. In a sector beset by competition from without, costs of compliance have long held unique significance—especially where the political prompt for the regulation arguably targeted risks to public health and safety that were smaller in magnitude than in popular dread. The "high hazard flammable trains" eventually the subject of the rulemaking could be handled in any number of ways to reduce the nominal threat. The regulators' selection of braking standards, and of a particular brake technology, focused the cost assessments and evaluation in a way that only design standards can. Without a legislative mandate to weigh costs, the ensuing rulemaking included these assessments and evaluations at the White House's behest, pursuant to the series of "regulatory impact assessment" (RIA) executive orders.

We have grown accustomed to RIA cost-benefit comparisons and much in the "bomb train" RIAs was unremarkable. As the focus was incrementally cropped to a particular braking technology identified and the unavoidable costs of its being retrofitted to existing capital and incorporated into future capital were evaluated, a great many variables seemed to enter the calculus. The disputes never were resolved about the unavoidable costs of the agencies' mandate. Two influences that became pivotal, however, were the economic structure of the industry—the distributed ownership of tank cars, locomotives, and other capital—and the sheer volume of legislated safety mandates that had come due at that particular moment in time. Congressional demands to automate train control in certain operations had put freight rail firms in a cost/technical bind. When the regulators' brake mandate materialized, they rushed to Congress. The overtly political methods of dispute resolution there radically transformed the role of uncertainty and its rational management.

---

11 *See* Chapter 5, Section 5.2.1.

We may never learn whether the enhanced braking required by the 2015 flammable trains rulemaking had within it the seeds of product quality improvement in the perennially ailing freight rail industry. All speculation aside, freight rail productivity continues to divide professional economists not least because transport's place in *production* remains contestable. Rail firms know perhaps better than most that their business partners are only too eager to cut the costs their services represent. If the flammable train braking rule's saga is any indicator, though, they have yet to learn what a strategic opportunity enforced technological diffusion can be for a vulnerable industry. Boom/bust cycles can obscure larger patterns, of course, and one pattern that the rulemaking record revealed was freight rail's long-term vulnerability to Congressional whim, erratic as that has been, and the sector's largest firms' relative inabilities to innovate their way to a better product that stimulates demand or dramatically lowers costs. The Department of Transportation's optimizations, especially its sustained search for the best braking technologies, were at least a minor public subsidy of sorts. And they may well have been a unique path to better profitability long term. Of course, a Congress too eager to react to the "political prompts" that rail risks seem to create can be bad for the industry sector's bottom line. But having Congress (indirectly) reverse the regulators may have been a short-term fix that came at the expense of longer-term prospects.

It is hard to derive an expression of popular will from legislation ordering regulators to further study a specific issue and implement their rule only after that study has been completed. It is even harder to do so when the study itself turns out to be too costly or infeasible (at least to the parties tapped to do it). That may all along have been a stratagem within the FAST Act. But if so, it is particularly noteworthy in what it does *not* establish about popular consciousness of risk and risk regulation's costs. Whatever the FAST Act's posture toward derailment risk in its requirement of the National Academies study of real derailments, that posture could not have been the discounting of the risks. In a frustrating and at times incomprehensible book, the philosopher Isaac Levi once confronted just this question: what choices mean when they are made under uncertainties that all would reasonably agree ought to be resolved before one knows what ought to be done.[12] Levi's basic answer was that such choices can never really *be* an expression of preferences, collective or otherwise. If this is true, the deeper meaning of risk-regulatory

[12] *See* Isaac Levi, Hard Choices: Decision Making Under Unresolved Conflict (1986).

delegations so common in our legislation today is tightly bound to those statutes' many and varied references to cost, cost achievability, and regulatory rationality. Indeed, it grounds their normative force as expressions of collective will in the search for social cost minimization over time. When innovation and technical change shift the landscapes on which regulatory costs are felt—or not—the people may just as well have asked for more of that as they have for "less" regulation. Only time can tell.

Index